Turn Right,
Turn Left, Repeat

Turn Right, Turn Left, Repeat

Life on the road for the Canadian indie band

Gern f. Vlchek

INSOMNIAC PRESS

Library and Archives Canada Cataloguing in Publication

F., Gern, 1966-, author
Turn right, turn left, repeat / Gern F.

Issued in print and electronic formats.
ISBN 978-1-55483-125-8 (pbk.).--ISBN 978-1-55483-144-9 (html)

1. United Steel Workers of Montreal. 2. Concert tours--Canada.
3. Music trade--Canada. 4. Alternative country musicians--Canada.
5. F., Gern, 1966-. I. Title.

ML421.U585F2 2014   781.642092'2   C2014-903295-1
                                                 C2014-903296-X

The publisher gratefully acknowledges the support of the Canada Council, the Ontario Arts Council, and the Department of Canadian Heritage through the Canada Book Fund.

Printed and bound in Canada

Insomniac Press
520 Princess Avenue, London, Ontario, Canada, N6B 2B8
www.insomniacpress.com

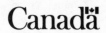

The Canada Council for the Arts since 1957 | Le Conseil des Arts du Canada depuis 1957

ONTARIO ARTS COUNCIL
CONSEIL DES ARTS DE L'ONTARIO

To Klara,
dreams will come and go —
start your life's work as soon as you can.

Ignace, Ontario

It hit me as we were traveling east on the Trans-Canada Highway (Highway 17) about twenty-five minutes before we reached Ignace, Ontario. I had it in my mind that I wanted to stop at Tower Hill Truck Stop. The tough part was making it past the Tim Hortons where everybody would want to stop to pee. I was thinking the food at Timmy's sucks: we would stop for a pee break, argue about eating there or elsewhere, and end up stopping later. That's two stops, and that would mean getting into Thunder Bay late, maybe too late to make it to the beer store. Someone (and I can't remember who) shouts out, "I have to *pee!*" It is always like that. First you think it, and then either you or someone else has to pee. This is the road with a band. The long hours, the fighting over radio stations or CDs, and the constant battle between getting down the road and the needs of everybody in the van.

Someone shouted again, thinking I didn't hear them, or more likely I didn't care. As we slid gracefully by the Tim Hortons, I said, "There's a truck stop just up the road, and I think it's getting close to dinner." Dinnertime with a band is not any particular time, just five hours after the last time we ate if it is daytime, eight hours after if it's night…but then that would be breakfast.

Chris pipes up, "Oh yeah, that place, didn't we stop there

on the way out?" I said, "Yes, I think we stopped there several times on our trips out west." And Chris said, "Yeah, you had the pot pie." Chris and I talked for the next twenty minutes, filling the cab of the van with talk about how we could remember almost every place we ever ate and what we ate during the entire six years the Steel Workers had been back and forth across Canada.

Herein lies the revelation. It was not just food that we could remember. It was food, restaurants, waitresses, gas attendants, shows, soundmen, other bands, club addresses, bridge tolls for two-axle vehicles, the sights, smells, and sounds of this long, thin road, this road unique to Canada. It's linear, and you are either driving east or west on it, and the more you drive the more incrementally successful you become. At that point in that trip, all those years back, we knew that road pretty well.

This book is not a flawless account of our tours, but I hope it is a surprisingly accurate portrayal of this drive to success for a working band.

As you head through Ignace, you think you've been through the whole town because it sprawls out in that Northern Ontario, single-storey way most of those towns have, with the businesses all pushed up close to the road and the housing back off the highway or on secondary roads a ways back, behind the used car or logging equipment dealerships. You make it through, and you're thinking, "Hey, we missed the truck stop" or, "Maybe I was thinking of another town, there are a lot of towns," and as you're running that through your head, you come around the corner to find a couple more businesses up ahead. The East End of town sprawls with truck depots, junk shops, those sorts of things, and just when you start to think that maybe the truck stop is in Dryden, there you are.

We pull into the lot fast, because now everybody in the van has to pee. Hitting the curb with a thud, moving it a couple of inches, bam, scrape, a perfect landing, the van disgorges us, and those who need to pee the most run towards the bathroom located at the back of the truck stop. That's the great part about stopping in the same place over and over: you know where the bathrooms are. The bathrooms have that truck stop smell that reminds you of urinating into a used tire, a memory you didn't think would ever come back. That memory, and the feeling of relief from the 1.75 litres of water you drank to get over that hangover from the gig at the High and Lonesome Club in Winnipeg, gets you through the bulk of that dirty bathroom feel.

As you banter with your bandmates, regular bathroom stuff, your eye pans the room, looking to see if any of your band stickers have been affixed to any of the walls or fixtures. You think to yourself, "Man, I should have those things in my pockets all the time." You finish peeing, and you immediately start worrying about table seating: will you get a window, or what mood is so and so in? Hope that table is full, and I'll sit with Matt, because halfway through he'll get up and eat his food in the parking lot anyway while talking on the phone to his girlfriend.

The Tower Hill Truck Stop belongs to the Northern Ontario school of independent truck stops. A mom and/or pop affair, built years ago and decorated for the mass media, seventies trucking craze that everybody got into back when

CB radios and *B.J. and the Bear* were everywhere. Aloft on high shelves that ring the entire baby-blue dining room are plastic models of trucks, the big rigs, in many makes and colours. The light blue and sort of dingy walls mix with trucks and prints of Elvis, all of which are discoloured and showing their age. I squeeze into my very small Formica banquette, which is pretty inadequate considering the average guy eating here is as big as me. But my dissatisfaction is replaced by the granddaddy of all truck stop experiences. There are two empty coffee cups on the table, turned upside down.

Years ago, before the years I've spent driving around as a musician, I spent time driving trucks, big trucks. I did it for a long time, and since then I have always wondered why all restaurants do not provide this service. Turning the upside down cup upright means, "Yes, ma'am, I would like a coffee," no pissing about. She walks over and slaps down some menus and fills your coffee up. Five-star joints could work like this. That system leaves me wondering if I could ever really quit drinking coffee. Oh sure, I could get away with it for a couple of months, but what happens when I walk into a truck stop and there's an empty overturned coffee cup there, the unspoken order as if you are a regular even if you live 2,500 kilometres away? I would surely break.

Halfway through my cup, I've scanned the menus and the dry erase specials board, and I am ready for sure to order the meat pie with mashed, and I'm trying to recall whether it was this visit or the one before when Filly got the way-too-big shepherd's pie. Filly, or Felicity Hamer, is the girl in the band who has to travel with five smelly dudes. She is small, much smaller than the rest of us, and in places like this, places with large portions, Filly usually finishes her food a day later, maybe at midnight. Moving on round the table, Matt gets the meat sandwich with a garden salad. That's easy because Matt has to eat that every day. There is always something of that sort on the menu, be it roast beef, hot beef, or beef dip, he always finds it. Chris (always the optimist) probably wanted the clams or something weird for way out here, this being 3,051 kilometres from any place that would have clams, but I think he relented and went for the special. Flipper would have ordered something weird too, weird for Ignace, like French onion soup. And, of course, Gus either got the pizza all dressed or the grilled cheese. There are two sides to this. If he gets the pizza, he'll hate it because he grew up in Montreal, and as all Montrealers know, Montreal makes the best pizza in the world. "Not true," shouts the world at large. But, hey, can't argue with the sons of Saputo. Montrealers love their pie. Sadly, they are the only ones who do. Gus also loves the grilled cheese but gets mad when the bill comes and the grilled cheese costs $5.75 even though it's two pieces of bread, some Kraft (or lesser slice), and margarine thrown on a grill for forty-five seconds. Not exactly the best meal deal going but always a good comfort on the road.

I myself order up the meat pie and mashed. Having learned on the way out west that the gravy at this restaurant smells like cantaloupe and has a strange colour, I decide to waive the gravy option and get by on ketchup. During the wait for our food, we note a boil water notice on the wall, and we discuss whether coffee makers boil water in the process of making coffee. In the end, there seemed to be no definitive answer, so we ordered another round. The food was good in a home-cooked sort of way, and what it lacked in subtlety it made up for in substance and satisfying bulk. Good road food gets you to the next town without making you sick, and should make driving just challenging enough to keep you awake. With Filly's one-third-eaten meal wrapped up, it's fill the travel cups and load up on smokes. It's only four hours and two pee breaks to Thunder Bay and a good night's sleep at the Apollo.

Newfoundland

The all-Canadian band experience is touring from coast to coast. Over the years we, the United Steel Workers of Montreal, have been back and forth across Canada about five times. Due to scheduling and the rigours of being indie and having to hold down jobs to keep things rolling and the rents paid, we did many trips in the early years that brought us just for a rip around Ontario and back. The Great Canadian Tour for us was usually broken into different segments: doing the east at one part of the year, the west a couple of months later, and, when time permitted, taking a run around Ontario. It wasn't until our sixth year that we undertook a full coast-to-coast tour.

According to MapQuest, St. John's, Newfoundland to Victoria, British Columbia is 7,238 kilometres. That's if you are using a fairly direct route and avoiding travel in the United States and considering that the Newfoundland ferry only runs Port aux Basques to Sydney, come off-season, which is when bands tour. Take into account that tours for bands are never in a straight line and there is always a bit of backtracking going on (well hell, a huge amount of backtracking) and that 7,238 kilometres gets up to around 11,000 kilometres. Returning to Montreal by way of Southern Ontario for a couple of shows,

I think we were close to 20,000 kilometres on that trip.

That's a lot of mileage. Our first time out, I think the tour took three months to pull off with maybe a week at home after touring the east and a few days off thrown in on nights when there were no gigs to be had. I looked at it then as a challenge and now look back with a fair bit of pride at pulling that off. St. John's to Victoria, now that's a tour. This book follows that route. To be fair and truthful, the stories that follow are an amalgam of the many trips we have taken. Please do not fret if the bass player's name changes often or the mandolin player is taller by the end of the book. The bulk of these tales do come out of that one long drive.

When planning our first trip to Newfoundland, I realized that I didn't know that much about the island and its geography. Living in Montreal for the last eighteen-odd years, the extent of my true knowledge about Newfoundlanders comes from the expat islanders who have found their way to Montreal, most notably Sean B'y Moore, our first multi-instrumentalist, a founding member of the band, and the guy who came up with our name.

Sean B'y is from the Goulds just outside of St. John's, and through his tales of home I found the idea of doing the Rock very intriguing. Truth be told, I also decided that coast to coast meant *coast to coast,* so let's start there. As with the start of planning any tour, I fired up the computer and started mapping it out. The first thing about Newfoundland is that St. John's is on the farthest eastern side of the island, and when reading the ferry schedule closely, you find that unless the trip is going to happen between May and September, you are taking the Sydney to Port aux Basques ferry and not Argentia.

That means a long drive after the ferry. Sounds like fun, except that not only are you not going in May or June, but also you have made the decision to go in February. The idea is that no other bands will be touring out there, so you will have it all to yourselves. Man, that is a long drive.

St. John's, Newfoundland

You enter St. John's at night. When you tour with a band in the winter, you get used to arriving after dark. You have only so much daylight and so much sack time in the hotel room where you've crammed six people before the cleaning staff kicks you out. It's winter, so daylight is at a premium. You're on the road, everyone having eaten breakfast at the crack of one p.m., maybe, schedule allowing.

St. John's will amaze you with its plunging hills and banked sharp corners. They stack the clapboard, multicoloured houses up tight against each other. It looks like the whole town is part of the structural planning for any given house. The anchoring of each of these buildings (set, I would guess, not that far into the bedrock) must rely at least partially on its neighbours' foundations to help keep it perched on its hill, like trees on a steep embankment with the intertwining roots holding them all together. No matter how you find yourself coming into town, the sheer gravitational force of St. John's will have you at the bottom of the hill before you find what you're looking for. In the gloom of night when reaching the bottom (that gloom highlighted by the glow of the sulphur lights), boats, big boats, seem to lunge out at you as you follow the road and veer to avoid the harbour. It is all mystifying until you've had a good night's sleep on some couch somewhere.

Re-inspecting the town by daylight, that question that has been nagging you for at least three months since first looking Newfoundland up on the Internet is answered. The question of course is why the biggest town on the island is so goddamn far away from every other damn thing in the world. The answer is the harbour. The wonderment of the town built on such a slope that you came across last night also makes sense.

St. John's harbour is the biggest bowl you will ever see. An incredible natural harbour, it was used by John Cabot arriving in 1497, Erik the Red, and of course the First Peoples thousands of years before that. Now, you get a good harbour and, man, you have a town. And what a town it is.

With a population hovering around 187,000 folks, the town can easily be called a small city. I've always been fascinated by small cities, having broken from the rural life somewhere around the time that I learned that drinking and driving is not a good idea, and that it is best to live somewhere where you can walk to the bar. Also, I've always liked any town that can claim to be the *magnetic* force for its surrounding areas, staving off the kids' dreams of New York or Paris. That said, St. John's has had a difficult time hanging on to folks over the years due to economic reasons, but is still what the Newfoundlanders refer to as "Town." If you are from Newfoundland and you're not from St. John's, then you're not from Town. Mind you, the locals say then you would be a "Bayman" and have Bayman powers, but let's talk about Town.

St. John's feels like a city to me. Having the university and the bars and the downtown core gives it a sophisticated feel that certainly goes beyond its population. It's the best of both worlds: the lefty, progressive sort of folks I am used to when in a big city, yet with a small-town homeyness that makes you want to stay.

The true magic of the layout of the town proper is its bowl shape. Someone decided to put all the bars down near the harbour and the houses all up the hill. When it's seven p.m. on a Tuesday, it takes no mental effort to get off the couch and go out for a beer because it's all downhill. Once there, the overwhelming thought of the trudge up the hill makes you stay for a couple more. Now, I've been to some hilly towns, but this place takes the cake. I wouldn't know from personal experience because we were always there in February, so everybody's geared up for the winter weather, but I suspect the average local must have a hell of a set of gams on them.

I've done the trudge uptown after a night of playing and then taking in a house party or two, and to be honest the walk almost killed me. I was like, "Hey, let's call a cab," and they're all, "Never mind, b'y, sure it's only six blocks," and they'd be smoking and carrying gear. Sherpas would be proud of this lot. It's winter, the sidewalks are slippery, and if the hill were any steeper, you would need stairs to climb it. They're a hardy bunch.

The bars in town are famous, and although we've only played a couple of them, we've drank in a few more. They all seem to embrace the pub atmosphere, smaller places, darkly lit. I'm sure somewhere out there there's a dance club, but I doubt if I'm going to find it.

The music scene is crazy there. First glance, it seems everybody plays in a band, on second glance as well. I think because pretty much everybody plays in a band, it's some kind of bylaw. You might think this would not bode well for an out-of-town band. You would be wrong.

Geographically speaking, St. John's is two days from Sydney, Nova Scotia, and almost three from Halifax. Not that many bands get out there, so when you hit town, you have them waiting for you. Besides, most people who are into live music seem to not mind going out on a Friday night and going to three different places to see three different bands.

Due to the distance, it's good to know that you can book multiple gigs during one visit when playing St. John's. This is not something you should do in most towns without checking first with the venue that booked you. We didn't get any flack from the venues we played for doing three or four nights in a row, even in different bars. If you started on a Wednesday or Thursday, then by the weekend the word is out about you, and if your band is worth its salt, then you're set for a jam-packed Saturday night show, maybe even a Sunday evening to boot. Keep in mind when looking at a $700 ferry trip plus gas across a barren land, it really is the only way to make it pay. (When I say make "pay," of course, I mean break even on the week.)

Things to know when going to St. John's

When saying, "Hello, St. John's," on mic, make sure everyone hears you say St. John's with the *s* at the end. There is a big thing about it being mistaken for Saint John, New Brunswick. If you f. up, the b'ys will call you on it. Second, Newfoundland is pronounced with the accent on *land. Fun* instead of *found* Newfun *land.* It takes practice to get it right. And the last bit of eastern tour band advice is: don't hold back songs for an encore. They want nothing to do with them. They go berserk all through even a mild set of tunes, and at the end, they clap for thirty seconds, down their beer, and take off for the next show. Don't get me wrong, they're the most appreciative audience anywhere. They just don't do encores, at all. It's neat because you just don't have to do those stupid ambiguous encores, and both you and the audience can just get on with the rest of your evening. It's play your set, thanks, and good night.

Noon the day after our gig at the Ship Inn on a winter tour, say, around 2009, we stumbled wearily back into the bar to not only load the gear out but also to have breakfast. Getting to load out and have breakfast all in one place doesn't happen often. Other than some fried rice at three a.m. on one trip, breakfast at the Ship is the only other meal I have eaten in St. John's that wasn't fish and chips. The bar staff and the opening band talked up the breakfast, and breakfast is the one meal that we rely on strictly local info for on the road. We slink into a big wooden banquette, still slightly sticky with beer from the night before, and order up the breakfast special. I think most of us had the egg and sausage. I was told the night before that their breakfast potatoes where amazing, so I made sure to have those too. With the order in, the big-ass clunky coffee cups arrive, and as is usual we grab our coffees and head out to the alley to smoke. A cold and dreary coastal morning awaited us in the stairwell alley that runs between the Ship's side-door entrance and some other nondescript building. The cold air hit my warm, cream-induced, phlegm-filled lungs, and I had a coughing fit that lasted most of my smoke, but when the cough subsided and the proper amount of spitting had taken place, I quite enjoyed the near morning on the stairs looking down on a mostly obscured view of lower

St. John's. Pretty much all the views around town will definitely give you the feeling that you are not at home but in a nice place.

Smoke done, we end up back inside as breakfast comes. Good eggs, okay (if not a little too Quebec reminiscent) sausage, and a big mound of cubed-up and deep-fried potatoes. You'll hear me go on about folks who have lost the art of cooking breakfast potatoes, and I warn you it is a big pet peeve of mine. That is not a home fry. No, that is a big ol', raw-in-the-middle, stubby french fry, mostly burned, and sprinkled with seasoning salt. Ick. Why did they catch on? I generally differ with the rest of the band on the issue of deep-fried potatoes. They are all quite a bit younger than me and do not remember when there were other ways to prepare a spud besides just deep-frying on max temp for forty-five seconds and sprinkling crap on them. Matt is the only one who relents and sides with me, given that he has some English blood in him and has spent some time over in the U.K., and knows the delight of a mushy french fry cooked on lower heat twice, in *lard*. Golden brown is for folks who aren't going to finish their potatoes. Breakfast potatoes have to be fried on a grill, or give me the leftover mashed.

By the light of day, and over breakfast, we witnessed the soundman loading his gear out a side door we had not noticed the night before. Bam…I found the alley he had been using and descended a very steep driveway and managed to park only feet from the door. We are a six-piece band, and a good load out is amazing. This easily beat the load in the night before when we were double-parked on busy Duckworth Street and had to lump down a long flight of stairs.

Fish and chips: the homeland but not the only land

Everyone who has ever ridden in a van with me will agree that I have a thing for fish and chips. If you ride with me on just one road trip, you will end up discussing fish and chips: it's a requirement. I think I am trying to make it back to that time in my life when I was, say, eight years old and living in Cobourg, Ontario.

Every Thursday, my brother Jay had hockey practice (I didn't play hockey due to weak ankles), so Thursday meant post-hockey fish and chips at Lakemens on King Street. It's gone now, but entering then through the steamed-up front door, the smell of frying fish and potatoes hits you and your eight-year-old stomach, and you know you've been so good about not whining about it all through your brother's practice. You go to the counter, two brothers in tow, and Mom orders four regulars. Before hanging up your winter wear, the most magical of eight-year-old magic takes place, and you get to go to the glass-door pop fridge and pick out your own pop. Years ago, all the pop came in those ten-ounce glass bottles, and let me tell you, nothing is cooler than laying your hands on that cold glass bottle of lemon-lime Crush and using the factory-installed bottle opener on the side of the fridge. The cap falling into the hidden compartment where all caps go, with a pop from the pressure release and a clink as the cap clicks its way to the never-seen storage compartment. You're good to go, just old-school pop, no twist-offs, no plastic bottles. You swing back to the counter and grab a straw from the box beside the cash and hang your coat on the coat rack beside your vinyl-covered booth. The three boys jockey for seating positions that eventually have to be sorted out by Mom, and about two minutes later, they bring you your meal.

This was a long time ago, so I don't remember, but I'm going to guess the fish was cod, a fair-sized square. The batter was close to tempura batter except darker, sort of puffed up like a pillow. All puffy and crunchy and light, and the fish was steamy as you bit into it. The fries were hand-cut, parboiled on a lower heat, obviously dipped in lard, and my guess is in a different fryer than the fish. The fries were definitely old-school, Protestant English chip shop stuff. Chewy on the outside, kind of mushy on the inside, but fully cooked, mind you, and nowhere near golden brown. Amazing! This is a lost art.

Here's the problem with fish and chips for me: all fish and chip experiences must live up to that. The state of French fries, vegetable oil, speed, and the depletion of the world's cod stocks have left that a very difficult row to hoe. So I've softened a bit. If they can get just one element of it right, I'm likely to go back, and in some cases I go back anyway.

I mentioned earlier that all band members have to have this conversation with me, but no member of the United Steel Workers of Montreal has taken up the quest for good fish and chips like Steve Brockley. Steve did a couple of road trips with us over the years. He was the fill-in electric guitar player for Matt Watson when Matt was off on paternity leave. Steve did two winter tours and was always on the hunt for fish and chips. After the tour, he went back out on the road with his regular band (the Steve Brockley Band), and his whole band took up the challenge to find the best fish and chips in Canada. They were a three-piece, so it was easier for them to accomplish this, having fewer arguments over eating. Steve and his cohorts are vegetarians. I've found even very   committed veggies tend to flip when touring the East Coast. I guess it's the abundance of fresh-caught seafood that does it. The argument I've heard bandied around is that you are closer to the folks that produce it, so it's less adulterated, more organic in nature. It's a palatable gimme on the road for vegetarians.

Now the big problem with East Coast cuisine is that bands tend to subsist on per diems. In our band, per diem was $20 a day, and out east smokes are, like, $14 a pack, so that leaves you $6 to eat for the day without breaking into your band pay piggy bank for the trip. You obviously do break into your piggy bank, but with an eye on the bill at the end. Most meals fall into the ten-dollar range. Not high-end dining, and let me tell you, the East Coast of Canada is not the place to be trying to find a $10 meal. Don't get me wrong, the food on the East Coast is great, but only great if you are spending $20 or more. Their fast food and diners are the worst on a cross-country basis. With all my years traveling out there, I can easily say that all the worst meals I've had have been on the East Coast with the exception of fish and chips, so let's get back to that.

It's a rainy afternoon mid-week in St. John's, in the middle of a three-nighter at CBTG's (Closest Bar to Gulliver's cab stand). We sat ringing the bar, killing the grey February afternoon drinking what would have been our comped beer for the night. The barmaid, Janet Lee, was great, as were all the staff in this rough-around-the-edges, punked-out club. We start prying Janet for local intel on the best fish and chips in town. "Everyone says Ches's is the best." There were others offered, but Ches's sounded the most like a chippie. We loaded up, and we were off.

I can't remember who came along, but I do remember we

had a remarkable amount of consensus on this issue. We headed up out of the downtown on our quest. We ended up at what had to be the original Ches's, 9 Freshwater Road. It looked like a diner, and it brought me back to my childhood memory. We were seated in the dining room portion of the restaurant, not the diner. We spent a portion of the meal discussing why we hadn't been seated there. There were theories about the food being cheaper over there, but we were a little too fixated on the food to find out. We went 'round the table, and this being touted as the best fish and chips in Canada, everyone got the specialty, all with chips. I remember there being talk about maybe getting ripped off on chips if you got the large three-piece meal. I said, "Best fish in Canada, you better make it a large fish, and chips be damned, plus a Coke."

The food arrived, and damned if that wasn't at least in the top two of the best fish and chips I've had in Canada. The cod (I think) was great, fresh, not even a little bit chewy, the batter not brittle but not soggy, just nice. The fries were, well, almost there, but a little too golden brown for my liking.

Ches's turned out to be in the running for the best fish and chips in Canada. I've eaten there again and had take out since, and I'd say on a good day they are neck and neck for the best. I will divulge the other contender later in the book. I'll give you a hint: it's in Ontario. What, you say? Ontario rivaling Newfoundland for seafood? No, I didn't say that. I said rivaling *fish and chips*. In the end, I really think it comes down to religion. Yep, it's a Catholic/Protestant issue really. In St. John's, you got the Catholics who are right there beside the cod (maybe), you just got to go out and jig it in the face and there you are, b'y, throw some batter on there, and that is that. Sure, but then you got the Protestants with all that chip shop blood running through them, and face it, they were just making fish and chips because there wasn't anything else going on in England during the war-rationing period, so they got good at fish and potatoes and lard. Skip forward, and let's look at Ontario. They have no fish anywhere near them, not since the turn of the last century when the lakes were fished out, and you are in a big old place filled to the brim with Orangemen wanting fish, and bam, they figure out how to cut a deal with the coast, and bam, they got the stuff, took 'er right off the Catholics, and, boy, are they good at cooking it.

In St. John's, I couldn't figure it out. Where the hell did they get that codfish from, anyway? I'm from away and not up on the local ways, but didn't they run out of cod? Either way, she was damn good fish even if it could have been catfish or farmed cod or something else. Hell, wouldn't it have been something if it were Pacific cod? Holy cow, talk about your Federal politics there, b'y.

Goodbye, B'y

It is a bitter pill to wake up on a grey Monday morning in St. John's and know it's time to load out and be on your way. In just one four-day stint, you've made a whole whack of new friends, got to hang out with some old ones, and in some cases, other bands (not ours, as such) have had to decide whether to stay and marry that girl from Saturday night at the Rose and Thistle. You load out, grab some coffee, and sadly hit the road, north or west whichever. Ah, the two-lane going thataway.

Dildo, Newfoundland

I'd love to say that we spent a lovely afternoon lounging on the shore of beautiful Trinity Bay taking in the many wonders the town of Dildo, Newfoundland, has to offer. We didn't. I merely mention it because of the funny name: sorry, Dildo. I'm in a band; we have little time to be tourists, so we ate at the Irving out on the T-Can, not even real close to Dildo at all. The only other noteworthy bit was that there was a picture of Mary Walsh on the wall of the restaurant. I love that old bird. She is on my list of people I'd love to get drunk with. Restaurant moguls everywhere: please keep in mind that it was this picture that made us stop at this restaurant for the second time, even though we didn't like the food. I'm not saying a picture of Mary Walsh would work everywhere, but you never know. What makes folks stop is always hard to define. You could try good food too: some places have made a go of that strategy.

Between Dildo and Gander, there are a lot of rocks and trees. There is also a big old national park, Terra Nova, but mostly it's just two-lane. Here's a tip: on your way to St. John's, the big thing for a band is getting a place to stay. Some bands will just hope that one of the lads gets picked up, and then everyone crashes on the floor of the unsuspecting girl's apartment, damn, sometimes in the room with them. Since the USWM was short on single members, this wasn't an option. Don't get me wrong. As it goes, St. John's is probably the best place to hold out for an offer of free accoms from some locals, cute girl or not. Everybody there owns a house because 'til about eight years ago, they were going for something just above dryer lint on the free market. So there are places to stay. The USWM (being a very large band) was always wary of getting caught out, so we booked hotel rooms for these stays. In the last year or two, we really started getting quite handy with online hotel booking, and Priceline got us some real great deals. To use Priceline, however, you need the Internet. One day, driving down the Trans-Canada about an hour or so north of St. John's, I saw this hotel with a big sign saying *Free Wireless Internet*. We pulled in to see if there was a password on their system, and because it's in the middle of nowhere, there wasn't. Perfect. We pull into the parking lot, park a couple of spaces away from the front entrance, and within minutes we are Hotwiring some accoms for the night.

In other travels, I've found that most GPSs will list the local library. Follow that to the parking lot, and you are online and sorting out your stay just like that.

Gander, Newfoundland: the gateway to the world

Gander, Newfoundland, is a town built on and then beside an airport that was once the last stop fuel depot for all transatlantic flights. Gander has seen them all: from kings and queens to movie stars and politicians. You name them, they have all stopped in this windswept town on their way to elsewhere. The town looks like any other pulp town anywhere on the Trans-Canada as you move west across this country. That is until you notice there isn't a pulp mill and it doesn't stink like sulphur and broken dreams. The next thing that hits you is a big old plane right up near the road. It freaks you out a bit, being red and damn near the road, especially if you're tired because now you're a ways into your day. This is the North

Atlantic Aviation Museum, the kind of place you would stop and take in the full glory of Gander's interesting and colourful past. Although I've heard rumours that Gander has a $300 Friday night gig, I've never found it for our band, and there being no gig there for us, there is no time. It's four and a half hours out of St. John's, so we eat. We pass up the Mary Brown's, the Jungle Jim's (more later), and we've struck Timmy's off of our list by now, so we eat at A&W. We get take-out, hoping to speed things along and sit in the van and fight about the merits of psychobilly music versus listening to the fifth in a series of documentaries by the CBC's *Ideas* on Darwin, this being the episode when he shuns the church and it all starts getting good. I have the Chubby Chicken, and we listen to the *Monster Mash* as we pull back out on the two-lane and Gander recedes in the mirror.

T-Can

There are three distinct vistas of topography to be viewed from the window of a moving vehicle during your trip across Newfoundland in the winter. In the east, there is that rocky, craggy coastal part as you leave St. John's, with trees, hills, and occasional beauty. In the west, there are the mountains. Yes, Newfoundland has mountains, and believe it or not is touted as having the best skiing east of Quebec. Here, as you leave Gander, you are running across the top of the island straight shot to Corner Brook by way of Grand Falls, Windsor, Badger, and South Brook, and it gets intensely forested. People have always referred to Newfoundland as the Rock, and I was not expecting it to have so many trees. Keep in mind these are trees perched up on top of a big old rock in the middle of the ocean, so we aren't talking grandiose redwoods here, just a never-ending tree line of softwood, sort of like Northern Ontario without all the chip trucks.

The Trans-Canada is mostly two-lane highway all the way across, and here is no exception. The miles bleed out as you ponder the reasons why folks have ended up living here, the interior of the big island. Gander has the airport, and now you see the trees playing out to the horizon along the road, obviously pulp and paper. Why folks live where they do has always intrigued me. I grew up in a rural part of Southern Ontario and have been left with the scars of isolation that only a young man without a car can bear. I always find myself asking why people would end up in these unlikely places. The outports of Newfoundland make sense. There was the fish, and you managed all your transportation needs by way of a dory. Man, when it comes down to it, you go where there is work and food. But there are still times when I just think to myself, "Wow, folks moved all the way out here just to work in forestry." It's a living, and I have met a few people in my time who enjoy living nowhere near town, so I guess that is the answer I come to as we cover the vast distance between St. John's and Corner Brook, a few houses and hamlets scattered here and there along the road.

As you tear your way across the top in winter, there are three things that you should be very wary of while driving these roads: moose, trucks, and weather. First off, you got the moose. They are everywhere. Moose are not indigenous to the island but were introduced back in 1904. Somebody thought it would be a good idea to have some moose running around so they had something to shoot at come fall, oh, and probably thought that it might be good to have something to eat come winter. It was a success: two bulls and two cows were released, and lo and behold, small gene pool aside, there are now over 150,000 of them, which means there is about one moose for every three people who live on the island. From a moose standpoint, this seems to be great, but, man, moose are big, real big, and take up room. So much so that they have spilled out of the woods and right into middle of the Trans-Canada. Spotting wildlife became a bit of a thing for our band. When traveling, you want to say, "Oh ya, saw a bear out west and a few deer through Ontario, killed a bunch of frogs and a bird," but when it happens, and you see that big old bull coming at you, it really gets the adrenaline going. For my money, if you're hoping to see a moose, then the trip across Newfoundland is a sure thing.

Now adrenaline and nature ogling aside, moose crush cars and kill people. They are like the Godzilla of wildlife, big enough to take out tractor-trailers, no kidding. Keep a sharp eye out, and avoid at all costs. On the couple of trips we took from Port aux Basques to St. John's, I think we had two sightings—both in the middle of snowstorms. Some handy driving and good luck had to take place for us to come out with no casualties.

Trucks are the other things going on this stretch of the T-Can. From 1898 until 1988, Newfoundland had a railway dubbed the "Newfie Bullet." It was a narrow-gauge line that was absorbed by CN in 1949 after Newfoundland entered Confederation, and it ran until twenty-odd years ago when it was abandoned and replaced by the Trans-Canada Highway. Although there is a ferry that runs to Argentia in the summer, trucks generally take the shorter, cheaper Port aux Basques ferry and drive over the top on the Trans-Canada. Combine them with the moose and you've got some white-knuckled driving going on as the trucks fly by you in a steady stream.

Then there is the weather. It's East Coast weather at its finest. You got the rain (which it does a lot); you got the wind coming down out of those mountains and mixing it up with the sea currents; and, believe me, you got the snow. We've plowed through some terrible slogs.

Putting this all together, I have a tip. One night, we were pulling out of Stephenville, Newfoundland, at three a.m. because we were not too impressed with what might have been our accoms for the night. Frankly, Stephenville on a Tuesday in the middle of winter scared us. Even though there was a blizzard going on and the snow was just coming down in blankets, we decided to make the run for St. John's and do it as an overnight trip. At any given time, there was almost a foot of snow on the road, and there were trucks, and we were all up on the dash of the van looking out for moose. When the weather was real bad, I was the go-to driver, leaning on my experience of being a professional truck driver, and I developed a system to get us through this unique set of circumstances. It's easy: find a truck and stick close. I figure, hell, they know the road better than me, they are breaking a trail, and if a moose jumps out, they'll get 'em first. The downside to this is you are only going to make the same time as the truck, but I know from years gone by that slow but steady wins. All you are going to see is snow flying around the back of a truck, and you will probably piss off the truck driver who's going to keep getting your lights all up in his mirrors, so keep your low beams on and try not to bug them too much, and then just hang on for thirteen-odd hours and you're there. It's not a great plan, but it got us across the Rock one night.

Grand Falls-Windsor, Newfoundland

We've passed through the old GF-W a few times on our travels, and it always struck me as extraordinarily big for being way out here. The town (established back at the turn of the last century) boasts a population of just over 13,000 souls. It had one main industry: a paper mill. On one of our last trips to Newfoundland, we happened to be passing through Grand Falls on the day that the paper mill had announced that after 100-odd years of being one of the biggest employers in the neighbourhood, they were closing down. It seems weird that, in all our travels, we managed to be passing through this town on such a sombre day, possibly the biggest news day Grand Falls-Windsor had had in quite some time. I remember they were interviewing a local gent who had been a mill worker all his life, and as a tribute to the news, he had written a song. I don't remember his name, and I'm probably going to get it wrong, but the gist of the song would be…

AbitibiBowater, why are you leaving,

AbitibiBowater, why, why, why,

AbitibiBowater, why are you leaving,

Why are you screwing with Newfoundland?

It seemed a bit of mournful lark of a song, but it stuck with us for quite a while, a real hit. A year or two later, for some reason (probably some news bit about pulp and paper came on), and Matt broke into the song, and everyone in the van started singing along. Everyone except Dylan Perron, who sat there in astonishment having only recently arrived to the band. When the fourth chorus finished, he asked, "Where did you get that song?" We explained about the news piece, and he said knowledgeably, "Oh ya, they are closing Grand Falls-Windsor and a bunch of other places, but the one in my hometown managed to survive the cut."

"Oh," I said, "that's the paper mill you work in when not touring?"

"Ya, that's it," he said in a "there but for the grace of God go I" sort of way.

This kicked off another rousing chorus.

AbitibiBowater, why are you leaving,
AbitibiBowater, why, why, why,
AbitibiBowater, why are you leaving,
Why are you screwing with Newfoundland?

Seriously, though, we have seen this sort of thing many times over: a town in decline and fighting to survive. I hope the folks up there are doing okay in the wake of the Abitibi-Bowater closing. Thank you to that gentleman for writing the song, which helps us remember.

Corner Brook, Newfoundland

Pulling off the Trans-Canada on a cold winter night, having hauled ass full tilt for the whole day, we descend into Corner Brook and make our way through the big-box store part of town on wide roads with all the conveniences that would be known to any fair-sized Canadian town. We stop for supplies at the big-box pharmacy, and the van disgorges us to buy cold medication and other sundries. Yes, it's early on in the tour and there are many months yet to go, but already it is time to start loading up on vitamin C, B complex, E, Rescue Remedy, pine oil, Halls, Kleenex, Neo-Laryngobis, Preparation H, and that green, yogurty drink. These are the things that bands run on to get them through the tour. Some preach vegetarianism, some do push-ups, some take stress meds, homeopathy, or swear off smokes before shows. But everybody over the age of twenty-four in a band van seems to have some health regime. The kids under twenty-four generally just drink their way through the tour and then quit the band at the end of the tour because they are scared they have become alcoholics, which of course they have. Those older than twenty-four are hard, act-touring folk, in for the long haul, and they fall into their own personal health life preservers when it's winter on the road and they are playing shows up to six nights a week.

As a vocalist, and being the eldest member of the band, and the most prone to ills and ailments, I have found myself on all manner of cure-alls. At one point, coming across the Prairies, I think I was taking something like twelve pills at a time at least twice a day for one thing or another. These were not the Michael Jackson speedballs of ketamine mixed with blood treatments, but just vitamins, cold remedies, and homeopathic fare, with maybe some Flomax and Advil thrown in. It takes a lot to get a gravelly voice through a long winter trip.

Meds acquired, we descend further into the residential part of town, and it gets quite quaint. With plunging hills and high, steep snow banks, it has a quintessential Canadian small-town winter feel to it. The town slants down towards the harbour, and you thank God they sanded the road, and you manage to stop before you find the West Coast all up in your cab. Hunting around town, you find your venue. We've played the University Pub and we've played Whelan's Gate. That night, we were loading into the Gate. The room feels like and reminds me of a very small hockey rink, with drink tickets and a soundman. Yay! It's mid-week, and even though we are not expecting a large crowd, the folks out here are very nice, so we don't mind.

Speaking of nice folks, our promoter, Neal Target, shows up. I'm not trying to give the idea that all promoters aren't nice guys and that this is weird because usually promoters don't come to gigs, but let's say them being nice and actually showing up at the club happens few enough times that this is a noteworthy event. Add to it that Neal is there before sound check and has a fistful of drink tickets and directions for how to get back to his house, where we are being put up, and you have a way to make friends in the industry and make folks feel welcome in a strange place.

Adding to the pleasures of the evening, Gwilym (our road manager) made us dinner in his pressure cooker that night, a soupy, chickeny thing with some rice and what-not. Home-cooked food on the road is great, even when cooked backstage before sound check. Gwilym was always good for that sort of thing. We only used him on the one big tour because having a seventh man around is a bit luxurious, and to be honest, we didn't think we were going to break even on the tour, anyhow. I think Gwilym got paid about three months after we got back from tour and had played enough local shows to catch him up. But for that tour, we had a driver, a cook, a referee, a merch girl, and a babysitter. We were sitting pretty, and there in Corner Brook, we were eating home cooking.

The night went well. We played the show behind this half wall: it was like playing from the bench of a hockey game, or worse, the penalty box. It gave me a funny feeling that they were trying to keep the audience away from the band. The stage had that chicken wire sort of feel. It was weird, but the small crowd we had out at The Gate that night did not try to bodycheck us. They were what we were getting to know as a typical Newfoundland crowd: nice, as well as into it. You could even say exuberant.

Corner Brook is a tough town for a touring band. A small town of, say, 25,000 people, it holds the record for having never grown. It has been 25,000 folks for almost as long as it has been a town, not getting bigger or smaller. Just nice enough so folks don't move away and not so great folks are streaming in. Stable.

The problem for touring bands is logistics. Road venues that are not in big towns have to face the realities of geography. For a town the size of Corner Brook (it being a mostly blue collar sort of place), the burgeoning ski industry notwithstanding, most of your best turnout is going to be on a Friday or Saturday night. The problem is that if you play there on Friday, that means you won't get to St. John's until Saturday. And the crowds that come out on a Friday night for a not-yet-established band don't make it worth missing Friday night in St. John's. It's a tough call, but I always figured doing an early Tuesday or Wednesday night show to fewer but more exuberant people (so we could plow through for a weekend on the east side of the island) would be our strategy. For regional bands that are going to make it out there more than once a year, maybe it's a better idea to mix it up and start developing the smaller towns right across the island. Keep in mind, bands who are already on the island or from the East Coast of Canada also face lower costs getting there, not having to drive all the way from the centre of the world, or at least just east of the centre of the world (which is Ontario). I would have liked to take two weeks to do Newfoundland and do all the towns. It was just never possible for us.

It does give me hope that with guys like Neal Target (and Mighty Pop, the promotion company he works with), perhaps we will see a day when this is all easier to pull off. If the folks in Corner Brook want to see more bands, maybe some work could be done to start booking Stephenville, Grand Falls, and Gander, which would give bands more of a reason to spend an extra week on the island. Towns or regions of Canada are successful at booking touring bands because there are folks like Neal making it happen. It takes years of organizing to build, and bars and bands are not the easiest groups to get to work and play well together. When things are happening somewhere, it can usually be traced back to a butt-load of work that one person or a small group of people have done. I see it starting to happen in Newfoundland. Mighty Pop, keep it up.

The next morning, we are up and back on the road.

Stephenville, Newfoundland

Stephenville, Newfoundland, has the bold distinction of having belonged to five different nations in the last 100-odd years, and they didn't have to move a foot. In the beginning, it was home to the Mi'kmaq, then was part of a colony of Britain, then it joined the Dominion of Newfoundland in 1907, and then in 1940 it became a U.S. airforce base, until they abandoned her to what had become Canada. That's a lot for a little town to go through in just a hundred years, and it has the scars to prove it.

To give the town its due here, I don't think February is tourist high season for Stephenville. As you pull in to this low-lying town built from cement blocks, the first thing you see is this big, life-size fighter jet stuck up on a pole against the backdrop of what looks like military dorms that make up a big part of the housing in town. Even the bright, multi-coloured paint jobs on those buildings do not break through the bleakness of a cold February late afternoon. Turns out that way back in forties, the U.S. government swindled the English into leasing the adjacent land to the American military for 100 years in trade for a bunch of mothballed warships. The Brits, staring at German forces across the Channel in France, reluctantly accepted the deal and, under American arm-twisting, threw in a few other island nations like the Bahamas, Trinidad, Jamaica, and St. Lucia to boot. The Yanks built a big old air force base right up beside the town of Stephenville and proclaimed it U.S. territory.

The town seemed to benefit in a weary sort of way from this arrangement over the years. There were jobs and U.S. servicemen spending money, and the population of the town doubled to reach its peak of somewhere around 6,500 people. The town and the Ernest Harmon Air Force Base have had a rocky history: servicemen were once discouraged from partaking in all the town had to offer, with the air force even specifying women, families, and businesses to stay away from.

We had our best luck stealing Internet from the local library, downloading our emails as we sat freezing in the parking lot. A population of 6,500 does after all have a difficult time supporting modern-day commerce, and after scoping out the available restaurants (two Chinese restaurants and a Subway franchise), we ate sandwiches in our van in the parking lot of the Sobeys.

It was at this point in our first trip that I realized that Subway has left a strange mark on the culinary makeup of Canada's small-town restaurant horizon. I have been back and forth across Canada several times over the years and have studied the phenomenon that is small-town Chinese food. If you have a town that has a population, or at least a surrounding area population, of 4,000, then you have a Chinese restaurant. I've always found it fascinating that Chinese culture allows for a family picking up from either Mainland China, or possibly Toronto or Vancouver, and heading out to the middle of anywhere Canada to open a Chinese restaurant. In these places they will be the only Chinese family in town. They arrive with enough start-up money to acquire a restaurant and then set out to expand the palates of the locals. They bring all the finest foods available, thousands of years of cooking history, and there in a small restaurant lay siege. The battle ends in a draw. The business becomes mildly successful (as it is, in most cases, the only restaurant in town) offering both full, sit-down meals and takeout, good for a Friday night first date, or a late-night, post-bar feeding frenzy. The two worlds battle, and the population eventually persuades the proprietors to boil their menu down to chicken fried rice and sweet and sour chicken (known locally as chicken balls), commonly known as Special Number 1. I have enjoyed this in almost every town we have stopped in.

Subway (the nationally recognized chain of sandwich stores) is in the running to unbalance this weird and cool demographic balance that Canadian culture and Chinese culture have struck dating back to the building of the railways or even to Confederation. The franchising of small towns has always been a numbers game. In 1978, when my hometown hit a population of 9,000 souls, the granddaddy of all chains anointed us with a McDonald's. It was a rush back in those heady days. I remember a line-up around the store for weeks after that first franchise opened. There were people standing in line for the better part of an hour to taste the wares of this big, modern, American invention. McDonald's came up with this population system: if you have the right number of people, we will build it.

Over the years, almost every other restaurant chain has implemented this system, all having different numbers with which to deem an outlet viable. Here's the rub: over the years, Subway has lowered that population bar to a level set just above that of the mom and pop Chinese restaurant. And I would say that this war has been brought to the doorstep of every Chinese family that has taken up the challenge of making a go of it in the wilds of rural and semi-rural Canada. Subway with its "fresh," or at least chemically enhanced and stasis-induced vegetables, its pre-prepared savoury wares, and below-belt taste sensations like chipotle sauce may have spelled the beginning of the end for the intricate and begrudging relationship we have had with Asian culture over the last 100 years. I myself am defending the Chinese-Canadian presence in small-town Canada by consuming as many chicken balls as I can in every town I where I find them, in the hope that this tradition continues and the "Man" that is Subway falters in this battle against locally cooked food. Support your local businesses and ask for duck sauce!

We finish our Sobeys dinner and head for the venue. Clancy's bar is in the semi-basement of a larger structure that seemed to house a dance club or a restaurant or something else that was closed while we were there. I would assume that it was an off-season sort of thing, or maybe even a mid-week thing. The upside is that we were the only entertainment that was going to happen in that town that night. I think it was Wing Night to boot. Wing Night can be a help or a hindrance: it brings out the people, but then they expend most of their energy applying ranch dressing to chicken products and consequently ignoring whoever happens to be on-stage. It was a mixed bag of an evening. There were quite a few people out, and there were more than a couple who were really into our show. Big thanks to the supporters of touring bands. There were folks out to drink as well, and this was the town that officially screeched us in. Somewhere into the third song, I looked over to see our road manager making out with a local girl he had apparently just met. It was heady times.

Being "screeched in" has many variables on the island of Newfoundland, and here in Stephenville, it was drinking shots of screech and then kissing a puffin's arse. It was a stuffed puffin, the kind you would get at a tourist shop down by the war memorial. Knowing these fine types of traditions from other towns on my travels, I knew that there was a great chance that the object to be kissed, as with the Blarney stone, could have been defiled by local youth who would go there in off hours to drink and piss on the stone to show their distaste for the tourist onslaught. I was justly wary of the puffin. For all I knew, they could have rubbed this stuffed puffin's ass on a real puffin's ass, or worse, on any random local's ass. But after one more shot of screech, I kissed it. The drinking went on and the shots of screech kept up all night for the band, accompanied by offers to lead us to the local whorehouse. For a town of this size, the claim of prostitutes galore to be had by folks who were looking for that sort of thing left me wondering if there really was a whorehouse or were they just mucking with us. We did not find out if these rumours of a den of iniquity were true.

Screech, for those who have missed being screeched in, is rum. It's high-proof rum from the days when the islanders did a roaring trade with Jamaican sailors. Fish for booze, now that is a great arrangement: turning over big, ugly fish for crazy-strong, mean-tasting booze. The transaction ended up making fish the national dish of Jamaica and screech the national beverage of Newfoundland. Rumour has it that American G.I.s named this rum *screech* after trying to shoot it like normal whiskey and ending up screaming when they noticed the difference.

Wreckhouse, Newfoundland

Winding down out of the Long Range Mountains, the highway starts to flatten out, as you are now rolling along the base of the mountains and it starts hugging the west coast of the island. The simple mass of the mountain range and its proximity to the sea causes a unique weather anomaly. Wind. Now some places got wind, and some places got high winds, but this place has what is known as *wreckhouse* wind. It's become a quasi-meteorological term meaning higher than most wind speeds. As you plow on through this area located just north of Port aux Basques, you see a sign that says *Wreckhouse*, so you think that you are coming into a town, but really it's just this flat bit of ground at the base of the mountains. I think there might be a wrecked house or two, just for effect.

As the story goes, there was this old guy who lived right around that area, for a real long time, and his sole employment was letting the Newfoundland Railway know whether it was windy enough to blow their trains off the track or not. He died in 1965 and his wife took over for a couple more years after that, but then they closed the railway and she moved away from that bleak old place.

Channel-Port aux Basques, Newfoundland

We're gong to detour to Port aux Basques here. Port aux Basques is the gateway to Newfoundland, at least in the winter when the Argentia ferry is not in operation. Standing on deck of the ferry on a blustery February evening as it navigates the outer harbour approaching the Marine Atlantic terminal docks, one is pummeled with the relentless icy winter wind and the term "The Rock" comes to mind with full force. Later on, you will find that Newfoundland has trees and mountains and moose and bars and cities, but as the ship docks, you are looking at Port aux Basques: a grey rock cut covered in snow, evoking a lunar station or an Arctic Circle base camp carved out of igneous, giving you the unfathomable idea that there is an entire group of 450,000 people who have eked out a living over the years standing in the middle of the ocean, perched on a rock.

You drive into the small, craggy town of Port aux Basques, a town that was built having never dug a foundation or blasted a hole in the ground. The small clapboard houses sit perched on top of rocks, and the streets follow the curve of boulders as you navigate the main drag.

It's a port town, the ferry terminal for the island. It's where all the trucks make landfall, and where Newfoundlanders say goodbye to home when leaving for the west and where travelers arrive. It's also where the first telegraph cable hit the ground back in 1865 as it headed east to be part of the transatlantic cable program. The Trans-Canada Highway also disappears beneath the waves here to continue in North Sydney, Nova Scotia. The town surrounds the deep-water port, which, although not attractive in the winter, bustles with ferries coming and going every day. One would assume most of the town's 4,300 inhabitants have something to do with the terminal and the comings and goings of people and freight.

As a touring band, we found a haven here in Channel-Port aux Basques: the Shark Cove Inn. The motel is located conveniently in the suburban part of town, which means you get to roll all the way through town before you get there, having stopped at the grocery store before getting into the downtown proper. Our van stuffed with provisions, we follow plywood signs cut out to look like sharks with their noses pointed mostly in the direction you would need to go to find the Inn. What a haven this motel is. To a band on the road for many a night, and this night being a night we do not have a scheduled gig, we are looking for the comforts of home, and the Cove provides. Pulling into a very wide parking lot covered in ice, we see three or four two-story buildings with outside balconies sided in painted plywood. We locate the office, and after some dickering and maybe lying about how many people we have in the van, we settle on a price and move into our digs.

Here we find a small three-bedroom apartment, fully furnished, including kitchen and utensils. That means we get to cook for ourselves and relax. The band fans out and rooms are claimed, roommates chosen. I grab the room at the end of the hall that isn't really a bedroom as much as a utility closest with a cot and no window, but the door closes and I don't have a roommate. This is the Holy Grail while touring in a six-piece band. I get my own room, and I heave my bag on the bed. This is our way of marking territory. We have this ritual in all hotels, and no matter how grand or cramped, the ritual is the same; you enter the room and heave your bag on the bed, where it stays awaiting dispute. It would be considered far too forward to strip down and rub your naked filthy body on the bed to mark your spot for the night. We developed the bag system instead. Those who perused my room decided having a roommate or taking the couch in the living room is a better deal than sleeping in the windowless room, and my claim goes unchallenged.

Rooms claimed, we start a pecking order for showers. Six folks, having driven hard and played every night, at some point pass on showers in exchange for more sleep, or maybe couch-surfing just doesn't leave enough hot water for everybody. As you savour your night off, you think, "Man, being clean for the first time in a couple of days is really quite appealing." The showers sched also makes room in the kitchen as everybody starts cooking. The KD comes out, the Rice-a-

Roni, the chili or pasta starts cooking, and the band settles in with a couple of cases of beer for a night off the road, and night of the board game Risk, which we find in a cupboard. A night when we don't have to get up in front of a bunch of people and hawk our wares. It's quiet even with the close quarters and a mild amount of bickering and disputes over board games. After a week of arguing about set lists, wakeup times, routing, microphones, monitor mixes, and restaurants, it's good to argue about something petty and unimportant like a board game.

Port aux Basques for us, as for thousands of Basque sailors over hundreds of years, is a haven.

MV *Joseph and Clara Smallwood*

It's rare in your travels that you're present to make history. Witnessing the closing of a venue that had been in operation for years, the opening of a new bridge, the closing of a highway, or in this case sailing on a ship that has now been retired and sold to a foreign nation to be run aground on the other side of the world (Alang, India). History cut apart and sold for scrap.

In our travels, I had the pleasure to ride aboard the MV *Caribou*, the MV *Leif Ericson*, and the MV *Joseph and Clara Smallwood*, and I must say the latter gets my vote for the best crossing of the Gulf of Saint Lawrence.

The six-inch-thick steel plate loading deck hits the dock, and the bustle of loading and offloading commences. Fear wafts over me as a newcomer to sea travel. You might have had a lifetime to come to grips with terms of buoyancy, even watched programs on shipbuilding and naval conquest, but it's not 'til you see that big thick steel plate hit the dock, and some guy in a hunting vest waving at you to proceed loading your van, and you look out towards the grey February horizon with the wind pulling up vast swells of the sea that you start asking questions. How can something made of steel and weighing 5,522,800 pounds (not including cargo and a crew of 106 people) float? The twenty-year-old, 180-metre boat is rammed head first, bow splayed open, and big old ropes hold her in place. The engine is engaged and idling way back at the rear of the boat, but you are still afraid that your wee little van is going to somehow move this grand lady. It doesn't, and the guy in the hunting vest steers you forward into a high-school-gym-sized bowel, which is the truck deck of the vessel. Our van is little in the belly of this beast but is still too tall for the regular car decks, so we get to park with the tractor-trailers and the 4x4s. The *Smallwood* has a capacity of 1,200 passengers, 370 cars, or 77 tractor-trailers. It's winter, so most of the cargo is tractor-trailers. There are a handful of 4x4s with ski-doo trailers, plus you, and a heck of a lot of trucks. After you park in your designated spot (trying desperately to remember the deck), you hike upstairs to the passenger decks to find that way up there the boat is mostly empty because it is the off-season. The 100 or so drivers and passengers fan out across the length of the ship to partake in her wonders.

The band, as is our usual MO, disperses, looking to explore mostly on our own, hoping to find adventures to talk about when next we meet up. The ship's crew quarters and off-limits areas take up a lot of the boat. Then there are sleeping quarters. These can be good for overnight trips but are generally used for the long, fourteen-hour trip to Argentia, which runs only in the summer months. From September to May, it's too rough to attract clientele or to ensure that the trucks don't move around in the decks to be a viable transport system. These berths remain mostly empty on this run of 180 kilometres from Port aux Basques to North Sydney, a six-hour trip if all goes well. Deck 5 has a bunch of great big old rooms with low ceilings and recliner chairs. Sitting in them, you realize they are not La-Z-Boys and are only good for relaxing under the most extreme circumstances. We find the bar in the middle of the ship's deck, but it's not open yet, so we find the lunch bar before running up another set of stairs to go outside on the upper deck to watch as the ship departs port.

It's something to see this massive machine pull a 180-degree turn almost on the spot here in this suddenly not-so-big harbour. I am one of a group of other newbies to venture to the front of the boat to make sure that they have closed the cargo doors and lowered the boat's formidable front visor. Folks who take this trip often trust the crew to make sure that all is buttoned up before leaving harbour. Then again, you remember that video about that ferry in Italy where they left the doors open and she went under like a stone, so it's good to maybe check the crew's work just to be safe. As the *Smallwood*'s bow comes around and aims her seaward, the wind starts hitting you real hard and cold, and you hold your hat as you bid adieu to the island.

It happens slowly as you get farther from shore, having retreated back inside where it's warm. You only notice the rolling of the ship as you walk, feeling as though you have had a couple of beers. You sit for a while, and then after about an hour of sitting in one of the chairs by the window (there are white caps), the boat really starts getting going. It's a boat, you're on the fifth floor, and this is a bit of shock, but it is February and you have been warned. It is not a storm like you see the boats on the Discovery Channel navigating. These are just some reasonably normal winds coming in from the Atlantic Ocean and you are in the trench, or *beam sea*. You start to think about all the advice your mom gave you about sea travel, as it is her wont to take cruises around the Caribbean. This is the Gulf of Saint Lawrence, and for the most part, this is normal. But Mom said you should try sitting in the middle of the boat and not near a window, so you go to the bar. I'm not sure if this was the reason for putting the bar directly over the keel, but it does help a little, and you get a beer.

A few hours into your trip, you decide to try out the cafeteria, and you finally get to sample a fantastic, if not the quintessential, version of CD&G. Yes, Newfoundland's answer to poutine is chips, dressing, and gravy. The dude food crowd in Newfoundland are rolling their eyes because I waited for this opportunity to mention CD&G, but it was on the *Smallwood* where I first had it, and I maintain I've had no better. For me, those McCain crinkle cut fries and that chicken gravy slathered over Stove Top stuffing, now that was the highlight. And for a reasonable price, something under $5, was the meal deal for the trip.

This meal deal came in handy later on. Herein lies tip number one for winter sea travel. Newfoundland ferries travel on their own timetable that is dictated by the sea. You've taken planes and trains and driven around a lot, there are cabs and buses and hitchhiking, but the latter is the only thing close to being as time reliable as the ferry. We learned on our way to

Newfoundland that the scheduled departure time for the boat can and does get changed at the whims of the wind and sea conditions. That left us driving full tilt across Cape Breton one evening having only late in the day checked the revised earlier departure time for an evening sail. We made it by minutes and were the last vehicle to get on the boat with the doors closing behind us before we even got the van in park. In winter especially, check the sailing times by phone. The boat may depart *hours* before its scheduled time.

Three hours into a very blustery, rolling trip on the way back to Nova Scotia, and just when you are getting tired of the pitching and think that for sure you will start to see land soon and be able to hold down dinner, the ship stops pitching. All goes calm and you think, "Hey, great, this is just nice," and then one of your bandmates walks up and says, "Hey, look out the window: *ice.*" You run up the stairs and out on deck to find that the wind has not died down, no, you're surrounded by ice. The happy part is that, yes, a big old foot-thick sheet of ice does put a damper on the waves, but it also slows the boat down. Suddenly, your schedule of just-on-time arrival in North Sydney and a quick trip down to Sydney proper for your gig at Governor's Pub goes out the window. As you lean on the rail, which has now attracted other spectators, you ask a local-looking guy, "Hey, ah, does this boat have a problem getting through ice?" The local says, "Well, she is ice rated, so she ain't gonna sink, but that doesn't mean she won't get stuck."

I learn about the Gulf of Saint Lawrence. It flows out into the sea, but come winter, the winds are coming out of the east, which means a lot of open water to rage across before reaching where we find ourselves now, here in the big old funnel that is the Gulf. The wind picks up the sea and propels it into massive waves and grabs any chunk of ice in the way and starts running it headlong towards the top of the Cape Breton, causing a massive ice jam that can extend for hundreds of kilometres. The bigger the jam, the more pressure it exerts across the jam. Our little boat goes slower and slower as the clock ticks toward sound check time.

After about another hour on the sea, or at least in sea ice, the MV *Joseph and Clara Smallwood* comes to a halt. We are now in full view of land. From the not so windy side of the boat, we have a great view of the top of Cape Breton, and you can see all the ice rammed into the bay, which is still maybe a good hour away in good weather. The ship's PA system booms with a message from the Captain, who takes only a few minutes to sum up that the pack ice has slowed and stopped our progress and we are awaiting the Coast Guard icebreaker to finish clearing the North Sydney Harbour, which is when they will come out and dig a hole for us to follow in. It shouldn't be more than a couple of hours. I look into my pack of smokes. I realize there's a problem. I had only planned on being on this boat for six hours.

This brings me to winter sea travel tip number two. Bring smokes and money. Ever since smoking rules started getting tighter and it started getting hard to find places to sit indoors to enjoy your smoke, it also started to be harder to find places to buy them. Back in the nineties, they started to ban the sale of them in pharmacies. Around then, they stopped being available on ferries as well. Here you are and your six-and-a-half-hour trip is now looking like a twelve-hour trip, and you don't have enough smokes. Fortunately, most of the other passengers aren't from the centre of Canada, so they have anticipated this and have brought extra, but there aren't a lot of folks on this boat and everybody in your band has just realized the same thing you did. You start rationing and going out of your way to strike up conversations with people who look smarter than yourself.

The other thing you realize is that you are going to miss your gig, and that means you are going to miss your free meal. There are bank machines on board, but this now means you are going to go over budget on today's meals. Dinner number two for the day is settled on, another dose of CD&G.

The cellphone reception you were expecting to have is not going to happen for quite some time. Fortunately, the other members of your band are not as dimwitted as you are and have cell coverage because their service providers have coverage where they say they do.

I am a pretty tech-savvy sort of guy. I can't figure out how to program a multifunction remote, but I show up on tour expecting to do a whole lot of tour management sort of stuff kitted out with laptop and cellphone. I am familiar with cell networks. You put up a cell tower and, depending on tower strength and altitude and land masses being in the way, you flick a switch and Bob's your uncle: coverage. This map is based on best-case scenarios, and if you don't have the brand new phone and it is raining or snowing or there is a forest fire in the neighbourhood, maybe that map won't be as accurate as it claims. My problem is not with the hardware and its deficiencies or this big old country with our very sparse population. No, sir, the problem I have is with that little faux-hawked brat from Dollard-des-Ormeaux, sitting in some cubicle, trying to sell me an upgrade to my current iPhone 4. I stupidly answered a call marked *Blocked Number,* and here's little Timmy taking over the world with hair products trying to argue that their plans beat all other phone providers in Canada. I retort that I just traveled five times across Canada and, yes, I do like my plan and I am very happy with the local service in all the major cities, but sorry, sir, twelve feet outside of any major town, everyone but me in our van (representing every cellphone maker and service provider in Canada) has cell reception. I yell, "I actually am that guy from the commercial standing in the field with the grey jacket and the black-rimmed glasses who used to be on that TV show *Two Guys, a Girl and a Pizza Place,* and he is saying 'Can you hear me now?' and in my case, no one responds!"

Rant aside, I find Filly, who is talking to the venue and explaining our situation. We have already missed sound check, and the opening band is tuning up.

Being stuck, we did the only thing we could do: we begged the crew until they let us sack out in the bunk section of the boat for free and try to get some sleep. This was an unsettling experience, lying with my head against the outside wall of the ship and listening to the boat scrape its way through the pack ice as it inched nearer to the Port of North Sydney with the assistance of an icebreaker, which was running backwards in front of us, trying desperately to chop its way through the pack with its propellers.

Missing a gig is not something the United Steel Workers take lightly. We have punched through blizzards, breakdowns, and poorly scheduled tours and have missed only two. The first one was in Luneburg, Germany. We did make it to that one, but when we entered the bar (which seemed nice enough at the time), we noticed that its clientele were all angry, post-World War Two types with Rottweilers who didn't seem to want us there. Sensing our brand of Americana was not going to sweeten their hearts, we beat a hasty retreat and headed for Berlin.

The six-inch loading platform hit the dock in Sydney at two-thirty a.m. just as Governor's was closing a twenty-five-minute drive away. There we are, a six-piece band in their van having made dry land. It's the middle of the night, we are out of smokes, and we are facing paying maybe $200 for hotel rooms that we will only spend a couple of hours in, and we need a saviour. In the dark, windy parking lot of the Marine Atlantic staging area, we find one.

Nova Scotia

Road saviours

I have a propensity to refer to men from the East Coast of Canada as *Jimmy*. This is because of a buddy back home named Brendan who puts on his *ah shucks* personality and goes on drunken ramblings, mostly in pantomime, about thick steaks, Indy pit crews, sauce vs. gravy, and how everybody on the East Coast is named Jimmy. We call him Jimmy, and so, for the purposes of this story, we will refer to our saviour as Jimmy, mostly because I have forgotten his name. I'm pretty sure it wasn't Jimmy and that I'm a bad person, but we move on.

We're sitting in the lot trying to figure out where to go because it's now three a.m. and it's, cold and staying the whole night in the van would be just damn depressing and more than a little uncomfortable.

This truck with four big lads pulls up next to us, rolls down the window, and says, "So, where you guys going?"

Jimmy is the middle-aged fishing boat captain I'd been bumming smokes off of all night as we watched the coast guard cutter chew ice. We reply that we are looking for smokes and I guess a hotel. He says, "I think I know where there is a convenience store. Follow me," as he passes us a mitt full of smokes out the window of his truck, which we gladly take and then follow him.

We drive around a bit in middle-of-the-night downtown North Sydney to no avail. Jimmy pulls up in front of a closed convenience store and we get out to talk. He says, "Well, that's her right there. I guess you've had 'er," or something like that. He thinks a moment and says, "I got smokes down in my hunting cabin 'bout a half hour from here. You can stay there too if you want. We are just gonna drive through and home to Lunenburg tonight, so there is room for all of ya." (Once again, I'm a bad person 'cause I don't think it was Lunenburg, and I should have remembered.) I think about it for about a millisecond and say, "Yes, sir, that would be great." We jump back into the van and we start following Jimmy and his crew, who look like big old guys raised on the sea, and I fill the band in on the plan as we roll out into the wilds of Cape Breton.

The band is a little undecided on this plan, having no real idea who it is we are following. We're all adults here and have gotten used to the old adage, "If it's too good to be true, then it probably is." At the same time, we are in Cape Breton, and everybody says these are the nicest folks in the entire world. And it would seem really dickish to just stop following him. And even if we did want to stop following him, how could we? Pull off the road? Where? How would that work? We resolve to follow him up a snow-covered dirt road and face whatever fate is waiting for us.

About a half-hour into the trip, we find ourselves up this winding one-lane back road, sitting in front of a small but cozy-looking cabin. Jimmy jumps out first and runs inside to light the fire. We all take a bit of time grabbing our bags out of the van and then shuffle on into the cabin. By the time we get in there, Jimmy's got the stove all fired up and he says, "Oh ya, smokes." He bolts into one of the bedrooms and returns a moment later holding two cartons of cigarettes. He says, "I got 'em on the rez. Five bucks a pack. Do you want Player's or Export 'A's?" We divvy up the smokes and he points out two cases of beer in the fridge. "Make yourself at home." And as quick as that, he says, "There's some KD in the cupboard, make sure you turn the heat down and lock the door when you leave. It was good meeting you. Let me know if you are playing a show down the south end of Nova Scotia. Maybe we can make it," and him and his boys jump back in the truck and they're gone. I'm not kidding. Gone. Just like that.

Now, here's the disclaimer: If some dude comes up to you in a parking lot and tells you to follow him up this dirt road for a half-hour or so and there will be beer and smokes and a fireplace, I'm not saying that you should go all running after him 'cause the Steel Workers say so. You never know what can happen. Chances are, if you follow that guy, it's going to end up like that scene in *Pulp Fiction* where Bruce Willis and Ving Rhames are tied up in the bottom of a pawnshop with things not looking so good. The way this scene ended for us was a surprise, and mind you, in ten years of traveling, we haven't been surprised all that much. It's a simple equation really. How bad do you really want to wake up five hours later, parked in front of a convenience store in North Sydney, feeling like someone has their leg up your ass, the van smelling of old band, cold and pissed off, staring at another day's drive to St. John, New Brunswick? Or do you want to risk being assaulted by fishermen, which could turn out real nice? I meant nice 'cause they don't end up assaulting you and instead give you smokes and KD. We rolled the dice and they came up Jimmy: the truest, best saviour we ever had on the road.

The next morning, we had KD for breakfast and did the dishes, turned down the heat, and left $40 under the empty beer case in the fridge, before locking the door and heading down the road.

Man, that was a good night's sleep.

Thanks, Jimmy.

Sydney, Cape Breton

Sydney, Cape Breton, or Nova Scotia. I say Cape Breton, 'cause folks around Cape Breton Island certainly give you the idea that they are not really from Nova Scotia at all.

Here's my take on this beat-up old town of Sydney. Mind you, I got most of it from a guy at a bar who could have been lying, but as the folklore goes, back about fifteen or twenty years ago, when Paul Martin was the finance minister, he shut down the coal mines on the island so he could then get the contract to haul coal to Nova Scotia Power from, say, Brazil, or some other place down around South America, say, Venezuela. That is all conjecture, of course, and here's some more that I heard sitting around bars or listening to the CBC: here he is hauling coal into Cape Breton and making a bundle doing it, his ships all flying the Panama flag, and at one point, his ship ends up with the Mounties finding 180 lbs of cocaine in the ship's locker, and before you know it, everybody is rushing around trying to figure out why nobody ever looked there before, and then the story just goes away. Like I said, I just picked up this folklore over the years, hanging around bars, and would be the first one to say there is no way that any of this could be true. And let's just be sure that no one even mentions or defames Brian Mulroney in all this, 'cause we all know what happens when you defame him, and more so, he had nothing to do with this, anyhow. The upshoy would be that Sydney, Nova Scotia, got the real shitty end of the stick here when they closed the mines and a whole bunch of jobs went out the window, or at least into the locker of a Panama-flagged ship.

You wind your way into Sydney, this town of around 30,000 folks. I'm guessing fewer now, since its greatest days are behind it. It must still be the industrial capital because I didn't see much industry in the rest of Cape Breton. There are no big mills that sprung up in Mabou or anything like that. The old days are gone, having left when the steel mill closed and the coal mines that supplied the mill shut down as well. Back in the day, say a hundred years or so, the mines and the steel and Sydney were a perfect marriage. You need coal to make steel, and there was iron ore in Newfoundland and a real nice harbour there in Sydney for shipping and water for cooling, and everybody seemed to have a great time making steel for seventy-five or eighty years, and now they are gone. Just like every other steel town where this has happened, man, did they leave a mess behind.

This mess is otherwise known as the Sydney Tar Ponds, which is the one end of the harbour closest to the old steel mill, and it's one of the biggest collections of PCBs (polychlorinated biphenyls, a known carcinogen) in the world. This isn't really the kind of thing that you go around putting on a postcard or on signs up by the highway, saying, "Hey, come see our PCB collection! No family holiday can be complete without seeing our sludge."

The Tar Ponds really brought down the property rates, so much so that even an only partially employed musician can afford to own his own home. Bam, before you know it, like nowhere else in the world, you have musicians running around living at the same standard as everybody else. I don't know if they *own* their own homes as such, but, hey, this is where The Tom Fun Orchestra comes into the scene. It's their hometown, and when they're home, they all seem to work at a smoke shop or convenience store or other bottom-feeding type of employment. Their mortgages or rent are cheap, and then somebody says, "Hey, let's go on tour." Everybody chucks a couple hundred in the bank, quits their shit jobs and bam, they hit the road. You come home broke two months later, get back your old job that nobody else wanted, and there you are: musicians' heaven. and there you are: musician's heaven.

The upside for us was that the Tom Fun Orchestra has a big old house with floors we can stay on, because they love us and they're cool. Keep in mind that if you are touring the east, the Fun are not contractually obligated to love you. I'm sure the Fun are not all that happy about living in a town that has a tar pond either. The folks in that band have hosted us a couple of times in Sydney, and we've done quite a few shows with them across Canada. They are this up-to-ten-piece bundle of energy that takes your breath away, on stage or just hanging around the green room. Don't invite them back to your hotel room if you're planning on getting any sleep. They talk fast, and someone in the band is always holding an instrument.

We arrive at their local Governor's Pub, and although they are not playing with us, they show up, and their friends Buck and Kinch open for us for the second time. This chapter is a little incongruent with the book because the first time we had Buck and Kinch open for us, we didn't make it. This installment of Sydney is from a whole other trip, so it was their second time opening for us and our first time playing with them. I get a chance after their set to mention that we are very sorry for not making it to the first show, and they say, "Ah, don't worry about it. The place was packed and we got to keep all the money, thank you, sir."

I feel less bad as we take the stage and tear through a set to a Wednesday-night fist-pumping crowd. I like Sydney. I've thought many times of selling up here in Montreal and buying some big old place up there and giving Governor's a run for its money. Sydney is a town that's on the main road to Newfoundland and not all that far from the mainland. I think that a medium kind of living could be made booking and hosting bands in this town full of hard-headed musicians, the capital of Cape Breton.

The turn that makes you a band (or a local)

As you make your way out of Sydney, winding your way out the 105, you pass through some hamlets and you get to see water, some of it the inlet from the ocean and some of it Bras d'Or Lake. Just after you pass New Harris Forks, you see a sign for Highway 312, which is how you get up to the Cabot Trail. When you're traveling across Canada in a band van, yes, you will get to see some beautiful scenery: the Prairies, the mountains, let's say the CN Tower. As you're tearing down the 105 and that sign comes up for the Cabot Trail, even though you know it to be one of the most beautiful drives Canada has to offer with its amazing vistas, and plunging coast lines, the mountains and the wind, you know you will pass it up because you are due somewhere and just can't afford the 200 kilometres out of your way worth of gas. You keep on the 105 and head south toward the next gig. This alone puts you in a small category of people akin to truck drivers. You are a professional musician and you are not on vacation.

Giving up the utter splendour of the Cabot Trail, you hit 105 for its length and take in all that the low-lying interior of Cape Breton has to offer. It's green and wet, and about halfway through, you are still beside Bras d'Or Lake as it winds in and out along your way, and at some point, the non-driver grabs the map and makes a mental note that land in Cape Breton is at a bit of a premium. Taking in the whole of the island, you don't really notice until it's pointed out that about a third of the whole place is Bras d'Or Lake, which leaves a big hole in the island, kind of like a donut, or a donut that you would make if you were drunk and it was late and you really didn't know that much about making donuts. You know they fry those things in oil? That's what Cape Breton looks like on a map. This alone gets you through the whole missing the Cabot Trail experience.

Baddeck, Nova Scotia

You check your pack of smokes, the gas gauge, and the time, and you're only an hour into your trip, so you slow down to fifty and just keep passing up another cup of gas station coffee.

Fun Fact

Did you know that showing proficiency on the fiddle (and Cape Breton traditional fiddle music) can get you a pass on the Nova Scotia driver's exam? Yes, since 1948, the Nova Scotia department of motor vehicles has accepted knowing how to play a reel as a practical exam equivalent to a road test. Since 1978, this is recognized only in Cape Breton proper because a dispute over allowable rosin nullified the practice in lower Nova Scotia. This explains how Ashley MacIsaac has maintained his driver's license over the years. Or that's as good a theory as any....

Port Hastings, Nova Scotia

Port Hastings is the gateway to Cape Breton. It's the sole fixed link to the mainland, and from there many choices arise. The entire road network of Cape Breton fans out from this point. I mention this because I have been at that point many times over the years and intended on each occasion to take a different route north (there are three to pick from), and I must say that today's Cape Breton travel tip is: you will probably f. up this turn. I'm a pretty good driver, and no matter which highway I take, I end up on the wrong one. Drive slow, breathe deep, and when it is safe to do so, turn around. You are not a loser. Well, you are not any more of a loser than I am.

Following the designated signage, you make your way onto the Canso Causeway. The Causeway has been open since 1955. It has marked the re-entry to the mainland lo these many years and has consistently confused tourists ever since. Tourists think that the town just on the south side of the causeway is called Canso. It is not. The expanse of rock and two-lane, which has a short swing bridge and a canal, was named after the Strait of Canso and not the town, which is about an hour from the Canso Causeway. I'm glad I got to clear that up. Oh, and when they built the causeway, it took the fish years to figure out how to swim around Cape Breton.

Auld's Cove, Nova Scotia

The Canso Causeway deposits you on the mainland at Auld's Cove, Nova Scotia. Auld's Cove isn't a big town. It's got the causeway, a big old gravel or maybe limestone quarry, a gas station, and a place just up on the left there called Auld's Cove Lobster Suppers and Pettipas Market. Caution! The boys in the van are still interested in getting some more East Coast seafood into them, and who doesn't like picking up some souvenirs. So Pettipas Market seems like the perfect match. You pull up in front of the place, which has a stunning amount of signage advertising anything from fishing nets to firewood. You see massive plywood silhouettes of lobster and brightly painted dories surrounding the parking lot, and you think: Who wouldn't stop here?

We pull into the lot, and a man comes running out of the store. At first we think maybe he is going to tell us get the hell out of here, because he is flailing his arms over his head and shouting as he makes his way quickly along the front railing of the store. He stops mid-rail, and there he places something and lights it on fire. We are dumbstruck by the fireworks display. Welcome to Auld's Cove, Nova Scotia.

We all shrink back in our seats, still having not quite figured out what to make of all this as the strange man runs up and starts banging on our windows, yelling, "Come in, come in." He drags us from the van like a man who has been stranded on a desert island for years and before your arrival his only companion was a coconut that washed away a few years prior. I mean, this guy is talking fast as he pulls and cajoles us into his ramshackle store. We sheepishly enter the hodgepodge of a market and start browsing for knick-knacks and bric-a-brac. Our host is relentless. I won't mention him by name, because although somewhere in the verbal hurricane of a welcome and the subsequent onslaught of one-way conversation he mentions his name, his moniker is no clearer than what he is selling. In the first three minutes, I donated to the Terry Fox Marathon of Hope, bought a sticker of the Nova Scotia flag, and gave up $5 to a fund that he started for a single mother who lives near by, I think, or maybe she lived in Germany. I'm not really sure. Upon having donated my $17 to the cause, I make my escape out to the van with his attention having turned on one of my colleagues. He is as good a hunter as he is a salesman and he finds me outside.

I'm holed up in the van with the doors locked, talking to my wife, Rachel, on the phone, and there he is pounding on the window. "Come on in! Your friends are staying for lobster dinner. It's our specialty." My wife is astonished because I was giving her the rundown on this place and its owner just as he started banging on the window. He could not be thwarted in his attempts, and me thinking the rest of them are now having dinner, I cut my call quick and re-enter. I get back inside to find my comrades as confused and mystified as I, being herded toward a table at the back of the store. We are ushered in and seated while a flurry of information about the Canso Causeway, the Nova Scotian flag, and just what a cod eats gushes from our likeable but scary host's mouth. We sit dumb-founded as he runs back and forth from the kitchen to the table. At one point, he pulls out a sword and dubs some guy who wandered in mayor of Auld's Cove. The equally disturbed tourist manages only to reply, "I just came in to use the bathroom."

Before you know it, we're fending off lobster dinner. I resign myself to eating a bowl of chowder but stand hard on not being able to afford the lobster dinner. Similar tactics were taken by the rest of the band, and we get away with two lobster dinners, four bowls of chowder, three desserts, and a random amount of coffee, no tea. We manage to dislodge ourselves from the grip of our welcoming and very happy host and run for the van. As we are locking the doors, the storekeeper is still trying to get us back in the store. Another car pulls into the parking lot, and the predator spins on his heels and makes for the railing to let off some more fireworks. We escape and feel sort of bad for the new prey that have found their way into the spider's web.

Ten minutes up the road, having caught our breath, we start adding up our bills. We went in to get some stickers for our guitar cases and maybe have some fries, and came out an hour later, the band wallets being lightened by almost $220. Wow, usually when we spend that much at a rest stop it includes 120 litres of fuel. I did warn you about this place, but at the same time, you really have to go there. Lock your wallet in your car and take a $20 bill with you. Walk in and say, "Hey, buddy, what can I get for twenty bucks?" and see what happens. I guarantee it will be worth it. What a barrage.

Defeated and sort of happy, we spend our time trying to

find safe places to put our recently acquired knick-knacks as the incident swims in our heads. And we try to reassess our finances for the day.

Antigonish, Nova Scotia

Antigonish is roughly taken from the Mi'kmaq word for "the place where bears go to tear off tree branches." From the Trans-Canada Highway (104), the town of just under 5,000 people seems like all others. You got the Boston Pizza, the A&W, a bunch of car dealerships, and a Sobeys. If you were to look past the mainstays of modern Canadian small-town commerce, you would also find a cozy downtown main drag as well as St. Francis Xavier University. St. FX boasts a student population that rivals the entire town's and was named the best undergraduate university in Canada by *Maclean's* magazine for five years running.

Even if you knew all that, you probably wouldn't know its biggest claim to fame is that it is exactly (well, close to exactly) halfway between Halifax and Sydney, Nova Scotia. As it turns out, that's the key reason (though it's a perfectly nice town) why you will never stop there. It's about a five-hour drive from Sydney to Halifax, and when leaving either town, everybody is already hungry and must eat far before you get there or has just had breakfast and is just not willing to spend money on food two and a half hours into the trip.

This brings us to Mother Webb's Steakhouse, located just a few minutes north of town on the 104. You will pass this very inviting log cabin diner with its numerous roadside billboards many times while traveling the East Coast. I like a good steak house, and yet it took years to align the stars just right so the band would all be hungry enough as we hit town to decide that they all wanted to stop and that they all wanted steak. Having been tantalized by its down-homey goodness and the promise of a $10 steak, we finally got to stop there.

We were playing the Stan Rogers Folk Festival a year or so ago in the town of Canso, Nova Scotia. That is when I was straightened out about the whole Canso not being up by the causeway thing. Its tiny population is inundated with folks over the festival weekend and isn't able to feed thousands of people breakfast on a Sunday morning. So, the band pulls out of town hungry, and we're heading towards home, which takes us directly through Mother Webb's territory, only 110 kilometres away and the perfect stop to meet an early afternoon breakfast-esque meal. Yes, steak is breakfast to me.

As you approach Mother Webb's, the billboards greet you early on, giving you ample time to prepare for your stop. They promise $10 steak, best steak anywhere, and instant service. We disgorge into her parking lot and immediately fling ourselves at the entrance and its hostess. The sign said instant service and, by Jove, they were right. The six of us were seated with menus and a promise of coffee as fast as a hungover bunch of musicians could walk, and then sit, all while deciding with whom to sit. The rustic charm of the place was only overshadowed by my spotting Mother Webb herself. She was (as expected) running around in a Mother Hen sort of way, shooing her staff and helping clear tables, and surely helping to make things run right. There was discussion about whether this was actually her, but in my heart of hearts, not unlike a kid's absolute and unshakeable belief in Santa Claus, I knew that, yes, this was finally Mother Webb herself.

Having left the vegetarians at home on this particular trip, we all ordered the steak special. Some chose beer, some, coffee. In my mind, Mother Webb herself took our order, her school marm charm kindly writing every detail with a love that guaranteed the finest steak $10 could buy. In reality, the waitress was in her mid-twenties, bored or mildly hungover, but a pleasant St. FX student who got almost everything right.

The steaks were, as promised, the best steaks around. Probably the most enjoyable meal I've had on the East Coast, or at least the most anticipated.

Truro, Nova Scotia

As you wind your way down the middle of the upper part of Nova Scotia, careening down Highway 104, you will get to the fork in the road. The Maritimes seem like a mostly flat chunk of land playing out in a fairly straight succession of towns. Only occasionally do you pick up the map to find that, no, that road turns a lot and those towns are fairly widely flung amongst the difficult topography of Canada's East Coast. Truro is one of those towns that points this out to you. It's here that you have to decide whether you are continuing east towards the rest of Canada or are going to head mostly south and take in the wonder of Halifax (and the lower part of Nova Scotia) or, stopping to visit this smallish but nice Eastern Canadian town.

We arrive at this once very important hub. It had been the branch point to many railways, highways, and hydroelectric transmission lines, and we arrive on Super Bowl Sunday. This trip had been booked a year before through an organization called The Atlantic Presenters Association, who had set us up with some really cushy gigs. Truro was no different: there was a rider and there were hotel rooms booked. Seven double rooms, a tour record. The overabundance of rooms was courtesy of our band's often misunderstood name. I believe the person in charge of booking us thought we were some musical offshoot of the United Steel Workers of America and booked enough rooms for a big showing of steel workers attending a convention. We took six of the rooms because it isn't very often you get your own room. We were nice enough to tell the front desk that we did not need the seventh.

There was great anticipation that this show was going to be big. The rest of the shows on that particular swing were packed, and the folks ate up our performances like Floridian retirees chowing down on peel-and-eat shrimp at a cruise ship buffet. We sold merchandise, we had great riders, and from the first four shows, it looked as though we could see the day when touring made sense as a lifestyle choice. This high-water mark in our career would take a blow on this Super Bowl Sunday.

We were booked at the Marigold Centre, a big beautiful theatre: a soft-seat gig. A soft-seat gig means that you are not in a bar and you will not have the advantage of the audience being drunk to help make your show seem even bigger than it is. You will be on stage with, say, 200 folks staring right at you and expecting the show to spellbind them. No distracting waitresses, no TVs going on in the background, no drunk, crazed fans dancing and shouting at you — nope, all attention is on you. It's a different gig than our normal affairs, but after getting a couple under our belt, we started getting really good at making it an event for any demographic that we were faced with. All of this is great if there is anybody in the theatre.

We arrived to load in exactly on time and were met by the new manager of the theatre, who had a chilly disposition. We loaded in and started sound check anyway. The sound check was grueling, having now pulled six nights in a row and everything hurt: fingers, elbows, and voices. We had learned over the years that when on these swings that this was normal and that it was necessary to play through these pains. The old adage is it will hurt until you start to sweat, so the idea is to plunge headlong into the pain and get those stage lights cooking and all will be fine. Add to this the manager's comments about there being only eleven advance tickets sold, and this was by far the worst sound check we had played in a while.

To all would-be booking agents and show promoters, here is the road tip of the day. If you plan on keeping your job (the person who booked us into the Marigold that night didn't), always take a look at the calendar before sending that advance cheque off to the agency. Never book a show smaller than, say, Paul McCartney or U2 on Super Bowl Sunday. There are other days of note as well, like any major city of Catholic origin on Easter Weekend or Christmas Day. But, yes, it is a good idea to find out what day the NFL is going to have their year-end big game. Our agent was trying to fill a Sunday night, which is usually impossible, so kudos to Rachel of UrbanHanded Works, and the manager of the club didn't look at a calendar, so here we are in an empty room awaiting our fate.

Twenty-three people showed up that cold February night in a room built for almost 200. With this and the pain of sound check firing up and a good amount of trepidation, we took to the stage and to our credit played one of the best shows of the tour. It took very little time to figure out that this was going to be a different show than we were used to, so I paused after the second or third song and started talking to the audience on a one-to-one basis. I started hassling them to sit closer to each other and talk between songs. The band responded with overly theatrical solo stances and really sent the songs home. The final song, "Place St-Henri," found me in the audience running from one group of folks to the other helping them to their feet and coupling them up with the other random folks in the audience until everybody, all twenty-three of them, were partnered up, and with great energy and surprise, they all slow danced to "Place St-Henri."

We took our bows and cleared the stage knowing we gave that small crowd the show they paid for. The upside is and always was that the cheque did clear and we got paid full price for the show. Very sorry to the girl who booked us and subsequently lost her job, but please keep in mind you made twenty-three people, and us, very happy.

Halifax, Nova Scotia

Halifax is the undisputed capital of the East Coast of Canada, a city in transition. We always enter Halifax by way of Dartmouth and the Macdonald Bridge. Halifax, being a very historic town, would beg you to imagine that the Macdonald Bridge was named after Sir John A. Macdonald, but it's actually named for a former premier of Nova Scotia. It's called the "Old Bridge," to distinguish it from the Murray MacKay Bridge, or "New Bridge," down the shore.

To make way for the new bridge, the city plowed down the Africville neighbourhood. The dislocation of all the inhabitants has been a thorn in the side of the black community ever since, and with respect for the loss of their community, we the USWM never take the new bridge.

The Old Bridge, the Macdonald Bridge, spans the better part of the Halifax Harbour and is one of the only places in Canada where you can see a submarine without getting out of your car. The Halifax Harbour is vast and abounds with activity. Ships large and small come and go and are moored here. I always try to not be the driver when crossing this span so I can enjoy the forty seconds it takes to drive across the bridge to take in the whole of the harbour and the city. It is one of the few places in Canada where I pray for traffic.

Descend the ramp at the far end of the Macdonald Bridge and it deposits you on Barrington Street, once the main drag of the town, which hosted bar after bar and, a real centre of nightlife. Years ago, a walk along this street actually guaranteed that by the end of the night you would in fact be drunk, have seen a great band, and been punched in the face while awaiting a donair at its many donair stands. Over the last few years, however, over-development has created a desert of call centres and condos. I don't think I've ever witnessed the destruction of a cultural landscape on this level. I've never seen an area get this broken up and die in just a seven-year period. I remember listening to a local musician a couple of years ago say, "Well you know where you're at when your music venues are getting closed down to make room for $7-an-hour jobs that no one wants to work and no one in the world wants to hear from. You are on Barrington Street, Halifax."

Now, not all is doom and gloom. At press time for this book, there are still some venues surviving in this beautiful city. As stated earlier, Halifax is a town in transition, and although the cool kids have all had to move away from downtown or at least anywhere near downtown, the town's position as a cultural mecca for the surrounding area, and having an art college, means that unlike the rest of Nova Scotia, which has lost most of its population under the age of thirty-five to the vast riches of Alberta and Toronto, there are still kids here, and, yes, still cool kids, so there are still noticeable cultural efforts.

For bands and fans alike there are still havens like the Seahorse, Gus' Pub, and at the newer end of things, the Company House. The Paragon still exists but runs on a weird reality where it seems to only be open for about an hour and a half a day. They manage to fill the room up at eleven-thirty at night, push two bands on stage, and then forcibly remove everybody after two forty-five-minute sets, usually removing people with such speed and physicality that it is impossible to sell them any merch at all. I think they should start their shows a little earlier: isn't that what an opening band is for? The Paragon is a weird place, but a decent room, if only for an hour and a half.

Our biggest show ever in Halifax was, of course, a Seahorse show we did a few years back where we actually sold out with 150 people standing in line. Very sorry to the folks who missed it. Wow, that was cool, even if the band The Grass overplayed their set by thirty minutes and we had to squeeze our headlining set into thirty-five minutes. But to sell out, that was cool: our first ever non-Montreal show to do that.

But, to date, the most important show we ever played in Halifax was our first, and it was at Gus'. Gus' is a little rough-around-the-edges, sort of a punked-out old man's bar, about halfway up the hill, and it has probably survived only because it isn't anywhere near Barrington Street. The bar is fairly well lit during the day, with many of its daytime regulars enjoying the finest array of video poker that one can imagine. The kitchen does a pretty good job of feeding the masses a decent fish and chips among other expected fare. Nighttime is ushered in as the doorman arrives around seven p.m., and he immediately makes sure that you have left nothing in your van. This is always a nice if not disturbing bit of advice from a local. You set up and do a sound check and wait for the headliner to arrive. It was our coup to have booked this show with the Tom Fun Orchestra. The show had been booked four months before, and in the interim, the Tom Fun had won an East Coast Music Award, so thus were splashed on the newspapers' front page pretty well for the weeks preceding this show, our first in Halifax, in fact our first trip to the East Coast.

This brings up today's tip: East Coast Fan Base. They are elusive at first. For all bands starting to tour the East Coast: you will find that on your first swing through her wilds, nobody will come. I mean with all the promotion and invites and press and friends calling and emailing their friends back home, maybe sixteen people will come out the first time you play. Those first eastern tours were really thin, but what we found out was that those first sixteen multiply, and that those first sixteen cool kids never let go. Years later and after many eastern swings, we still recognized those first fans. As well, those folks have friends who rely on them to tell them who is cool and worth seeing, and they tell their friends, and the whole thing, although taking a huge amount of time, eventually pays off in spades, because once any of these people have seen you, they always come back. I am of the belief that the USWM could lay it completely low for the next twenty years and reform to mount a very successful eastern Canada tour.

Now for us, when it comes to Halifax, we got very lucky and by-passed all that by getting to open for the Tom Fun. They had a huge following even at that time, so we got to play in front of a ready-made fan base right off the bat. From then on, Halifax was to be our anchor for any trip taking in the entire end of the country. Thank you, Tom Fun.

Now Gus' packed out that night. The sound was bad, but the crowd didn't care; they jumped up and down and they drank and cursed, a true forum for our band. The coolest thing about the whole gig was the fact that I noticed at around midnight the trio of, say, aged late sixties staff, still wearing the black and white service uniforms of, say, the seventies— white shirt, rolled up cuffs, black trousers, and an apron. That trio had been our servers when we first arrived at three p.m. and were actually still on duty. Now I'm not sure they are still staffing there all night, but at that point it would have been weird to see even a young staff member pull a stuffed bar on a thirteen-hour bar shift, and all of that with smiles on their faces. I've done a lot of bartending over the years, and I must say that my hat was off to this unlikely trio.

The show in the bag and having added 150 new fans to our East Coast base, we did what all Haligonians do after the bars close: we went and got donairs. Now donairs, or, as everybody else knows them, gyros in pita, are that meat on a vertical spit that you shave with what looks like a set of barber's clippers. The long, thin strips of meat are then shoved on a pita and garnished. Halifax claims to have invented this

Lebanese delicacy. This is very much in dispute by many Lebanese communities all over North America, if not say Lebanon, but Halifax does have one claim to fame, which is the sauce they use on their "donairs," and maybe the entire experience of eating them when drunk.

Now the sauce: well, it's kind of this honey and cream-based sort of thing. I've tried it many times, and I think they make it by mixing non-dairy creamer with some non-honey, honey-flavoured ick, and add some fat of some kind. You end up with something that would be great as an industrial lubricant or maybe for smothering forest fires, but not for putting on meat, even low-quality meat. With all my heart, I cannot suggest you try the sauce. Ask for tzatziki, or ranch if you have to. Ooooh, I just got some bad press in Halifax!

The next thing to know is that these pitas, or donairs as they are called, come in different sizes: small, medium, and large. Keep in mind that the actual size of the pita bread does not seem to change, they just put a ton more meat on the bread and most of it spills on the floor of the restaurant. I must say I think this is great — nothing like excess at three a.m. Now, the final problem with the whole experience is the crowds you will encounter after the bar. For your first donair experience, maybe you should try it in the afternoon. But the wild at heart and the really adventurous should try walking into a donair shack around 2:15 a.m. You line up to the counter in this very crowded, brightly lit room, and the lineup takes on the formation of an offensive line in position to hammer home the third down and goal. Shoulders locked together, there is pushing and shoving and men eyeing each other up, trying to get the upper hand with intimidation.

Cheerleaders scream, "I need a Coke." The skirmish is set into action by the man behind the counter yelling out "who's next?" and a volley of orders takes place. There is much more pushing and shoving and catcalls until, about fifteen minutes later, some guy hands you a piece of foil dripping with meat fat and a white viscous goo. He relieves you of the better part of a $20 bill and you make your way to the door.

Stupidly believing it will be better outdoors, you emerge right into the middle of a post-bar fistfight. Two lads have squared off over some drunken damsel who is being consoled by her friend via cellphone as she staggers around trying to figure out why her bulletheaded boyfriend is so mad at her again for making out with this other dude. You get shoved by one of the dudes, and most of the meat falls out of your foil wrapping and lands on the other dude's new runners and you somehow make it out of there alive. You sit on a curb a couple of blocks away and enjoy what's left of the fruits of your labour and wish you had got tzatziki sauce instead of that goo.

Before departing Halifax, I must say that this last bit about the donairs is not to be taken as my putting down the city and its rambunctious residents. It would be more than fair to say there are a lot of towns in Canada that have this sort of post-bar frivolity. And overall, the average Haligonian, drunk or sober, has a generally pleasing disposition; they are definitely the hipsters of the East Coast. Halifax tip number one: Don't get the sauce. To leave you on a better note for your trip to Halifax, let's have Halifax tip number two: If you find yourself with the afternoon off, one of my favourite things to do is to take the ferry. Some folks love to walk the Citadel and be scared when they set the cannon off at noon.

Or is it one p.m.; I'll let you find that out. I find the Citadel to be more for the non-smoking crowd, all that walking up hill, and those paths and stuff, is just a little too much work for a day off. However, being as the Citadel is a hill, it will eventually find you looking for Chinese food down the hill. Gravity expediting the trip, you will eventually end up on the waterfront looking to check out some boats, because who doesn't like boats, eh?

Well, just completely by accident, I found that there is a ferry service that runs from the downtown waterfront to Dartmouth. For the price of a transit ticket, you can take the ferry out across the harbour and get a real good look at the city, and of course the boats. The fare is, I think, $2.50, and if you stay on the boat at the other end, which you probably should because there really isn't any big pull to Dartmouth, then you have the cheapest touristy thing you could do in Halifax, and for less than a lousy cup of coffee.

Prince Edward Island

As you bank your van down the on-ramp to Highway 16, you realize at some point you have left Nova Scotia behind you. You have looked at the map and, yes, you do realize that there is a whole lot more to Nova Scotia if you just run south out of Halifax for a ways. We have done some shows down that way in Lunenburg and Little Brook, but for the most part, there is just not a lot for the usual bands down in that part of the country. As I mentioned, Nova Scotia has lost a lot of her younger population to the wilds of western Canada and it makes the southern part of the province, although very beautiful, kind of lonely for a band. Please let other bands know if it turns out I am wrong and there are tons of gigs I haven't found.

So having given New Scotland everything you had, you wind your way up Highway 16 towards P.E.I. In earlier days, I would think that this part of the trip would not have been possible, sitting around waiting for the ferry and in the end having only a small number of gigs to take advantage of. But, alas, it is a new world, or more to the point, since 1997, there has been a bridge.

It was built with much controversy, since a fair chunk of

the island's population actually wanted life to remain as it had been since before the bridge. A quaint, cut-off, rural existence where the idea of heading for the big city was measured in how many hours late the ferry would be. The countering opinion was to throw open the doors to progress, money, and possibly the invasive species it would bring. The federal government, as it does, used its might as well to sway the discourse, looking forward to the day it would not have to subsidize the ferry. The discussion eventually led to a plebiscite on the issue, with 59.4 percent of the populace of the Island deciding to be fixed to the mainland for the forseeable future, at a cost of 1.4 billion dollars. Four years of construction and the fixed link became a reality. It would later be named The Confederation Bridge, because to some it sounded prettier than "The Fixed Link."

The bridge stretches 12.9 kilometres out across the Northumberland Strait, and in winter it kind of just looks like you are crossing some snow-covered field. This bridge is magnificent in length if not beauty, and although it doesn't make the list of the ten longest bridges in the world, it is still impressive, and comes top of the list for being the longest bridge over ice (small yay!). The other cool feature of this bridge is that it is free. Well, it's free if when you get to P.E.I. you decide you like it so much that you buy a small home and get married and never leave the Island again. I have thought about it.

If that doesn't work out, it's $44.50 to get your van off the Island, which does make it the most expensive toll bridge in North America. Hey! A real record! Big yay, sort of. It's the pay-later approach that the tourist board adopted to trick people into going to the Anne of Green Gables museum. They said if you could find where Lucy Maud Montgomery hid her whiskey bottles they would let you off the island for free. Hint: look in the leather-bound edition signed by Megan Follows.

The grand bridge drops you in Port Borden, and right away you realize why your western shows are so populated by folks from P.E.I. It's because the Island is kinda just a very small, flat prairie. Not a ton of topography going on here, and so you just start following the signs for Charlottetown, which is just over a half-hour drive away. The Island unfolds along this drive as a mostly agricultural endeavour, with a small town after small town charm to it. P.E.I. has the potato, and it has the sea, and it has the wind, all of which they capitalize on. The new bridge has brought down the cost of shipping potatoes and seafood to the mainland, so even though the spud has been a mainstay of the local economy forever, it has once again taken a jump forward and is responsible for a steady incline in its importance.

Lobsters abound, or try to bound from coolers in many more car trunks these days, and lastly, the bridge now makes it easier to haul wind turbines onto the island. I believe P.E.I. holds the record for the largest percentage of locally produced green electricity in Canada.

Charlottetown, P.E.I.

Although the bands in the know may find that there are quite a few small gigs located around the island, for the average "come from away" band, Charlottetown is the usual stop, a smallish college town, home to the University of Prince Edward Island. The university makes this the main cultural town on the map of this dot of land. A small town with a population just over 32,000 souls, this being the big town on the island gives it a slightly larger feel.

Charlottetown bills itself as the birthplace of Confederation, having hosted the Charlottetown Conference way back in 1864. So, if you are looking for ground zero for all that Canada has been responsible for, look no further than Charlottetown. This is where to send all your complaints about softwood lumber disputes, the tar sands, the closing of the wheat pool, Ontario owning everything, Aboriginal disputes, Tim Hortons, no cod, asbestos, the Toronto Maple Leafs' bad Stanley Cup record, Tim Hortons, and the fact that they fudged the numbers on the whole Newfoundland referendum. Take all those concerns and pen them into a letter and send it along to the Chamber of Commerce in Charlottetown and ask them why they keep bragging about starting all that. I myself find it ironic that P.E.I. only got bamboozled into Confederation to begin with just so old John A. Macdonald could distract people from the fact that he was taking bribes from railway moguls. The ruse worked to get P.E.I. on our map but failed John A., who had to step down as leader of the Conservative Party. Unfortunately, he did eventually make a comeback, setting in stone Confederation and our ability not only to tolerate scandal but also eventually to reward it. Put all that in your letter too, maybe suggesting that they shouldn't go around blowing that particular horn so loud, especially when they have all those beaches to talk about. Sorry, I rant, but, man, they name everything Confederation around here.

The main drag is rich in Victorian architecture, or at least what I believe to be Victorian architecture, with tons of those big old clapboard houses that we all secretly want to own so we can roast chestnuts over the hearth with a dog at our knee. Well, the secret is out because I really want to own one and thus save myself the $44.50 return bridge fee. The picturesque housing that catches your notice gives way to a downtown that is a complete mix of Commercial Victorian but leaning towards Americana (think Mayberry) and new concrete and glass "we are the capital, and have government money" (think Ottawa). It's not as unpleasing as I let on. It's a pretty and clean provincial capital and you find your venue at Baba's on the main drag.

Baba's Lounge, once described by *MuchMusic* as: "the world's biggest little rock and roll bar!!" is, in fact, all that. It's located over Cedar's Eatery, which makes it a second-floor load in, always a trial for the working band. But I must say, as many times as I've loaded up rickety spiral staircases (check out the load in at Club Lambi in Montreal, sometime) covered in ice, Baba's isn't so bad, and it's worth it just to play there. Baba's is an intimate venue—it only holds around fifty people on a good night, but we've had great luck packing it out even on a Tuesday. Although, that happened after we'd played a couple of closer-to-weekend gigs there first. The bar has a small but mostly well-equipped stage, and the last night we played there we had the soundman who actually looks like Hugh Laurie. He acted like Dr. House too, all gruff and spiteful, mostly after I mentioned he looked like the guy from *House*, which I'm pretty sure he gets four or five times a day. No, really, just like Hugh Laurie! The place is small and kind of looks like a dining room with walls covered in posters of past shows. Baba's glories in having booked bands such as the

Trews, Wintersleep, Slowcoaster, and eventually us. I remember thinking how cool it was, the last time we played there, that we had finally made the wall on a permanent basis.

Baba's also has one of the only enclosed smoking rooms on the Island. Now, that might not sound like much, but, man, these days it's real cool to have a smoke and sit with your beer. The room is a closed-in patio, and in winter it's as cold as hell, and it smells like the arse end of an ashtray, with a hint of black lung thrown in for good measure. I'm sure a non-smoker would throw up if they happened to wander out there on a show night, but we dying breed have to take what we can get in the small comforts these days. It makes a great wind-down room after a show, everybody sitting around smoking and talking about the show—just like the old days when everybody was forced to get cancer.

I should admit that I now enjoy and even flourish in a smoke-free environment. I remember a couple of years back playing in Belgium, the only smoking show we had done in over a year, and, man, I almost died trying to get through the set. I mean, when it comes to playing a show, I guess you just can't go back to the smoky rooms that we played for so many years. That said, it really is nice to have the best of both worlds: play a show smoke-free, and then have a smoke after.

The room sits mostly empty on an early Tuesday night, but we are expecting a pretty good crowd. With the help of some local friends, the recently defunct Grass Mountain Hobos, we had a pretty good following in Charlottetown, and Baba's generally brings them in. Eleven p.m. and seemingly the door swings open and thirty-five-odd people walk in. This room always seems to fill up late, but the crowds seem to visit every time there is a decent show going on. I love clubs that have that ability to draw all on their own. There are bigger places in town, probably not a bad deal if you are there on a weekend, but this smallish place over a Lebanese restaurant gets my vote.

A few words here about the Grass Mountain Hobos. Chris Reid, our banjo and mandolin player through the period around and after our third album, is from Charlottetown, and he got us hooked up with the Hobos. They were his high school buddies and are still great friends. When it comes to hookups on the road, you will often get hooked up with bands who are friends of friends, or friends of someone in your band, and it usually works out okay, even though in a lot of cases the match-up is a bit of a stretch. But the Hobos hit us bang on. One of the best bluegrass bands Canada has ever produced, in my reckoning, winner of a couple of East Coast Music Awards, and hard-working tourers for a couple of years, these guys brought it on. They were fast, slick, and sometimes crass and in your face, but they always gave me the feeling I was watching the way old-time bands actually played live shows back in the day. No smooth traditional boys here. They played it like their collective pants were on fire and it meant something. The other thing worth mentioning is that they, and their immediate circle of friends, are probably the funniest bunch of sons a bitches I've ever met. With a weird and highly addictive country drawl, they did impromptu skits that would have put the Kids in the Hall to shame on a good day.

Now mind you, this is all backstage stuff. Onstage, there were quips thrown back and forth on mic, and they could make the audience laugh, but for the real show, get stuck in a hotel room with them sometime. I once witnessed an entire thirty-five-minute, off-the-tops-of-their-heads, skirmish involving six characters that were all being sold an investment scheme, involving moving their savings from the unstable banking system and investing heavily in the new world of Video Lottery. The thing is, it wasn't any one of them in particular, it was one guy feeding a line to the next as if this bit had been done before, but throwing in a left hook to keep everybody on their toes. I've never seen anything like them, and I've never found anyone on the road since that stands up to those boys.

It was with great sadness that I heard about them hanging up their road boots. They handed us a lot of good shows over the years, and it really is a toss up as to whether we owe them or Tom Fun the greatest amount of thanks for all the folks they introduced us to. We once spent a cold and snowy end of weekend with them holed up in a house they were all renting together. I slept on the unheated third floor: it was cold, but it was far enough away from the party that I could sleep when I wanted. Down on the first floor, over a three-day period, we saw a non-stop procession of local musicians roll in and out. Not a big party, never more than six or eight people, but it just didn't stop, an open jam that ran around the clock swinging from rock to old-time to punk and back to country. Sequestered upstairs, I would go down every so often, and there would be another three or four guys playing a whole bunch of other tunes. They gave me the feeling that these guys, in or out of the music business, would be surrounded by music and comedy the rest of their lives. I look forward to playing with them again someday, or even just some of them.

I look forward to investing in Video Lottery as well. If ever you run into a guy called Thomas Webb standing in front of a video poker machine and he offers to give you half of his winnings if you stake him with a dollar, take it! That lad knows how to pick THE HOT MACHINE! He can feel it. He can feel it from way out on the street, through a wall: "If that there bar has a Hot Machine in it, it pulls at me from across the street way down the block. I've had to move farther from the bar just so I can get some sleep."

New Brunswick
(McIrvingland)

Forty-four dollars paid to cross back on the Confederation Bridge, and you are plunged headlong back into New Brunswick, formerly known as the Colony of Acadia. Originally the home of the Acadians, who were French colonists, then the British came, and then no Acadians. Some returned from exile and some resurfaced, and then they all became New Brunswickers. Then, the Irvings and the McCains bought the whole place, and there you go: McIrvingland. It is estimated that one in ten New Brunswickers work for the Irving family in any one of its many concerns: logging, pulp and paper, radio, wind farming, ship building, oil refining, newspapers, or schlepping food in one of its many Big Stop locations.

It is also said that the rest of the population has never eaten a potato that did not pass through the actual hands of a direct descendant of Harrison McCain, founder of McCain Foods, the largest producer of frozen french fries in the galaxy. Between these two family-run, mega-giant businesses, there just isn't all that much left of the province for the average New Brunswick citizen to wander.

With the exception of some cleaning crews, the entire population of the province is forced to live on three reserves of land know as Moncton, Saint John, and Fredericton. The rest of the province is completely private land. Yet, the privatized wilds of New Brunswick unfold as you wheel your way towards your next destination, once a huge shipbuilding and railroad town: Moncton.

Moncton, New Brunswick

A once proud and bustling wooden shipbuilding centre, Moncton was almost brought to its knees in the late nineteenth century by the advent of steam-powered ships. This incredibly bad fortune was short-lived, however. Steamships led to steam-powered trains and bam! This centrally situated community got another 100-odd years at bat. A very important eastern hub for the Canadian National Railway, the city grew by leaps and bounds. Unfortunately, the eighties came along, and along with Disco, casual sex, and V8 motors, the party was over.

The town rebounded in the late nineties, and business is booming once again. Moncton commands a growth rate that western Canadian cities can only dream of. Mind you, most of the jobs out west pay you $78,000 a minute to do something cool like push pipe on an oil rig, and in Moncton you get to swill beer with the other office workers at the end of the day and talk about how you fixed that cable billing problem for that guy in Wisconsin, "and, boy, I know I'm glad to have a job, but call centres?" The town's large bilingual population makes it a veritable hot spot for phone service. It would seem that Indian companies are still having a hard time with the New Brunswick accent, but this drawly mix of Franglais has saved the industry and beaten back outsourcing. Yay! We *gagnon!*

This hard-beaten bunch of folks have really grown on me over the years. There was a time when I'd just give Moncton the big miss because just didn't seem to be a base for us to work with. There was this big old club downtown that you wouldn't even think of booking unless it was a weekend, and even then, nobody would come, except some folks from Bathurst who always seemed to come see us, no matter where we played in New Brunswick. It was for them that I decided to book Fredericton instead. In the end, we returned there this year, having heard good things about a new club, and, yes, it came true. Plan B: the first believer club on this tour.

Believer Clubs: if you build it, they will come

This is what makes a believer club:

- A booker who answers his email on a daily basis
- A stage and PA system
- Beer, preferably free for the band
- On-site accommodation (although a good deal at a local hotel works too)
- A good load in (no stairs if possible)
- A wall of fame, or a guestbook
- Staff who know music (preferably musicians, but not necessarily)
- The ability to hang posters on walls (or in some cases print or even make posters)
- A media presence: web, Facebook, calendar, email list
- And a reputation for having a non-stop line up of

music that you will never hear on the radio
- Lots of patrons willing to show up six nights a week
- Some arrangement to make selling merch possible: even a dedicated table helps
- Someone to work the door and parking, because getting up in the morning to plug a parking metre sucks!
- Safe gear storage or the ability to leave your gear in side, out of the way, and get it in the morning, this usually requires a cool cleaning staff
- Food, or, at a minimum, a deal on food
- And if you can get your laundry done and stay an extra night, say, if it's Sunday and you have no gig, then that is the real deal

It was quite a while into our touring that we started to see what I have dubbed "Believer Clubs." I got the term from Dan Kershaw of the Brothers Cosmoline but never really witnessed it until we reached Groningen, in the Netherlands, and checked into Club Vera, during our first European tour.

We'd never seen such a place. We arrived the day before our gig hoping they could suggest a place for us to sack out, and give us some local intel on hotels and such. They said, "Hey, why don't you stay here? Pull around back and we will lock your van in our garage." They showed us to our rooms, which were kind of hotel-esque — very clean, cable TV, balconies for smoking and they handed us keys for the back door so we could go out and find beer and food, and left us there till sound check the next day.

On the day of the show, they fed us a big home-cooked

meal as we gazed at the wall of fame, which ran back thirty years and had bands such as U2, the Pogues, the Planet Smashers, and the Hanson Brothers. We played in front of a crowd of about sixty-five people on a Wednesday night, having never set foot in Holland before, and spent the after hours drinking free beer with the manager of the club, who had been booking it since the late seventies. He told us that U2's first time there, they had only three more people show up for their gig than we did. Nice. We slept soundly that night, gear all locked up safe. They parked our van for free, and we even stayed the next night, I believe. Overall, we made, say €400 playing the gig and selling merch, but got probably €400 worth of accommodation, €100 worth of parking, €50 worth of food, and maybe €100 worth of beer. All this at a greatly reduced cost to the venue, and we left happy having covered three days, worth of very expensive traveling. As well, there was a pizza place ten feet from the club's back door that had the best pizza I ever ate. Get the four-cheese extravaganza.

When playing a club, the biggest pains in the ass are going to be security of your gear, a place to stay, somewhere to park, and getting your gear in and out. Only after that do you start thinking about: Is anybody gonna show up? Is there beer? Are the staff cool? The places that take care of those variables start to get bands lining up to play there, giving the club first dibs at booking the best touring bands on the road. It also makes booking faster and easier because folks are calling you first, way in advance, and you can juggle your sched to meet your own needs, the bands not being locked into a specific dates yet. As a result of all this work, the local community would start coming out several nights a week to see bands, it being better than staying home and watching TV. That's the great thing about these places. For the folks who run them, they are a sound business move. They, in most cases, make money because there are people there every night drinking and spending money.

I have been measuring all clubs by that experience at Club Vera ever since.

With all that said, we pull up in front of Plan B in Moncton. It's a small place, kind of a café/bar. The first thing I notice is the posters in the front window. There are a lot of them, and everybody we know from the road as well as our hometown is playing here. For a small club in a town that, until a couple of years ago, couldn't seem to get folks out on a Friday night, these guys are doing multiple shows a week. It's a simple place, and when we played there, it had a grungy, eight-channel, powered Peavey PA, with a couple of beat-to-shit monitors and some bent mic stands. If I remember correctly, the sound was rough, but at the end of a jumping night, nobody in the band was bitching about the sound. It was our first decent show in Moncton, we were tired from playing hard and a little drunk, and after signing the wall of fame located just over the entrance to the men's room door, we crawled upstairs and slept on the floor of the soundman's apartment. Now this might not sound fabulous, but to a great extent, all our needs were taken care of. The gear stayed onstage, we parked the van in their driveway, we stayed upstairs for free, thus saving $150 easy on hotels, and had sixty or seventy people jumping up and down in our faces loving our music, and buying our CDs and T-shirts, in a town that had paid us no attention before this. That is what gets you through a tour spiritually and monetarily.

Behind the bar work various local musicians, and the clientele is lousy with players as well. We got to hang and trade tales with the guys from the Divorcees, who are a great shit–kickin', chicken-pickin', roadhouse country band. Best honky-tonk I've heard in a while.

That, by the way, is another sign of a good club: getting to know some local bands and swapping stories, strategies, and lies always makes a great time at a club.

The night ended at four in the morning with a boot toss competition started by our banjo/mando player, Dylan Perron. I believe he won the boot toss but lost the parking metre vault when he got himself hung up on a double metre. Ow…. This would be one of the things bands do to unwind after a show. Well, it's what our band did while I sat and watched. Having suffered many band-related accidents over the years, I was generally discouraged from such extracurricular taunts at good health.

Morning came, and we loaded up our gear, which was safe and sound locked in the bar all night, and went out to find an Irving's Big Stop to get some breakfast.

Big Stop breakfast

Sliding down Highway 2 towards Saint John, the brown and grey splendour that is this part of the world rushes by as the band grips the seats in anticipation of the ultimate band longing: breakfast. Finding a parking spot this cold but sunny Saturday morning wasn't easy because the lot was filled almost to the brim with locals. Everyone wants eggs.

It's a big truck stop parking lot, but nobody wants to park

way over by the tractor-trailers and hump it across to the restaurant. We wedge into a spot between two 4x4s and the band carefully disembarks trying not to slam the doors of the van into the late model hunting vehicles, a skill we've learned over the years. The van is high off the ground, and climbing out can be a bit of a frenzy with everyone pent up inside. The smokers want to get out first and get a half a smoke in them during the walk across the lot.

We are at the Irving. I've taken quite a bit of the piss out of the Irving family over this chapter, and I won't stop now, but in their defence, their restaurants have been a lifeline to us over our trips: feeding, fueling, and even clothing us on occasion. The bigger truck stops can be a real one-stop shop for most of our needs, be it gas, food, smokes, munchies, and, in some provinces, beer. The Irvine Big Stops kinda hit that middle ground of convenience, and now they have started moving from their homeland in New Brunswick into Quebec, so on our trips east, we find ourselves in a lot of them.

They are all pretty much the same: their French fries are always frozen, their fish is tough, and the coffee is warm. But, nevertheless, on the road, you stop where you know, even if you know it isn't all that good. Some people might say we should look around and take chances and search out those mom and pop places to get good food. They would be right, but in the van, with six people all wanting to eat right now, and nobody having any better ideas, you eat where you have eaten before, time and time again.

We walk in to find there is a line, which for a Saturday late morning isn't at all surprising. Truck stop convenience comes into play here, and we all have coffee right away… that helps a lot. Menus are pondered over, as though there will be something different on this one, and eventually everybody has decided, the waitress takes our order, and within ten minutes our food arrives. The potatoes are cubed-up, deep-fried chunks of starch, the eggs hard, and the sausage tough and deep-fried. All of this is to say it is exactly what we ordered, and, with ketchup, we dig in.

Man, I've gotten to the point where I just hate breakfast. I think the next part of my life is going to find me sleeping later and eating less. Gone are the days when potatoes were fried on a grill, with the eggs and sausage. It was greasy, but no greasier than now, and there was life to it. Every breakfast place had a slightly different way of doing their home fries, and the egg depended on a skilled fry cook to turn out right. Sausage changed from region to region, some places better than others, but still they all had a characteristic to them. But on the road over the last ten years, we have witnessed the end of breakfast in Canada. In the Midwest, and the South, breakfast still lives: grits, biscuits, gravy, home fries, hash browns, the lot. But here at home, it is with sadness that I have witnessed potatoes cubed, bacon deep-fried, and sausage resembling low-grade filler stuffed into a condom and thrown in with the fries to die a greasy death.

"This all sucks!" I scream in my head as I stare at my singed eggs, and then look plaintively around the room to see if I am the only one who is outraged. If my counterparts are concerned, they don't show it. They just slurp up their side of fruit pieces and leave half of their food on the plate, having decided that this is breakfast. The most depressing part is that we all expect it and just don't finish breakfast anymore.

Saint John (the other)

Entering Saint John by way of Highway 1, you are taken by its dirty, rundown port-town exterior. Oil refineries and post-industrial lands take up a lot of the view as you plunge into the downtown area. Oh wait, no, it's the uptown area. The downtown part of Saint John happens to be perched on a hill, so the locals all refer to it as uptown. On a dreary February evening, Saint John can be just a little more so. The fog coming in off the Bay of Fundy, via the main harbour, can give it the atmosphere of Victorian London. The streets are downright eerie, the faux historic streetlights actually giving it a spooky feel. This town, having now survived 100 years of decline, hangs on, and the last census showed that its population has risen for the first time in decades.

The town boasts of being the most Irish city in all of Canada, with more than one third of its folks considering themselves of Irish decent. I picked that up from the Internet, and it surprised me because I never really got that feel from Saint John. Unlike St. John's, Newfoundland, where it seems as though 96 percent of its population just got off the boat.

Saint John claims to be the oldest city in Canada too, and inhabitants will tell you so, right after meeting you, just before apologizing that no one is going to come to your show. As if this historic tidbit is going to make up for nobody coming to your show. Strangely, it kinda does.

The promise of a mostly deserted city always sets my mind to work trying to figure out how, if things were different, I could fit in here. I find Saint John reminiscent of nineties Montreal, before the condo generation. I've probably given this town more thought over the years than most. Unfortunately, I've probably missed the boat, because in the last couple of years, the real estate prices have bumped out of reach finally, as I thought they would. This town is on the incline, and it will probably be unrecognizable in a few years.

Because it's always been easy to book and it's not that far off the beaten path to Halifax, our band has played Saint John many times, and with the exception of our last two shows—one being on the waterfront on the eve of Canada Day and the other at Peppers Pub, located in a kind of mall — we have always played in front of almost no one. This is a college town, and it has always blamed its lack of musical support on the fact that the university is located quite a way out of the uptown area. Students prefer to stay home and video date instead of supporting clubs like Elwoods, the A Khord, or the Blue Olive, and when they do come uptown, they seem to not be able to go anywhere but those boom-boom dance clubs located in the mall.

I am making it sound like all is doom and gloom, but we did keep coming back because the support that we had in town, small but enthusiastic, was worth showing up for. For most of our shows, we played Elwoods on Prince William Street. I was bemused recently when a local mentioned that Elwoods turned into a "Gay Bar." He used the whole "air quotes" movement and everything. Now, herein lies my love of Saint John. Anywhere else in Canada, when a local refers to a bar as a "Gay Bar," it usually means that they sell chilled vodka and have a dress code of some sort, and maybe a gay person went there once and didn't get beat up. But in Saint John, I was surprised to drive by Elwoods and see it adorned with rainbow flags. Lo and behold, it does seem to be catering to the gay and lesbian community. All right!

Saint John, along with being owned almost entirely by the Irving family, has a huge crack problem, industrial decay, a dead live music scene, and a heck of a lot of fog. But in its favour, it actually has a large enough gay populace to support a gay bar. It really does have its big-boy pants on, as far as demonstrating that it is not such a backwater. If you throw in a couple of independent news publications, a shuttle to the university, and a decent stage, they are about a year from having a nightlife.

I get the feeling this town has a real up-and-coming undercurrent of culture that is just not accessible to the likes of me at this point, but it's coming. It makes the list along with Hamilton as far as a town that could really actually eclipse its larger neighbours culturally if the right folks keep fighting the good fight.

We eat at the most convenient restaurant in the uptown core. It's right across from Elwoods, and even though we've eaten there before, we do it again. Sound check over, we scramble a bit to get some food in us and maybe some digesting done before we have to play. Nothing fits this bill like Jungle Jim's. I believe this restaurant is owned by Westinghouse as part of an experiment to prove that fine food can be prepared using nothing but a microwave. I imagine the kitchen of gleaming white, and stainless steel counters, not a fryer in sight, or a stove, just a big freezer and a bank of microwave ovens. You enter the front lounge, which abounds with bamboo and tiki, and are escorted to your table by a very likeable hostess. Drink orders are taken, and you are at first excited by the fact that it is Wing Night. Wings arrive, and immediately you are amazed that they somehow managed to get a chicken out of the egg, get its little feathers off, and nuke it into death. Man, those are some small-ass chicken wings there, complete with individual portions of Kraft ranch dressing on the side in those little plastic packets. I can't believe we have eaten there three times, and once at their branch in Corner Brook, Newfoundland.

Dinner finished, we retire to the van, feet up on the dash, to smoke for a couple of hours until it is time to play. There is a crowd of, say, fifteen or twenty folks, including the opening band, Green River Killer. The show goes well, and we load out on to the cobblestone streets and pack the van.

After many very small shows over the years and managing to get non-stop play on the local college station, our efforts in Saint John came to fruition finally when we were asked to play the eve of Canada Day concert on the boardwalk. Finally, after years of banging on this town, we got to play in front of something like a thousand people. In fact, most of the folks had seen us before, but I guess they had just all seen us fifteen or twenty people at a time over the years. I guess the message here is, keep coming and eventually it will all work out fine. Thanks, Saint John. You rule…eventually.

The night road

Having finished our lightly attended show at Elwoods, and having spent hundreds of dollars previously on hotel rooms in the Saint John area, we trek out into the wilds of New Brunswick on the infamous rural night drive to parts more welcoming. The last few times we played this area, we ended up opting to drive on to Fredericton to take advantage of a deal that the Capital Bar set up for us at a motel there, rather than brave the meagre motels in the Saint. There are some seriously bad motels in that town.

Now, as you travel the historic Highway 1 west, it's a two-lane affair that does its fair share of winding and mounting hills, more of a back road than a highway. It's four a.m., it's snowing, and you are trying to make time. Every so often you see the speedometer hit eighty-five and you think, "Oh ya, we are making good time here, Gern."

It's at that moment that your headlights reflect eyes just off the side of the road, and your knuckles grip the steering wheel, and your knee flexes wildly as you back off the accelerator and poise to jump on the brakes, which is a bad idea on snow-covered roads. You zoom past the threat and are back on the accelerator. This dance goes on for a couple of hours, New Brunswick not being the safest place to be on the road at four a.m. in the winter.

You start thinking about what you could do in Saint John. All you would need is about $500,000. Looking on your computer earlier today, there was a massive building on Water Street for $300,000, and the way your brain works at four a.m., you are able to push away the reality that the band made only $250 tonight and your take was a $20 bill. This leaves you a bit short, but never mind.

You see musicians' lofts on the fourth floor, a youth hostel on the second, a café/bar venue, and maybe a convenience store on the ground floor.

It could work. You see the youth hostel bringing the black underwear crowd from all over the world, attracting college students to hit on the European women in the café. Open mic on Tuesdays would bring in musicians who would eventually need the studios on the fourth floor. And there you would be, tucked up at night in your bed on the third floor, peacefully dreaming of the end of the Irving family's stranglehold on New Brunswick.

The dream unfolds between dodging deer and dogs on Highway 1. I love night driving: anything can go through your mind as you wait for something to come through the windshield.

St. Andrews, New Brunswick

Tonight's destination is the outport of St. Andrews, New Brunswick. This beautiful enclave is located on the border with Maine, U.S.A. Here's the first tip for St. Andrews: always pay attention to your phone service when entering town. It is so close to the U.S. border that on many occasions, using my cellphone, I find out way too late that I have just made a long, distance call via an American cell provider. It ended up costing me $12 to make a three-minute phone call to get directions to our gig. Always check the corner of your screen to make sure it does not say AT&T.

St. Andrews is a small place, kind of a summer town all laid out on a big grid of low-density housing, some of it quite charming. Our only show in this town was at the local community centre. There are two bars in St. Andrews, and we had a night off and can tell you both bars are not bad for a town this size.

On our arrival, we were greeted by local businessman and music lover Jamie Steel. We load in to the small auditorium with a rudimentary PA system, and the sound is bad, but we pull off a great show in front of seventy-odd folks in a small town on a Tuesday night—magic. We finish up and head toward our accommodations for the night, the jewel of St. Andrews, Salty Towers.

This B&B, owned by the aforementioned Jamie Steel, is one of the most unusual places we have ever stayed at on the road. A rambling turn-of-the-last-century clapboard, with a wraparound front porch, it's summery-looking even in the dead of winter. You enter through a dark front room resembling an antique store and are then ushered upstairs. You have the choice of many rooms, the first choice between heated and unheated rooms. The choice to take an unheated room is boosted by the fact that I get to have my own room. It's small and paneled in wood, has a creaky bed and a light, and not a lot else, but it's all mine.

Waking from a deep sleep the next morning, I notice that a small ridge of ice has formed on the edge of my blanket located just below my nose. It's early and I have to pee, so I run to the heated part of the building and find a toilet. Relieved, I run full steam back to my rapidly cooling bed and force myself back to sleep for a couple more hours, taking full advantage of the day off.

Shaking myself awake around noon, I make my way downstairs and find the communal kitchen, where some of my bandmates are making breakfast. Tea is made, and then, post-toast, we explore the house. Off the back of the house there is an entire closed wing of what must have been dorms once, with small beds, two per room. These rooms look as though they've been untouched since the sixties. We find a third floor that is similar but partially gutted years ago, possibly in an abandoned attempt at remodeling. Having exhausted our nerve, since I'm pretty sure we weren't actually supposed to be wandering around those parts, we end up back in the living room and lounge as we drink tea and check out the wide range of kooky decor. We while the afternoon away in the knowledge that we have another day off, and we are in a good place. Much better than hanging around a motel room! The band members noodle away on guitars or read magazines as the February sunshine bleeds in through the window sheers.

That night, we sample the downtown bar scene, stopping first at the Red Herring, where it's open mic night. The bar is empty and yet nice, but empty bars usually stay that way, so we eventually find ourselves across the road at the Kennedy Inn. It's karaoke night, and we tie into pints, and I spend most of the night fending off offers to get up and do a song. I've never been a karaoke kinda guy. I think I just sort of feel that if I got up and sang, I might just find it a lot more fun than doing the work that is involved in playing in a band. Steve and Filly lead the room in a duet, maybe "Islands in the Stream" or something, and we get blotto on Alexander Keith's.

Later, back at Salty Towers, Jamie Steele and one of his friends are making food in the kitchen. Over salad and guacamole, they tell us stories of the house and we trade ghost stories. This place is spooky, but I've always found haunted houses feel really safe once you are in there. Jamie makes us feel really welcome, and we have some more wine and beer and then retire to the splendour of our rooms for the night.

Salty Towers is one of those places that you look up on the Internet and the reviews are exactly mixed. Half the people just hate it because they want recently refurbished bathrooms, cable TV, room service, and the like, and the others fall in love with the place, as we did. It's creaky and at times disheveled but very homey, and you get a sense that Jamie has invited you into his home.

Bands passing through the area might want to check out some of the local bars for gigs. My guess is that they only book the weekends for shows, but I have known some friends' bands to get some okay Saturday nights in St. Andrews. Keep in mind when in the area that Salty Towers is there, and Jamie likes bands. Treat his house with respect, though. Don't be a dick: this is his home even if it is a B&B.

GPS

I was once a professional truck driver, and I have found that tour management requires many of the same skills: a great sense of time management, the ability to keep an eye on where north is, and knowing how to read a map.

Fewer people now can find their way through the world with a greasy road map half unfolded across the steering wheel of a moving vehicle. This is a shame, and I do believe that there will come a day when the GPS systems around the world, which depend on poorly maintained satellites, will come into crisis. Then, we will be f.'d, because there will be only a few Luddites around who can navigate the world without digital assistance. That said, the GPS is an essential band tool, as important as a cellphone and a laptop to the unsigned band and traveler.

Our first GPS was acquired quite by chance when Filly purchased a new couch at Brault et Martineau, a Montreal furniture chain who were giving away GPS units as part of a promotion.

When we started using it, everybody was a little bit freaked out. I remember Matt yelling from the back seat, "Don't follow the machine. It doesn't know where we are going!" We eventually got used to and then relied heavily on this wee bit of nouveau tech gear. To this day, GPS's still have some factory-equipped glitches to work out, and one of them is in New Brunswick. There is a big old chunk of Highway 2, south of Cabano and north of Fredericton, where the satellite just doesn't recognize that they built a new highway about fifteen years ago. The machine says you are driving through a field for two hours. You learn the deficiencies of your individual unit quickly when touring Canada, and then it becomes indispensable.

These damn things work wonders. You think it is just gonna show you where to go, which it does, but the best thing we found was the reverse kilometre clicker up in the corner. With that little ticker going, there are precious few calls from the back of the van, asking "How much farther?" or "Are we there yet?" As a passenger, you can snooze away, drifting in and out in that uneasy 100 kph road sleep, and awaken without bothering to even interact with your fellow man to have the answer to your groggy question. We are 276 kilometres from home. So you shift your weight, shut your gob, and go back to sleep.

Another indispensable feature is *find gas*. Rolling through the hinterland on empty in a part of the country that you've never seen before, this feature will save your life. No, I mean it will *actually* save your life. Plug in *nearest gas station* and drive. Using it in conjunction with a trip metre to monitor known gas consumption can make it possible to decide whether to drive out of your way to get gas or stay the course. After a few trips, you get really well acquainted with how far your van goes on a full tank of fuel. Our 2006 E-350 would normally go 720 kilometres on a 120-litre tank. On a few occasions, we have managed 780 kilometres, but that was coming across the Prairies with a massive tailwind for the entire tank, and the last 50 kilometres were white knuckled.

Before the GPS entered our life, we had rafts of dirty, half-ripped, unmanageable maps cluttering up the van. We used to need a Canadian road atlas and still had to make time to stop just outside of town to buy a local map for the towns that were big and confusing or call for directions. It took a lot of time. Now we just plug it in and drive. Miss that right turn in Halifax, and bam! It resets and you are able to find the revised route to where you are going.

Finally, when you are late for your gig, because you slept in, or had to stop at Magnetic Hill and get ice cream, it helps you more effectively to lie to the club owner on your phone. "Oh, hey, Jimmy! Yeah, we are going to be a little late. Had some van trouble. We should be there in, say, an hour and a half." You say this as you stare at the ticker that shows you have a full 200 kilometres left, but an hour late for a band is well within belief to most hosts.

This all leads me to a travel tip: when leaving St. Andrews for Fredericton, if that is the way you are going, punch in Fredericton to your GPS and follow it. We did, and the damn thing took us on a "as the crow flies tour" of rural New Brunswick and, I think at some point, Maine. We were really scared about getting busted by Homeland Security or U.S. Customs for having illegally crossed into their territory. For much of the time, we were also worried driving on some neglected roads, mostly following skidoo tracks and a steady trail of discarded beer cans. We made it to Fredericton on time, though, and took in some nice scenery too. Keep in mind that these were some pretty tiny back roads we ended up on. If you have a really crappy band van, you might want to stay on the main roads, but if you have the time, a good van, and no illegal substances on board, give it a try.

Fredericton, New Brunswick

Fredericton, a city of about 50,000 people, is the capital of New Brunswick. In spite of its status, when you get downtown, it really does feel as though you have arrived in a small town. On your way to the business district, you pass through a belt of low-density housing laid out in that Middle-American way that Canadian towns of this size have. Tree-lined streets, quiet backyards, and a school thrown in here and there. Downtown is laid out on a grid that reminds me of some small western towns in Alberta, except for the hard left turn you must make to avoid the Saint John River. Before you know it, you are at the back door of your venue.

The Capital Complex, which is located on Queen Street, gives you the feeling that, "Hey, this place looks closed." It is a storefront, but upon further investigation, you find the bar or the complex that is the Capital actually faces in towards a courtyard of other bars, which gives it a bustling sort of effect on spring and summer nights. This massive outdoor courtyard bar, of course, competes with your show on nights when it is nice outside and the terraces abound with drinkers but the room you are playing is dead empty. This small venue has always gone a long way to make us nervous about turnout pre-show but always seems to draw the folks in right at show time.

Sound check is always quick and goes fine, and then you spend a few hours lolling about on the deck outside worrying about turn-out. As is usual, the bar is dead empty right up until you take the stage. So here is today's tip: have a really loud and extended tune-up before your set. If you really tele-graph your start, by the time you've fumbled around on stage for five minutes, all the folks hanging out back and upstairs at the dance club will have figured out that you are going on and rush the stage. You tune, and bam! They are there. Well, if they are going to be there at all, they are there just as you finish tuning.

Our key biggest surprise about Fredericton was their knowledge of Canadian music. Being a university town, this place is wired up. The kids are on the cutting edge of band knowledge. They have taken to the Internet for their music well in advance of most other towns, and rely on sites such as CBC Radio 3 to get their fix of music. We were amazed, the very first time we played the Capital, that halfway through our first set they were singing along with most of our tunes. This floored us. We'd never played here before, so how could they possibly have heard of us? This instilled a love for the town that has lasted throughout the years.

A tip of the hat goes to the bar itself, because they use Radio 3 as their house music, which means that during the regular run of the day, the bar plays nothing but current Canadian music. Now that is knowing which side to butter your bread on. It seems weird that nobody else has figured that out: as a venue, you should and can play a steady stream of songs by bands that will eventually wander through your front door, which creates an audience for this music far in advance of its showing up.

Now lots of places play good music and even, if events allow, preview the bands that will be rolling through, but I must say that I was amazed at the way they had worked this out. I was also amazed that the folks in the audience seemed to know the lyrics better than I did. (The band was not surprised by that since I'm kind of famous for not remembering lyrics and making fumbling sentences up to cover that fact.) I would say that over and above my co-singer Felicity Hamer's many great attributes, her top talent was in fact to anticipate my screw-ups while she sang backup. She, having noted I was stumbling over lines, would wait on her harmonies just long enough to figure out what was coming out of my mouth and then sing that harmony over it. Often the third verse would come out where the second should have been, or a complete mangle of made-up-on-the-spot lyrics, and she always seemed to cover it. She was amazing at that. I can't remember a single time she didn't manage to cover for me. Plus, she never dropped a line; she had a great memory for lyrics, thank Christ for me.

Now the other thing that Fredericton served up to us, and that we took major advantage of over the years, was their deal with the Prospect Inn. I've stated before that a really great thing for venues to do when the bar cannot offer accommodations is to have a deal worked out with a local hotel. In this case, the longstanding accoms for a show at the Capital has been the Prospect Inn. Located at the corner of Woodstock and Prospect, sort of on the far edge of town, this simple motel has been a safe landing for us many nights. If you book early, you can get the rooms on the ground floor, which are right off the parking lot, and you can back right up to your door for a very easy three a.m. load in. The downside to this stop is that the motel is a little on the rustic side: the smoking rooms are very smoky and the non-smoking rooms only a little better. The place could use a remodel, but the TV works and there is generally hot water.

The staff are great, the breakfast special is definitely worth getting up for, and with the deal we got through the venue makes it a great, safe, cheap place to sack out in.

One thing to keep in mind about the Prospect is that the walls are paper-thin, and many a band argument has been started by band members bitching about the other band members in the next room, and them hearing you, or, in this case, me. I must admit I've been busted myself. Shhhh.... Go out for a smoke if you want to bitch, take a walk down the road, or lock yourself in the van.

I've always found that bitching is the cornerstone of all band relations, allowing one to get things off one's chest, but just keep in mind it is not all that helpful to getting down the road if the folks whom you are bitching about end up banging on your door, and then it's a fight and not just bitching. Bitching and fighting are usually two separate events, and steps should be taken to keep them apart. Bitch on the road and fight when you get home, if at all possible.

For some reason, New Brunswick has been the scene of the overwhelming majority of our most serious band squabbles over the years. I've checked with other bands, and they mention an increased amount of fighting when within the borders of this mostly innocuous region. Is it the lack of good food, the long night drives, or just its being at the end or beginning of this leg of the tour? I'm not sure, but thicker walls would help, and maybe a good club sandwich could go a long way to soothing tensions on a long drive.

More night driving

Since Fredericton is only a ten-hour drive from our home in Montreal, we found that we ended up doing a lot of night driving in New Brunswick. Either rushing straight out of Montreal heading to a Thursday, Friday, Saturday trip out east or finished on the East Coast and trying to save money on accommodation by heading straight home after a gig. The after drive is a grueling one. To start with, someone has to stay sober all through the gig, which isn't the biggest problem, except that it is usually the last gig of a trip, and who doesn't want to have a little bevy on the last stop of the tour? It usually comes down to a coin toss: the loser pulls the first six hours, drinking a very large coffee while the other members sleep it off in the back. As well, tearing straight home gets you home sometime around two in the afternoon on a Sunday. It's always snowing or raining on that day, and then you just go to bed, only to wake up at two a.m. Monday morning with nothing to do. I hate that run, but we always took it. Didn't matter how many times—it was hell.

Highway 2, the Trans-Canada, is a challenging four-lane road in the middle of the cold dark night. Challenging due to the fact that it is really uneventful, 110 kph speed limit, fewer but not non-existent deer, and a sporadic parade of Irving-owned transport trucks going by to keep you awake. The fact that the trucks come in two different colour schemes, the yellow ones being Sunbury and the green ones being Midland, does little to interrupt the boredom. I've thought many a time over the years of coming out here to play that I got totally hosed during my driving career because I didn't get any East Coast runs at all. That's a shame because these roads are built for the long-haul driver. They have hills but not large ones; once you get south of Quebec, it's mostly four lanes, and there are just enough properly spaced truck stops to keep you in coffee, and there really isn't a lot of traffic. Damn, after running the eastern seaboard of the U.S. for ten years, this is trucking in God's Country. To a professional truck driver, boring is good. To a sleepy guitar player at four a.m., it could be a little less boring if only just to keep you awake.

On the ethereal trip that is this book, and in a perfect world on a perfect tour, you would not be driving all the way home. On the tours that will be planned later, due to my experience, we will be heading north to Bathurst.

Bathurst, New Brunswick

When touring, how do you fill the off nights? It is reasonable to expect to play Thursday through Saturday. If you don't, then you just don't actually have a tour. As your band gets a little bit more exposure, though, it can be expected that you reach the level of filling Wednesday or Tuesday easily. Once you get more known, you are more sought after, and clubs are willing to book you on a Tuesday night, figuring that even though it is an off night, they can get folks to come out because everybody has heard about you. Real big bands don't have this worry—you know you have made it in Canada when you can book seven nights a week without batting an eye. After ten years together, and the last six or so touring, we got to being pretty able to book Tuesday nights with an okay show, generally depending on what club and what part of the country. And to give dues to our agent, we occasionally actually got the elusive Sunday gig. But that still left Mondays, and the Sundays and Tuesdays were still sporadic.

So, how do you kill those dead days when it's too far to drive home, there is no gig to be had, and it generally costs the band a couple hundred dollars a day to be on the road, so you are also losing money? Well, when out west, it is easy. Wednesday to Saturday, you play one area, all the shows are not more than five or six hours away from each other, and then on your off days, you drive to the next area, like, say, Edmonton to Vancouver. You can kill two days easily on that run.

We would always finish up in Lethbridge on a Saturday night and then spend three days straight running back to Ontario, arriving there Wednesday night just in time to play a show. The east leaves fewer chances to arrange things this way, actually making it harder to figure out a decent tour, because it's too close most of the time to justify staying out for an extra week.

Over the years, however, swift tour planning has come up with great answers to this problem. Sometimes, you manage to stay with friends. If you are lucky, it's in a cool town, like Halifax or St. John's, but sometimes we have holed up in farm-houses in the middle of nowhere, or worse, Antigonish.

We have also had good luck "Pricelining" these off days.

I know we got some great three-star accoms in Halifax on the off Monday night for something like $50 a room. "I'll take three, please." I even got a Toronto three-star hotel downtown for $40 a night once.

On one occasion, we found ourselves coming out of Cape Breton on a Sunday with two days to kill, so for the first time in our East Coast history we actually back-roaded it. Yep, jumped right off the Big Road and took a detour up along the coast of the Northumberland Strait with no purpose but to kill time and see some scenery. Gone were the uneventful highways of Nova Scotia and New Brunswick, and we finally got to see a little bit of the beauty that everyone raves about, even writes songs about. Yeah, it's a nice drive that eventually leads to the unlikely destination of Bathurst.

Bathurst, New Brunswick, is a quiet town of not quite 13,000 souls, resting on the shore of the Baies-des-Chaleurs. It's a sleepy place. Kids from here used to come and see us play in Moncton, Fredericton, and even Halifax. That's because Bathurst is one of those towns that we could never really get around to playing. It's small, and the only shows that are available are only available on, say, Friday nights, because this blue-collar town is just not going to bring enough folks for any other night of the week. And even then, if we did play it on Friday, not only would we have a small turnout, but it would also mean backtracking quite a ways to get up here. The town has size and geography playing against it.

For bands able to overcome this geography, you might find a small group of soon-to-be-your-biggest-fans. There are reportedly two places to start looking for a gig, but according to some local kids, one is really filled with "skids" and the other is just a "blow joint." You can go to Bathurst sometime and maybe you can figure out what that means, because really I just shook my head.

This brings up a really interesting part of this region that is typified by Bathurst: the language. It is unique. I've heard it in patches because upper New Brunswick's key export over the years is its young people, and I've picked up on it in the bars. They seem self-conscious about their language and will only speak it in hushed tones and only with other Acadians. It is a complete mix of French and English, which I find amazing. Any sentence spoken amongst friends will start in either French or English and then switch several times by the end of the sentence. Now I live in Montreal, so I hear a lot of folks whose conversations switch back and forth amongst the two languages in the course of a regular conversation. The true Montrealer is very picky about which language is used to speak about this subject and which subjects require the other. It's nice, and knowing a wee little bit of French, I find it makes me proud to live there. Well, in the right parts of New Brunswick, they take this to a place that is just not witnessed anywhere else. For example, two girls are talking to each other, and one says, "*Hey, j'aime t'skirt com l'way c'hang.*" Roughly translated, it's "Hey, I like the way your skirt fits you," or "I like the way your skirt hangs on you." Now, that's language. The other thing that this little tour out of the way taught us is this section's travel tip: when touring New Brunswick, you will find all the hotels and motels to be very expensive; even shitty ones in shitty towns will be up around $100 a room. That is until you make it off the beaten path and start running into the mom and pop motels. Once you get off the main highways, you will start running into small town after small town and, they all have these private, non-chain, no-frills sort of places. We found this in Beresford. Out on rue Principale, we pulled into John's Motel. The name says it all: no frills, just John's. It was clean, they had TV and Internet, although bring your own USB cable, and there was a pool if you happen to be traveling in season. We got three rooms for under $150, tax in, and spent a night off watching Discovery Channel while drinking beer and eating pizza. A great night off.

While checking in, I got the chance to experience one of the best things that can happen to musician who is in a mildly famous band. Someone recognized me. Here in a town that we have never played before. I'm sure that getting stopped on the street could get old real fast, and for the truly famous versus, say, us at the time, being small "f." famous, it was just a nice thing to have happen. I had just finished checking in, and the guy (who denied being John, although I had my doubts) was asking what we were doing out here. I mentioned we were on our way up to Carleton, Quebec, to play a show. He asked what the name of the band was, and he gave me that "never heard of you" that you will generally get if you play in a band in Canada. He didn't sound uninterested, he just hadn't heard of us and had been kind of hoping I was the drummer from April Wine, and I wasn't. So I had just finished talking to him about that and was waiting for him to dig up a USB cable, when two more folks wandered in off the road, having hitchhiked here. I knew this and was a little ashamed because we had actually passed them two hours before and didn't pick them up, figuring we were quite packed in there ourselves and there just wasn't the room.

I struck up this conversation with the guy, trying to divert my guilt for not having made the room, and he said, "No problem. Hey aren't you the lead singer from that band the United Steel Workers?" I glanced back over my shoulder to see if the John was suitably impressed, but I think he just thought it was a set-up, and proceeded to check them in. The long and the short of it is that being in pre-fame and on the long, hard road, it was just nice to have someone mention they have noticed your work. Now, if I can just get that stalker who works at the dep down the street from my house to back off a bit, that would be good too.

Bienvenue a Quebec

As I see it, here is Quebec as it pertains to Canada with respect to the music scene. In a nutshell, here goes. First off, you have the Canadian music scene, and then you have the Quebec music scene, and it would seem that the two never talk to each other. The English-speaking agents out of Toronto won't call Quebec clubs to offer shows, terrified that someone will pick up the phone who doesn't speak English. The French-speaking Quebec agents, who all speak more than enough English, won't call clubs in the rest of Canada, I think because they are just not sure whom to call, or they fear their bands don't have a market there. The labels don't know each other, the distributors run in different circles, and left in the middle are the bands and the fans. There are precious few bands from the other nine provinces who would even think to play shows in Quebec, apart from Montreal and maybe Quebec City. Add to this that most English-speaking bands in Montreal identify themselves with the Canadian music scene and not the Quebec scene, and so mostly they don't play around Quebec either. They choose to drive an extra five hours out of their way to pick up a gig. The French-speaking bands don't really think they will do well in the rest of

Canada, so they stay in Quebec.

Now the great thing for those French-speaking bands is that there are a ton of gigs within the borders of Quebec, so they stay home. These two solitudes add up to a really shameful lack of cross-pollination, and it is this situation that is dragging down the entire industry. For non-Quebec Anglophone bands, there is this big long hole in the middle of the country that you drive through on your way to Fredericton. You stop for a poutine, and get a speeding ticket, and you just keep driving through. It's a big gas suck, and makes successfully playing the East Coast even harder to pull off. For the Quebec bands, it becomes a little too much of a backwater and limits their success. The Quebec bands are very well supported by fans, radio, media, and government money, but it would seem they lack the momentum that would propel them much farther, to the national or world stage. Now some French-speaking bands have pushed their boundaries, and they have found that there is a place for them in the Canadian and even American scenes.

To understand today's touring scene, we need some history here. Back in the sixties and early seventies, someone invented motels. Well, okay, motels go back farther than that, but it was in the early seventies that they started showing up on the outskirts of every town in dCanada. What happened over the years was that those motels started cutting into the business of the local hotel. Let's understand the local hotel. Every town in Canada with more than, say, 2,500 people had at least one, and in most cases, a couple of them. They were those big old Victorian jobs, three or four stories high, and they marked the downtown core. In a lot of cases, they sat in state at the main intersection, a real cultural anchor to every downtown sector. It was in these hotels that you could rent a room, get a bite to eat downstairs, usually even a beer.

The trouble with those places, however, was that usually they were built pre-modern-day plumbing. They were retro-fitted later on, but back in the day, that generally meant there was one bathroom per floor, which meant you had to share. Well, this is where the idea for the motel came from. It was an easy sell: you could stay in your own room and use your own bathroom, and there was little to no chance that you would even have to interact with your fellow travelers. This is actually hitting the people were they live: in real life, folks don't want to meet other travelers. People are generally scaredy-cats, and certainly if they can avoid it, they do not want to share a bathroom. The private bath was a smash, and people stopped using the local hotels as a means of accom-modation when traveling for business or pleasure. This left the local hotel desperate to find other income. Most of them had already been supplementing their hotel business over the years by having a bar on the ground floor where their steady stream of guests provided a good base for a restaurant and bar, with locals wandering in to drink and mix with the travelers.

But with the travelers now being attracted to the more private motel, the local hotel had to rely solely on the local townspeople to keep afloat, with the upper floors of the build-ing going vacant or catering to locals who needed low-cost, short-term housing. This wasn't that profitable, and one of the schemes that took hold was the hotel bar hosting strippers. This worked well and brought in all sorts of folks to the bar but also went a long way to making the hotel bar a little less welcomed by the average townsfolk.

Another saviour for local hotels was live music. Most of these towns didn't really have a large music scene, so a circuit developed, and bands were paid pretty well back in the day to truck from wherever they called home to some bar somewhere and set up for the weekend in your "local," now referred to as "The Hotel." This scenario was a good deal for the bands, well at least from our point of view. Blow into town on a Thursday afternoon, the bar put you up in vacant rooms and probably fed you, and I'm sure gave a bar tab. At the end of the weekend, you got paid.

Now I know there are a million stories about bar owners screwing bands over, but for the most part, there were lucrative three-night gigs all over small-town Canada. Bands started up all over the place to fill this need for live music.

Most bands toured regionally, within a four- or five-hour drive from home. You really didn't go beyond that because what would you do between Sunday and Thursday afternoon? You finished up on Saturday night, got drunk, stayed over, and in the morning headed home for a couple of days. Come Thursday morning, you headed out again. Mostly, Ontario bands played around Ontario, and western bands stayed out west. You did this till you got noticed, and you got noticed by doing this week in and week out. Once noticed by labels, you got a record deal, then airplay on the radio. You did a bunch of blow, your record company stole your money, and your wife eventually left you because she found out you were sleeping with strippers who were staying across the hall from you in what had now become a sleazy hotel.

That was the seventies, at least as far as I have been able

to put it together from musicians who are ten or fifteen years older than I am, as well as from my own recollections of my local hotel back in the day.

When the eighties came around, someone invented the franchise restaurant chain. These strip mall oddities, located just out of the downtown area, between downtown and what would become the "new mall that was killing downtown," went a long way towards helping towns abandon their main drags. These new restaurants offered casual dining. They had names reminiscent of Irish pubs, such as O'Tooles, Flanagan's, O'Hara's, and Copperfield's. They weren't pubs, but they were trying to play off the huge business that pubs were doing back then. They had family dinning up until nine, and after that, they turned into bars. They popped up all over the country and did okay restaurant business for a while. Then someone figured out that you could pay the guy working door, the skinnier one who you hired because he was related to someone and wasn't really big enough to effectively beat people up, $50 a night to bring his late-model record collection in and spin dance music.

Dance music brought in a slew of the ladies who found these old hotel bars to be sleazy and a little scary as well as now run-down. This new suburban type place offered clean bathrooms and dance music, and the ladies came running. All good bar managers know that when you get a room full of ladies, the guys start showing up to fight over buying them drinks. These places killed the local hotel bar, and they did it faster than you can "spin right round, baby, right round." By the mid-eighties, the hotel bar scene collapsed, and gone was a whole music era. The road bands had no place to play or people to play for, and they quit touring every weekend and the interest in live music outside of major cities pretty much blew away. So did most of the homegrown music.

Without the steady stream of musicians rolling through town, getting paid and getting laid, to influence the younger kids, those kids stopped putting together bands because there wasn't anywhere to play. And then they all moved to Toronto instead, taking the last bit of culture most of these towns would see for years with them.

Hard to believe this was all caused by the invention of the private bathroom and subsequently the invention of Wing Night. Yes, I'm saying one directly led to the other, and then caused the collapse of live music in small-town Canada. My own hometown of Cobourg became a complete dust bowl of culture for about twenty-five years, and only now, with the advent of cafés, has the town started to see the resurgence of people playing music again. An entire generation of musicians was lost or at least dislocated from their hometowns.

In the years since the seventies, there have been some exceptions to all of this. Some local music scenes survived due to their proximity to universities, or perhaps the towns had the wrong demographic to entice these restaurant chains and so the local bars survived, but gone were the majority of those sweet three-nighters that paid well. What was left was a patchwork of places to play that spanned Canada—enough for a band that wanted it bad enough to string a tour together, playing one-nighters and moving on to the next town, hoping to fill those holes in the schedule, and they did. Back before cellphones and Internet, they rallied and took to the roads, sometimes driving from town to town just hoping that nobody had been booked there yet — showing up and walking in, and asking if the bar needed a band to play for the night.

I heard a story once that there was this guy in St. John's who, for business reasons, used to buy all the Canadian phone books, and every spring, his office was awash with bands borrowing phone books so they could cruise the Yellow Pages and look up gigs to book a tour. It really amazes me that this is generally how it went back then.

Now, when booking a tour in an unfamiliar area, the smarter bands just go on line and look up a band that sounds similar to them and see where that band is playing. A quick search and you are sending an email asking to play. It's still tough work putting a tour together, but, wow, it's a lot simpler than it used to be. With that said, it's been a tough situation that is only now really coming together after thirty years.

Now what does this have to do with Quebec? Well, Quebec, due to its speaking mostly French, really did not develop in the same way. They had motels just like us, and that did seem to kick off regional playing, and that still continues. What they missed out on was, no, not dance music, because they do have that, but they just didn't get those damn Tipsy McStagger's casual dining joints with the Thursday night Nacho Platter deals the way the rest of Canada did. With the exception of Tim Hortons, Quebec has never been terribly friendly to chains, and I think that is why small-town Quebec still manages to have bars in most towns offering live music every weekend. Because it didn't go away, they still have a heck of a lot of folks who go out every weekend expecting to hear live music.

The French-speaking bands that have toured east or west

have been quite surprised to find out that there are a heck of a lot of people in Canada who want to hear their music. A lot of folks outside of Quebec speak French, and there is a pretty healthy Franco music tour circuit that spans Ontario, Manitoba, and well into the west. Add to that a lot more English-speaking folks who are interested in hearing French music and have enough high school French to get them through a set, or just take the music at face value. If it's good, they like it.

On the flip side, our band was from Montreal and believed that the French-speaking population was just not going to respond to our English repertoire, so we avoided playing outside of Montreal and Quebec City. We were stupid. It was not until a few years ago that we were swayed into thinking it could work for us. Friends of ours, a local Montreal band named Lake of Stew, started touring Quebec singing pretty much only English music, and by all reports it went over well. Lake of Stew was kind of swift that way, saying, "Why would we drive all the way to Ontario to play a show, when we have French-speaking people showing up at our Montreal gigs all the time and they aren't getting mad because we speak English?" It was smart. As this was starting to take root in our heads, we had been invited to some festivals around Quebec. We realized that the Quebec audiences weren't hung up on our inability to sing in French, and it dawned on us that more and more French-speaking people were coming to our Montreal shows. So we started to explore Quebec. It is sad that even with all this, we did our first proper tour of Quebec only in the last year our band was together.

We discovered that English bands were welcomed with

open arms to the province and its many, many gigs. It helps if you have some folks around who can speak a little French, to help with the booking, and trying your bad high school French on mic does go a long way towards bringing the folks eye to eye with you. The biggest problem I had in the band while touring Quebec was that everyone in the band spoke French better than me, and I was the front man. Two members of our band at that time were actually francophone Quebecois, but with great trepidation I sucked it up and just started berating the audience with some of the worst French they had ever heard. The band moaned, but the crowds loved it. "*La prochaine chanson, se c'est un chanson du oiseau blue dans la fenetre.*" It was a great tour and we did very well. We sold record numbers of CDs due, in part I'm sure, to the fact that the folks wanted to take the music home and sit down and try and figure out what it was we were going on about onstage for an hour and a half.

French crowds love to hear English music, and English crowds love to hear French music, so let's swap gigs and everybody start touring the entire country, coast to coast, with no holes in the tour map.

Carleton-sur-Mer, Quebec

First stop on the Quebec leg of the tour, if you're coming from the east, would be Carleton. A small town with a population hovering around the 4,000 mark, Carleton is a welcoming community of farm, forest, and fisheries workers. The town was the first in North America to offer thalassotherapy, a treatment invented in Brittany, France, in the nineteenth century. It involves healing using sea water and salty mud.

The mud, along with a big old wind farm, has diversified the economy and brought this picturesque town into the twenty-first century.

The microbrewery Le Naufrageur has also helped the town move ahead. A range of full-bodied ales, and generally enthusiastic staff, make it popular with brewing enthusiasts in the Gaspé region. They have also made themselves into a pretty decent stop on Quebec's folksy music circuit.

They put us up in a camper trailer behind the brewery and fed us pretty well on bistro pub grub. The PA and soundman were on the temperamental side, causing us to actually play our last song acoustically, but certainly the crowd of forestry workers who came out heard no problem and danced from almost the first song til quite a while after we actually finished playing. This is something you're going to see a lot of in rural Quebec: dancing that could go a long way toward putting Newfoundlanders to shame. Those tree planters with their big over developed calf muscles could dance any band into the stage. This club showed us that the Gaspé would be worth playing again.

The Gaspé is very much a tourist area, so during the season, gigs will go to poppier bands, or those who can cover well-known Quebec pop stars. But off-season is when the real rootsy bands are going to grab the attention of the locals. Under the right circumstances, some places are great in the off-season, and Carleton is one of those places, hosting country, alt-country, folk, roots rock, and the like.

On this leg of the trip, you will find out why the good folks of Quebec go on and on about the Gaspé region. Man, it is all that! Rolling hills, seaside beauty, and small shore towns abound on the Rose, which is the tourist route that runs all the way around the Gaspé Peninsula. Coming late to the Quebec touring circuit, we never really got to explore its full splendour. Besides Carleton, our only stop out there was Matane.

Matane, Quebec

If Matane were a city, it would beat Chicago for the title of the Windy City. The gales almost took me and my 280-pound frame sailing down the street. This is a reasonably barren place in the early, early spring, when the wind howls in from across the open water of the Gulf of Saint Lawrence, hitting the wind farm at the western end of town with full force. There are more than fifty egg beaters cutting through the skyline in all its Euroesque splendour.

Our band has a fixation, no, a mania, with windmills, wind farms, and wind culture in general. We play a game, sort of inspired by punch buggy, the childhood car trip game played by punching your sibling in the arm and calling out the colour when you spot a Volkswagen Beetle.

I don't quite remember exactly how the game started, maybe it was Felicity or maybe Eddy Blake. There certainly is no hitting involved since we don't want to make our band relationship any more physical than it already is. We use a points-based system awarding bragging rights to the most observant.

At first, each person had a different thing to collect, and it was up to their bandmates to spot them before the "owner" did. Our road manager, Gwilym, was collecting hydroelectric dams, Eddy Blake was collecting the elusive nuclear power facilities, and I started collecting windmills. Over the years, the game started to boil down to windmills, with everybody in the van putting an inordinate amount of effort into claiming windmills before anyone else saw them. It really did pass the time, and as one of the chief drivers, I usually had the upper hand. The driver, or at least a decent driver, should be scanning the horizon in search of things that might go wrong up ahead, and generally just be very aware of his surroundings. I really did develop an ability to see and identify windmills, even wind farms, that were really very far away. The Prairies were good to the younger members of the band, folks still retaining the ability to see twenty miles to the horizon, so being older and further from my years of 20/20 vision, I relied on my knowledge of wind farming, gained from the Discovery Channel. Discovery building and engineering programs taught me to keep my eyes peeled when around the base of mountain ranges or near large bodies of water, places that are inherently windier than others. And, in the end, a keen memory of previous trips and just being more awake than anyone else in the van seemed give me a big advantage. In the latter days of our travels, it must be said that when touring the East Coast, that part of the world being fairly behind in wind technology, the game further devolved into spotting decorative yard-based windmills, pinwheels, and later into weather vanes. It must be said that the term *roof cock* was heard many a time in the last few months. This was our term for weather vanes, made honorary windmills for the purpose of the game.

Over the years, we became fairly well known in Matane. I'm not sure how this happened since we had never played within a hundred miles of this town before our first show there, but never underestimate the rural Quebec music consumer. Unlike other provinces, Quebec really does have an underground community of music lovers. I think it was probably the tree planters who originally brought the knowledge of our band out this way.

Band travel tip: promo CDs to tree planters. Tree planters traverse the globe and, not unlike Typhoid Mary, spread many things across this planet, like STDs and cultural info. From tree planting has come our knowledge of vegetarian cooking and left-wing politics, and a fairly useless acquaintance with rock climbing, the fanny pack, and those funny Indian hats everybody was wearing in the nineties. Along with these earth-changing things, we also discovered Michelle Shocked, Billy Bragg, and the good people of Matane, Quebec got to hear about the United Steel Workers of Montreal. Our show there came about because some ardent fans who lived in Matane decided that they wanted more live music in their town and got together to make it happen.

There was a recently opened *brasserie artisanale,* or brew-pub, there called La Fabrique, and some local folks got together and pitched the idea to the bar. They fronted the money for the sound system and came up with the guarantee to pay us. They set the cover charge at $10 and then hassled all their friends to show up and pay to get in. The whole thing worked, and the place was packed. There were some sound issues, such as the air conditioner causing a major squealing sound in Matt's guitar amp, but turning the AC off during the show seemed to fix it. This also made the audience sweat more, thus making them believe they were having a much raunchier time than they were. There was also a very large bottom-end feedback problem. Halfway through the set, I noticed the newly constructed stage was built to unintentionally mimic a bass bin. In the middle of a song, I actually jumped off the stage and moved all the cases and coats away from the bottom edge of the stage thus allowing the bass frequencies to escape and stop feeding back through Flipper's standup.

We got wholly drunk that night on homebrew and wobbled out to the cab at two a.m., vowing to play this town again. I think the homegrown aspect of the folks who brought us there added a lot to the event.

Shows like these have really started to become part of the touring experience. Our band, having come late to this party, never really got onto the house show circuit that has flourished in the last four years across Canada, but I must say that these types of shows arranged by private citizens are a nice transition from standard club-booked shows to the full-on house concert idea. Bully for the folks who do this stuff: it really is starting to fill in the blanks for touring bands. Keep it up!

One final note: there is an abundance of restaurants in Matane catering to a tourist class of traveler, yet every restaurant seemed to offer the same menu of seafood, Italian, and Chinese. For a late-night romp, Dylan and I got takeout from the Palace du Chine. I "think" I had the chicken balls and fried rice, and Dylan got the cashew chicken and noodles. My meal was exactly as I expected it: dark brown fried rice and dry, hard balls of deep-fried chicken with red sauce. Dylan's dish, at first glance as seen through a plastic top, looked as though the entire dish was made up of cashews, but upon removing the lid, he was very angry to find that it had maybe three cashews, two pieces of boiled meat, soy sauce, and an entire aluminum foil plate of elbow macaroni. I've seen Dylan angered over food before because it's kind of his thing to get real mad about bad food, but here in Matane, as we made our way across a parking lot in a 60 kph wind, his hair blowing almost straight out to the side, holding his $11 plate of elbow macaroni with grease soaking through the bag, Dylan spewed a tirade of franglais about wind, macaroni, and Matane. It is one of my favourite memories of touring with him, but unfortunately, it was the last time he ever consented to go out for Chinese with me.

MV Camille-Marcoux

The grande dame of the St. Lawrence estuaries, the big boat that traverses the river at a point where you can no longer see the other side, the *Camille-Marcoux* has been plying these waters since 1974. This boat is the weirdism that makes it possible to put together a winter tour in Quebec.

Looking at a map of the province, Quebec is geographically cut in half by the St. Lawrence. Half the gigs are on the South Shore and the other half on the North Shore. In the off-season that means that most tours must backtrack to Quebec City to cross the river because most of the ferry service is seasonal except for the Matane-Baie-Comeau ferry. This boat also crosses to Godbout, Quebec, but as far as I know, there really isn't any gig up that way. There's nothing past Baie-Comeau, unless you are thinking of going towards Sept-Îles, but the roads actually run out not far from there. I hear there is a highway out of the Baie that runs to Labrador City, but as far as I know, few folks have mounted tours that take in the grandeur of that area. If someone was willing to take the trip, I'm pretty sure they'd find some really appreciative folks.

The ferry between Matane and Baie-Comeau is named for Camille Marcoux, the first doctor from the Lower North Shore. For his merits, they have dubbed this fine sailing ship after him.

The deck plate hits the wharf with a thwack, and our van slowly plunges into the interior of this aged vessel. The interior looks as though it was serviced by pre-schoolers, with endless coats of oil-based paint giving it the look of Plasticine. The moulding joints of the walls and ceiling seem to form rippling cracks that give you pause and leave you searching the decks for a certificate of seaworthiness. It's slightly encouraging that the locals and the service people seem unconcerned by the state of this vessel, so we lock up the van and ascend to the upper decks.

Taking this ferry saves several hundred kilometres on the trip to Lac Saint-Jean, but still, I do wonder why this ferry runs year round and many of the others don't. The other ferries stop during the winter, but the weird part is that those ferries can see the other side, but for the *Marcoux*, it's a two-and-a-half-hour trip. You can't see one shore of the river from the other. I don't know why the crossing isn't upriver at, say, Tadoussac, but, hey, that is for the *Société des traversiers* to have worked out, and I'm sure placing the winter ferry here is probably the only reason Baie-Comeau is still the town it is.

On a windy March day, the water is angry, grey with large, low swells and hints of whitecaps. It's the big old river meeting the sea here. Fresh water mixes with salt water, and if you keep an eye out, you just might spot whales. Tadoussac, which is a

100 kilometres upriver, is actually known for whale watching, so it's possible you'll see them here too. The cold wind does eventually drive you inside where the low ceilings make the rest of the trip feel claustrophobic.

One of the cool things about ferries in Eastern Canada is the ship models. Located somewhere around the middle of the *Camille-Marcoux* is a glass box about eight feet long, encasing a scale model of her. You can see what she looks like below the waterline, and the ship takes on new dimensions when viewed like that. The overall impression of this vessel is sturdy but old.

The journey ends as she enters the harbour in Baie-Comeau. Like the other RORO, or roll-on/roll-off, ships in her class, her nose lifts up as we dock, exposing a forward loading deck. Rolling out into the parking lot, I felt a certain amount of pride having now become a veteran of sea travel.

You pass through Baie-Comeau on your way upcountry. This picturesque town of 20,000 is actually the hometown of our beloved Brian Mulroney: feel free to hock a loogie out the window, or stop and pay homage, depending on your political bent. The non-homaging will exit town by way of the 138 and start rolling over some rough-looking countryside.

I suppose this part of the trip is far prettier during the summer. As you head upstream, you will pass through a whole lot of quaint little seaside towns, and if you keep your head turned to the left for the whole journey, you will enjoy the scenery. The problem is, for a lot of this trip, and especially in the off-season, looking to the right, or, say, looking north, you will just see a whole lot of brown scrub that used to be forests, or at least brown scrubby forest. It resembles the drive across Northern Ontario, a drive nobody is ever in a hurry to take. But when it gets too bad, just do a neck stretch and look south and to the left. Oh! I think I see a whale.

The town names will play off in succession over the next hour or so, and if you are Montrealer, you will finally be able to put a place to the names that you have heard on the nightly broadcasts of the CBC Quebec regions. The news stories usually concern mill closures, forest fires, murders, school closings or openings, and land settlements. The trip really did open up for me a working knowledge of the province that I previously did not have. It's either my failing memory or my lifelong bout with dyslexia, but I need to have traveled through a place to actually remember where it is on a map. This alone, for me, was a great reason to finally have mapped the Lower North Shore in my head.

About ten kilometres before reaching Tadoussac, you find that the GPS says to turn north on the 172 to head for Chicoutimi. The rigour of the band schedule dictates that you make this turn, a sad turn. I've never done the drive between Tadoussac and Quebec City, and I bet that a whole bunch of folks reading this are now groaning quite loudly that we have just missed the best part of the North Shore. In the meantime, we head north on the 172 and things get rocky. The road winds, and gets hilly, and nature abounds. It's a real rock, trees, and fish sort of drive, craggy nature at its best.

Lac St-Jean

In Montreal, whenever you ask where someone is from, if the answer is "Lac St-Jean," then the words are always accompanied by this knowing nod. "But of course he is from

Lac St-Jean." I never really knew what all the nodding and knowing glances were until I made it up here for a show.

Chicoutimi is the centre and the bigger part of the amalgamated town known as the Saguenay. In 2002, Chicoutimi, La Baie, Jonquière, and a bunch of smaller places were shoved together to make up the new town of Saguenay. This sprawling small city of around 140,000 folks is a little more town than first meets the eye.

We arrived with an invite to play the Jazz Fest, which is run out of the Chicoutimi Hotel, a grand building that has survived the years and still keeps watch on the main drag of the downtown core. The festival is held around the month of March, so it doesn't feature the usual big outdoor stages, but the organizers have a couple of venues set up and a rotating roster of an eclectic mix of musicians traveling through town over the weeks that make up the fest. We played a basement restaurant, and I wowed the crowd with my broken French and antics including humping married men in the audience, and generally amusingly confusing the crowd.

Today's safety tip: keep in mind that humping the crowd is the kind of shtick that must be honed over years of practice, so please do not attempt to hump just any audience member. First, make sure that you are not in a biker bar, and second, try and find some rube that is definitely married to a woman and not out with his homophobic buddies.

Surprisingly, physically attacking members of your audience seems to work best while they are eating: it would seem their inhibitions are down at a low level while digesting food. It seems counterintuitive, but it works. Possibly, the slowing of my victim's metabolism may hold the key to why I did not get punched in the face during our set.

The crowd sated with food, wine, and entertainment, I ducked outside for a smoke, my usual sweaty, disheveled, post-show respite. It's a time for reflection on the show, a moment to catch my breath, and in most cases, to touch base with the local smokers and the early birds leaving the venue. Located under an awning at the exit door on a cold March evening, I proceeded to talk with quite a few locals in my very imperfect French. Most of the folks were actually surprised that I could speak French at all, based on the act they had just witnessed. It was through these conversations that I found the answer to the knowing look I had been getting all these years when being introduced to people from Lac St-Jean.

They were a weird mix of rooties, intellectuals with a common trait: it seemed that almost everyone had at one time lived in Montreal for a period of time. I mean, I talked to twenty-odd folks that night and every one of them had spent time in Montreal, either for school, work, or for a relationship of some kind, and all of them had moved back here.

This is different from most places. I myself grew up an hour and a half outside of Toronto, and the pull of the big city for economic reasons, social reasons, or just fed up with home reasons spirited away half my high school graduating class. This is not surprising: small towns are populated by the next generation of students, children, and folks who have convinced themselves that a 130 km drive to work is in fact a reasonable commute. But here in Chicoutimi, I found that the magnetic pull of this town seemed to bring them home again after a short time away. Possibly all it took was two years in Montreal's urban splendour to convince them that all that, plus the mountainous beauty of the Lac St-Jean region, was the better deal. So I figure that knowing look to a Montrealer translated as a sort of comment on the fact that that person from Lac St-Jean was not going to stay here, so don't go giving them too much of yourself.

As for the rest of the town, I must admit I was impressed by the local's heartfelt ease with their hometown. The other thing I found about this town was that it was quite devoid of nightlife. I quizzed the locals to no avail because I was hard pressed to find a depanneur that was open after seven p.m. Cruising the main drags, I was surprised that for love or money there were very few places to spend even a modest amount of money in this town once the evening rolled in. In most places we play, this usually means that there is not a hope in hell that anyone will show up for a gig, but, in fact, the gig was packed. One of the francophones in our band assured me that they had played the rock clubs in this town and that they were good gigs. I really do hope that at some point I will get up there again and give those clubs a try. With a wink and a knowing nod that I just may have imagined, Flipper, our bass player at the time, said, "Oh ya, you know the folks up here, they are from Lac St-Jean. They really let go when there is something to see." Hmm….

Quebec, Quebec

Whisking your way down Highway 175 through the heart of the Grands-Jardins National Park is a beauty of a drive for those who love mountains. It's not the grandiose beauty of the Rockies, but nonetheless it's beautiful and a shorter drive for eastern bands who maybe want to see some scenery while they are out on tour. This two-and-three-quarter-hour drive proves that, yes, it really isn't that far up the road to service the Saguenay region.

Pulling into Quebec, let's first deal with the name. In English, you would refer to this provincial capital as Quebec City, but in French, it is simply referred to as Quebec. This is a city of a half a million people, the second largest city in the province. A nice town, very historic, the *vieux Quebec* part of town dates back some 400 years, making it one of the oldest towns in all of North America. Historic, but, in fact, life rarely happens in places where tourist hang out. The real life of the town happens outside the ancient walls and sprawls into the newer city. As far as the Quebec music scene goes, the majority of it happens in Lower Town, or *Basse-Ville,* located downhill from the historic walled city.

There is, in fact, nightlife in this town, although it is seemingly fleeting. Quebec can be a hard town to get a gig in, and although there are actually a couple of decent places to play, most are a bit of a challenge to get folks out to. I suspect that Quebec's proximity to the larger city of Montreal makes it difficult to hang onto musicians, but the fight goes on, and it would seem that recently there is the burgeoning of a local scene here. One of the great proponents of this town's nightlife has been a club called L'agitéE, roughly translated as "the agitators." This club has always impressed me. The club is in the low end of town, and, to my knowledge, the place is a co-op, run business, a makeover from an old-man bar, or, as they were referred to ten or twenty years ago, a "tavern." Most of these taverns, historically located in or near residential areas, until not that long ago catered only to men. Most of these places with their marble floors, musty beer fridges, and shabby bathrooms have gone the way of the dodos. Their location close to residential housing usually pressed them to turn into more family-friendly affairs, especially when the liquor laws were amended to remove the distinction between the men-only saloon bar and the lounge for ladies and their escorts. This tavern has been saved and turned into a music venue. The L'agitéE folks are good folks, offering shows ranging from rock to folk and it's a great place to play.

Located just five or six blocks from L'agitéE is one of Canada's unique culinary experiences. If you have the time before your gig, you must take the pilgrimage to Épicerie Économique. A grungy little depanneur located at 293 Saint Joseph E, it's rundown, it's loud, and it's rife with arguments between its shopkeepers and the immediate homeless population, but it has steamies for a dollar. As well as being a convenience store, the place also offers a range of quick eats, but its specialty is the dirt-cheap hot dog. As with most other places in the province, Quebec has a complete moratorium on outdoor food vendors (although this is changing slowly), citing numerous reasons for this from cleanliness to competition for local restaurants. Municipal governments across Quebec have squelched the obvious need for the street meat, and here in Quebec City, the result is Épicerie Économique. Here you can buy smokes, beer, batteries, and the renowned version of the hot dog known as a steamie.

Okay, the easiest way of describing the steamie is: go to your freezer right now and take out that freezer-burned package of Oscar Mayer wieners that have been mouldering since you last had fifty people over for a BBQ and mentioned maybe folks should not only bring their own beer but bring some meat as well. At the end of your evening, having started to clear the empty beer bottles, you find a half-finished bag of weenies and foolishly toss them into your freezer. Okay, take those freezer-burned weenies out now and steam them back to life along with a very soggy white bread bun, and *voila*, you have produced the Quebec Steamie. Hurray for you!

Now, in case you have never had friends, so thus never had a BBQ and do not have weenies frozen to the back part of your freezer, or if you are in a band and are still pretending that a day's worth of food can be had for under $7, then you make your way to this fine establishment. After coming to near blows with other customers in the lineup to the cash, you then exit the store to eat your five steamies in relative peace on the sidewalk of a fairly busy street, your meal being only occasionally interrupted to fend off people trying to bum smokes. No, I'm not kidding—eat here, it's awesome. Remember, though, don't get mustard on your stage clothes.

Heading out

Your gig played, the gear repacked for the umpteenth time and secured in the back of your rolling stock, you head out into the night and smack into your first argument for this leg of the trip. Now, we were from Montreal, so the less than three-hour trip home at three a.m. was a given. We never made enough money playing Quebec to willingly lay out for accoms, and so, loading into the van and then loading into the accoms just to get a few hours' sleep, when you could just make the drive home instead, always lost the contest. That, of course, is not the argument: making your way out of town, the big question is to take the 40 or take the 20? Now, the 40 is a very straightforward piece of highway, very few towns, little traffic, usually better weather, but a rough old girl. The road seams every so many feet remind me of being on a train: the clack-clack of the seams in the rails, except in this case, in between the clacks, there is not that weirdly smooth rail surface to lull you. There are potholes and lots of them. The potholes are about all there is to keep one awake.

The 20, on the other hand, is a little more winding, a little busier, mostly with tractor-trailers at four a.m. The 20 being below the river and in its lea usually means more weather. It seems counterintuitive, but I always choose to take the 20. The distance is almost equal on the two routes, and for us, getting into town via the southwest was always a better option. Here's your challenge: try both, the 20 on the way out and the 40 on the way back. You will be surprised that after doing this you will be no farther ahead in the argument you will have over this issue years from now, even after having done this trip thirty times.

The definite upside to taking the 20 is that while exiting Quebec City you will get to cross the river on the Pont Pierre-Laporte, the longest main-span suspension bridge in Canada. It's a spectacular vista and worth the drive to see it. The bridge was named after Pierre Laporte, who was kidnapped and died, or was murdered, depending on which side of the political debate you were at the time. This happened during the October Crisis in 1970. Laporte, the Deputy Premier of the province at the time his death, was killed by members of the *Front de libération du Québec* (FLQ). Naming the bridge after him seems quite fitting when taking into context the view. To the immediate left of the Pierre, you will see the most striking bridge you are likely to see in Canada, the Pont Du Quebec, and it dwarfs the Pierre in beauty and design, especially at night, when you don't see how rusty it is. In its beauty there is also a bleak history. This nearly 100-year-old bridge, which still holds the record for the longest cantilever bridge in the world, was built in 1917 at a cost of $25 million and the lives of eighty-nine workers because the damn thing fell down twice during construction. Just remember when driving out of Quebec in the wee hours that these two old girls of architecture are actually the headstones for ninety-odd people. This is a fact that will spook you out just a little bit at night.

Now, peeling off the ramp of the bridge and onto the 20 west, keep in mind that a Quebec band tradition is just ahead. It's late, the band is still a little keyed up from the show, and you are just about ready to bear down on Highway 20 for the long trip back to Montreal, but to your right you see, in all its glory at exit 311, parking lots gleaming invitation, Ashton's. You, the driver, swerve to make the turn, having taken no poll or asked permission to stop. It's open late and the argument is clear: it is far easier to make this trip once everybody in the van has filled up on poutine! You will be remarkably surprised that no one will make the point, "Hey! We just ate a few hours ago, and, man, we are just a few hours from home…." No, without discussion, the van will just disgorge its passengers without a word, and everyone files into Ashton's. This stop is just *fait accompli*: you are a band; it is late; excluding the driver, you are all drunk; let's eat.

It is very brightly lit, and the folks behind the counter look more tired than you do. The food is not the best, by far, but I make the argument that when folks from Quebec shout, "Poutine! We invented it!" this is what they mean. This *casse-croûte* (snack bar) serves the usual Quebec fare of steamies, burgers, sandwiches, and the like, but, come on, it's four in the morning and everybody, without exception, is getting the poutine. With at least six types to choose from, in varying sizes, the pull of fries, cheese, and gravy is just too strong. As is my wont, I order the *Galvaude*, which is chicken, peas, cheese, and gravy, and please err on the smaller side of things. Keep in mind that everybody is just half asleep and worn out, and you really are not going to eat a big old meal here. If you do, the chances that another member of the band is going to overorder is a sure thing. Get the small, and eat what, say, Gus can't finish. He'll invariably get the large hotdog poutine because he's drunk. At the end of your small order, you can decide whether you want to finish his or not: you probably won't.

Now, poutine is one of those big arguments here in Quebec. It was, in fact, invented here—some say in Drummondville, some say elsewhere. I believe that, yes, this is the birthplace. Outside of that, however, I must say I've had better poutine in almost every other province in Canada. Folks are going to be mad at me for saying this, but in my own defence, I must say that I am a student of gravy. I love gravy in all its forms, and it would seem that over the years of Quebec dominance in the poutine market, they have lost their foothold here. From one end of the province to the other, it would seem that everybody is using the same gravy. I think if you made your way into the back kitchens of this province's *casse-croûtes* and restaurants, you would find a big shelf filled with four-litre cans of something marked *gravy*, maybe even marked *Quebec Gravy* or *Provincial Gravy* or even *Gravy du Patriot*. They all get it from the same place: it's thick and blackish brown, and it has a weird BBQ sauce back end to it. If you were to investigate things too deeply, you just might find out that there is a sinister backing to this anomaly. I blame the Mob — yes, organized crime. I really do think that fast food in the province must be controlled by some kind of a syndicate. From one end of Quebec to the other, everybody has the same hot dogs, the same buns, the same fixings, and, yes, the same gravy. No, not similar, but the same—exactly the same. It is impossible that there is not a single renegade in the fast food community who will go outside these walls and make their own gravy, unless the reason is every time someone tries, they are beaten into submission or blackmailed by unseen forces. All of these places also seem to stock Saputo cheese, but I'm sure that is just coincidence.

All of that said, I tuck into my *Galvaude* with gusto, the pride of Quebec drizzling down my cheek, a long viscous string of cheese running from mouth to plate with that awkward, polite frenzy of trying to break the cheese string off with your fork and get the whole of its messiness in your mouth before anybody else sees you and gets grossed out. We load back into the van thirty minutes later, happy and more than a little bloated, fighting off the rounds of gas that try and make their way out of your body. In a quiet van, on that long night drive home, that is the experience of late-night poutine.

Late-night eating, although obviously practiced all over Canada, is more common in Quebec than most places, shy of only, say, New York City. But here in the *Belle Province*, it seems not only just a time-passer, or a tradition, but also a way of life. In Toronto, if you hit a breakfast joint at three a.m., it always seems like you are cheating by having a club sandwich and a coffee before crashing into bed to sleep it off. Here in Quebec, it doesn't feel like that: it is three a.m.; you have been drinking; you eat! And you eat stuff that is bad for you and satisfying. Thank you, Quebec, for inventing poutine. Thank you, Ashton's, for making poutine available in a pre-breakfast format.

A bright light on a dark road. . .gone!

Located just an hour up the road from Ashton's, for years, a gleaming light would appear in the distance, a thirty-foot-tall, gleaming light, flashing its message of welcome. *Food!* flashes, and after a pause, *Gas!* and, wait for it, *Motel!* And finally, *WE SPEAK ENGLISH!* Yes, it's the Monster Truck Motel, or as the locals call it, the Madrid. Looking it up on the Internet, I find that I am too late in mentioning this Quebec landmark. It was torn down in 2011. This awesome landmark offered life-size plastic dinosaurs and some of the biggest monster trucks ever. As you drive along Highway 20 at St. Léonard-d'Aston, please remove your hat as you pass by.

I remember passing this truck stop/hotel many, many times over the years, the forty-foot-tall monster trucks parked up by the fence as an allure to the traveller to come sample the wares, flanked by dinosaurs, and a big flashing sign. This reoccurring moment always brought discussion as we passed it, although we never stopped there over the years because it was too close to Quebec or Montreal to warrant gas or food. Steve Brockley would wax poetic about how he was going to take a date there sometime. "Ya, man, just a date, a little overnight excursion with some special lady. Just imagine your first date: you jump in the car and drive an hour and a bit out of town and pull in next to the monster trucks, go in and have some pizzaghetti, with the *table d'hôte*, and who knows? There is a motel upstairs: anything could happen."

I regret that we never stopped there, and we push on.

Trois-Rivières, Quebec

Not that far after the site of the Madrid, you will pass the turnoff for Trois-Rivières, a town we only played once. If you've never been there, you must go if for no other reason than to take another bridge, and this is a big 'un. The Laviolette Bridge was opened in 1967 and cost $50 million and twelve workers' lives. The workers were killed when a caisson imploded during construction. Man, it sucks to work on bridges in Quebec.

The land is kind of flatter out this way, so the bridge actually has to go pretty high in the air to clear the tops of the boats on the Seaway. For the folks like me who get the fear of heights in them, this bridge is breathtaking.

The bridge dumps you on the other side of the river, and you steer downtown. This old and touristy little town will actually remind you of all those small towns you see across Ontario, with its four-storey buildings all kept up and looking like great places to buy knick-knacks and postcards. This town really is quite beautiful, and they seem to shut the streets down to traffic whenever they can to allow a festival to run amok, which is why we were there. Years ago, we played Le FestiVoix in Trois-Rivières. It's the only gig we ever played there, but it left me thinking we should have gone back. It was a Thursday night and we had a pretty good turnout for our show, which was in some hall up on the second floor above some café that I can't remember. What I do remember is that we were up against The Tragically Hip, who were playing the main stage down the way a bit, and we actually still drew a crowd. Yay! I like Trois-Rivières: nice job dissing The Hip and coming to our show. This town just might harbour some sweet weekend gigs for the band that is willing to seek them out.

On a windmill side note, it must be mentioned that this place is the holy grail. Not that we saw any windmills while we were there, but it is where the Marmen factory is found, which employs more than one thousand "Trifluvians" to manufacture the towers that make up all those windmills you have been counting across Canada.

Back over the bridge and through Bécancour, and you are back on the main line heading for Montreal.

Saint-Hyacinthe, Quebec

I must admit that I have seen the name of this town over thirty years of travel but never actually put it together with its pronunciation. Spoken in English, it really is an unattractive name, *Saint Highasinth*, which is how I always had it in my head. I never put it together with the town that I would occasionally hear referred to on the radio, correctly, as *Sainteeasaint*. Man, that is a pretty-sounding town. *Sainteeasaint*. Who wouldn't want to go there?

This town of around 50,000 taxpayers was named after Saint Hyacinth, an eleventh-century strong-man whose miracle was that he was able to carry a very heavy statue of the Virgin Mary away from an attack by the Mongols. I am left trying desperately to find a segue here that makes it fitting for this town to be named after him, but really I think they just chose it because his name came out of the bingo tumbler. Nice name, nice town.

The streets are small and the buildings close together, which is a problem with most small towns in Quebec, the usual small-town architecture being really hodgepodge. But here in Saint-Hyacinthe, it hangs together, it's clean, and when the weather is nice, the streets are crowded with people and motorcycles.

This is a great time to mention Quebec's love affair with the two-wheeler. Standing out front of the club Le Zaricot, you will see a constant parade of motorcycles, a lot of them Harleys of all shapes and sizes. I must admit, having been an enthusiast years ago, I was very surprised to find how popular bikes are in Quebec. Just go out into the hinterland outside of Montreal in season, and maybe stop at an ice cream shop or something at some crossroads, and just watch. Man, they love their bikes here. The province has always supported a hefty number of outlaw-type bikers, going back to the wild days when Montreal was a wide-open town at the mercy of the gangs and mobs and paid-off police. This history means the last thirty years have left it more vulnerable to bike gangs than some other places, but here on a warm, early spring night in Saint-Hyacinthe, you are likely to see the more middle-class rider. The bad guys were mostly chased off their bikes by the cops at the end of the biker wars in the mid-nineties, and those outlaw types now ride in Beamers or some other flashy car instead. The folks out on the roads now are just crazy for loud pipes, flashy paint, and cruising.

Grabbing a bite from the terrace side BBQ of Le Zaricot, the sun is out and you tuck into a burger post-sound check. This club tried to book us years back, but we just never got the time to get down here, even though it's a forty-minute drive from Montreal. We were crazy!

Le Zaricot feels a little like a theatre and seems to be the place that did everything right. A few years back, they organized a country show that was televised monthly on one of the Quebec networks, guaranteeing them a place in the hearts of the folks in the area. The sound is pretty good here, the staff are super nice, and the place is known for putting on a show. This means folks come out. People are willing to pay good money to see a good band, and the staff treat the bands very well: there is beer and food and smiles and true enthusiasm. Tip of the hat, folks.

Home (Montreal, Quebec)

I'm going to have a problem writing about Montreal, my home for the last twenty years. I know this town well, and I love this town over all others. How do I do it justice? How do I encapsulate it in one short chapter? I will try.

I am an immigrant here by way of Toronto, Cobourg, and Akron, Ohio. I live here by choice, and it's the only place I have moved to on purpose. I moved here for love and found it in a city. Like many people, I moved here in the hopes of cheap rent, three-storey walk-ups, beer in corner stores, and a chance to be part of a city. Coming from anonymous Toronto, my thought was that things here in Montreal were going to really take off and I could be in on it. And *la grande ville* did provide. I arrived to 30 percent vacancy rates and beautiful yet cheap apartments in small neighbourhoods with truly diverse cultures.

To understand Montreal over the last two decades is to understand world politics and the fluid dynamics of populations and cultures. I arrived speaking no French in a town where you really do need to speak the native tongue on some level in order to make a living. I floundered for the first couple of years, picking up a tiny amount of French and working as a truck driver, my trade at the time. I became part of the working class. The city was seemingly sparsely populated at the time, with vacant apartments everywhere. It was a quiet time, with streets to be wandered and dreams to be dreamed. Everywhere I looked I could see the unexploited buildings, streets, parks, and businesses. I just couldn't really figure out why everybody wasn't moving here.

Little did I know that things were afoot in a far-off land that would change everything. That land was China. So here is my narrow view of how it unfolded. In the mid-nineties, Great Britain's lease came up on Hong Kong, and the landlord decided to not renew the deal. In the last years before reversion, the folks from Hong Kong started to look elsewhere to avoid returning to Chinese rule. One of the first stops was Vancouver, B.C. Now, Vancouver had been the hotbed of all things cool since the eighties. Pre-Homeland-Security, it had access to the United States West Coast folks in the cultural industries, and artists and bands did a great cross-border trade. From beer to coffee to indie media to bands, this was the place to be. But, come the late nineties, with all those Chinese streaming in—and, mind you, we only let in the folks who had a big chunk of change — the rents went up due to lack of space, and *voila*, Musician/Artist Q Public said, "I have had enough. I play in a band and wait tables four nights a week to pay my $1,200 a month rent. I can't afford to pay $2,000. I'm out of here." And away they went, collapsing the Vancouver arts scene seemingly overnight. Sorry, Vancouver.

Passing right by expensive old Calgary, the first stop was Winnipeg. The truly connected tried Toronto, and the rest of them, driving their U-Hauls crammed with djembes and amplifiers, drove across Canada listening to the CBC. They heard all the stories about how Montreal was the cheapest city in the Western world, a safe haven for the artist, a promised land. It was the Dirty Thirties in reverse. Instead of homesteaders and farmers in broken-down farm trucks with all their household wares and families tied to the back, it was musicians in third-hand station wagons, the dashes strewn with Starbucks cups.

They arrived to find a struggling arts scene hanging on here in Montreal, awaiting reinforcements. They took up residence in previously vacant lofts and lived like true hipsters for a couple of years, their travels piquing interest across the country, building a wave.

When we first started our band, back in the early two-thousands, the hardest part of the entire endeavour was that we had to share our rhythm section with five other bands. This made the rehearsal schedule almost impossible, getting half the band to dance around the drummer's and bass player's other rehearsal scheds. In the end, we spent the last eight years of our band without a drummer. We just said, "Screw it: it's just too hard to arrange. Let's go ahead without one."

In the interim, all these guys started to show up on the scene from points west. In the migration, it seems all the guitar players went to Winnipeg, all the singers went to Toronto, and we got all the rhythm sections. I can't really statistically back all this up, but within three years of Hong Kong reverting to Chinese rule, everywhere you looked, there was a dude with a stand-up bass here in Montreal. Six years and a hell of a lot of work later, Arcade Fire came out of nowhere to become the biggest band in the universe, and everybody was looking at Montreal.

Montreal, formerly the largest city in Canada, and now the coolest city in North America. A city that is a far cry from those early days, packed to the gills and bustling with life. Although the rents are higher now, they are yet still below the national norm. Montreal is one of the most livable cities in North America. Even though it must be said that we now cower slightly as a cultural war takes place, with the condos encroaching on our venues, this still-vibrant scene lives with the memory of the fall of Vancouver and Halifax.

As an "in the know" local, I enter the city via my all-time favourite route. This route works well for the purpose of this book, since on this tour, we are coming from the East Coast. Arriving in town from what is known as the South Shore, the best way to be welcomed to Montreal is by way of the Victoria Bridge. Please keep in mind, though, that between the hours of three and seven p.m., the bridge is closed to north or inbound traffic so that the suburbanites can flee to their bungalows and backyard swimming pools. You negotiate the maze of traffic cones and barriers and find yourself travelling on the east-side roadbed of the Victoria. Don't look down because you are driving on a steel-mesh road with a very good view of the water. An entrancing view that may cause you to have an accident. From the east side of this 150-year-old train trestle, Montreal's downtown skyline unfolds, and this three-kilometre, route allows you the perfect vantage point to get accustomed to a beautiful city. The skyline looks a bit like many erect penises lying at the foot of the mountain. The foreground is taken up by post-industrial Griffintown, and on the mid-horizon, the glowing red lights of the *Farine Five Roses* sign flashes in welcome. This sight is best viewed at night when the overall vista glows in an otherworldly way, but on a beautiful sunny afternoon, it does distract you from the knowledge that you just crossed over a very big fast-moving river.

On the other side, you are deposited in the once-thriving neighbourhood of Goose Village, torn down in the mid-sixties to accommodate visitors to Expo 67. This now semi-vacant business park unfolds into Griffintown, yet another of the city's *villes* that are being run over for the sake of major development.

Now that you are in Montreal, I must take this time to hit you with today's travel tip, *possibly the most important travel tip of this book from the point of view of a band.*

TRAVEL TIP: as you tour Canada and the world, it is very unwise to leave your gear in the van. In some parts of the country, this rule can be overlooked because there is a small possibility of robbery. But here in Montreal, I will stand up and shout! *DO NOT LEAVE YOUR VAN UNATTENDED WITH ANYTHING IN IT!!!*

Now, all bands have had run-ins with thieves: to be in a band is always to balance the need for security with the need to stop to eat, or sleep or play a show. You are always trying to figure out if it is safe to leave the van and all your gear in a parking lot while you run off and do something? Well, as many, many bands have found out: In Montreal, it is never safe.

Here's why. In most towns, it is unadvisable to leave your stuff, like, say, behind the Horseshoe Tavern in Toronto, or beside Pat's Pub on East Hastings in Vancouver. That's because a crackhead will break your window just to see if that bag left on the dash is a purse with enough money in it to fix for just one night. In Montreal, it is different. They are organized. I believe that there is actually a team of bottom-feeding dudes who read the band listings every week, check out the bands' gear on Facebook, and make a shopping list. They do the circuit every night and pull up in front of the numerous venues around the city, looking for band vans. We all know what a band van looks like, and Montreal's thieving class does too. Band vans stick out like heat-seeking missiles and are usually parked within five parking spaces of the venue's front door. Being near your gear will not save you: you must be watching it at all times.

Unload as soon as you get into town, make sure that your gear goes onstage, and make sure the stage is nowhere near the front or back door. If the venue has a lock-up, use it. This goes for gear and personal effects. These thieves know that as well as guitars and amplifiers, today all bands also carry laptops, hard drives, cellphones, and an array of sexy underwear. They also know that it is easier to move a laptop than a classic guitar, but please keep in mind that they will, of course, take that too if given the chance. When it comes to this sort of crime, the truly worst part is not losing the guitar that you have played hundreds of shows on and wrote all those love songs with. No, what really hurts is that you lose your guitar and the soulless dude who went to all the trouble to steal it probably only got $45 for it. That is the ultimate insult.

When you pull into town make sure you unload first, and even when unloading, make sure that someone in the band is always standing beside the van. Before going into sound check, make sure that all your gear is either safely locked up out of sight or is removed. Keep in mind, bags that contain dirty laundry or empty merch cases look like they are filled with cash when viewed through a dirty window. Don't lose a $700 side window to your van just so the creep can find out you haven't done your laundry in a month. As well as the cost, there is the frantically running around trying to find an auto glass repair place to get your van fixed. Running around the city mad, trying to get back on the road, instead of enjoying Montreal.

Some folks will go even farther than that to get your stuff, too. In some cases, they even follow the band back to where they are staying so they can rip them off. One band lost their entire van and fully loaded trailer which had been parked in front of their friends' apartment while they went upstairs to get a couple of hours' sleep. Came down in the early morning carrying only their sleeping bags to find an empty parking spot. Their guitars, amps, clothes, laptops, gone. Tour over, take a bus home. It happens to everybody, even Iggy and the Stooges. They lost an entire twenty-four-foot Ryder rental truck filled with all their vintage gear. The dudes just walked in, started the truck up, and drove out through the main gate, giving the guard a wave as they left. These guys are relentless and brazen. Ask anybody who tours, and they will tell you how they got ripped off in Montreal.

All that aside, Montreal probably has one of the best music scenes in Canada. Diverse, from indie rock to spoken word and everything in between, and in two different languages to boot. Herein lies the problem for a touring band. You can see a great show seven nights a week here. No matter what you're into, you can see it most nights, and the thing is they are all good, almost all unpretentious, laid back, and supportive. Problem is, with that going on, there just isn't a lot of room for bands from, say, Regina. It is sad, but if they haven't heard of you, it is very tough to get folks to come out.

The usual method for booking Montreal for a road band is this: find a band that plays pretty close to your genre and try and get them to do a show with you. The local scene is real tight here, very supportive, with all the bands playing with each other a lot. If you want to get on a bill with someone, you have to give them a huge amount of notice, usually more than three months. Over the years, I have been trying to get the local bands to be more welcoming to out-of-towners, and in some cases, this has caught on. It really only takes two or three plays in town to build a following, so hang in there. Great clubs to play here are, for different reasons, le Divan Orange with its medium room and cool staff, Casa Del Popolo for its commitment to out-of-town bands, Barfly for its shady dive-bar charm, L'Esco for its middle-of-the-scene location, and Grumpy's for their built-in crowd. There are many more clubs than this. The scene is quite large, so look up your favourite Montreal band, and when they can't play with you because they are way overbooked, ask them who else you should be playing with and where.

The sweaty show complete, the music done, the drinks drunk, the rider plundered, the feeble amount of money split up, the band goes in search of late-night eats. I know this town well, and narrowing it down is real difficult. Montrealers are all about the late-night food. For my pick, I'm going to say go to Schwartz's. Everyone from all over the world has heard about it, and they make the world's best smoked meat sandwiches, bar none. If you don't know what smoked meat is, well here goes: you take that big chunk of meat up near the front of the cow, right between the legs. It's kind of a tough part of old Bessie, but you have a plan for it. Take that big old "brisket" and dump it in some brine for a couple of weeks, then take it out and cover it in peppercorns and smoke the crap out of it. Take as long as you want, maybe a week, say. Then toss that piece of meat up in the window of the shop for a while until you need it. The day you serve it, take that slab out and throw it in a steamer for a while. When some-body yells, "I'll have a medium," you get to work and plow off an unreasonable number of thick slices with a big old knife, toss it on some rye bread with some yellow mustard, throw a pickle on the side, and you, sir, are in heaven.

Pay attention here because all the Montrealers in the room are now yelling, "Hey, Schwartz's is not open all night!" Yep, that's right, it closes early, and when it is open, it usually has a lineup way down the block, the inside of the store is packed, and the staff do a remarkable job of pushing you through very quickly. It's kind of cool, but if you don't want to go through all that, you are standing in front of Schwartz's wondering why I sent you there. Well, it's because if you look right across the street, you will see my favourite restaurant in all of Montreal. Shining like a beacon from God, a light that cuts through your drunken haze, located at 3864 Boulevard Saint-Laurent, is the Main! Go there: their smoked meat is almost as good—I mean like 95 percent as good, but no line, cheaper prices, nicer staff, and, yes, open all night! Your first time, get the smoked meat sandwich with cheese special, the one that comes with a poutine, and make sure you get the Cott's Black Cherry Cola to drink. To the return visitor, please keep in mind that the steak and smoked meat special is probably the best $15 you will ever spend at 3:30 a.m.

If you are smart, you played Montreal on a Saturday night, and if you are lucky, you stayed at a friend's house. Road folks from around Canada probably do have friends here, Montreal being the place everybody moved to in the last ten years. So if you are lucky enough to have saved hundreds of dollars on hotels, because they are really expensive here, you have woken from a drunken sleep, back kind of done in by a second-hand couch. Or worse, you got the floor, or worse, you got the kitchen floor. On a nice day, the sun is streaming in the window, and you are trying to remember that girl's name from the bar last night and wondering if she really was going to check out the band's Facebook site. You are hungover and slightly in love. You've worked out a deal with the bar owner about picking up your gear later in the day, and you wander into the streets of Montreal.

The all-time best breakfast anywhere can be found at 5843 Sherbrooke St. West, and unless you stayed in the neighbourhood of Notre-Dame-de-Grâce, or, as the locals call it, NDG, you will probably be back in the van to find it. The restaurant is called Cosmo's. All the folks in "The Deeg" are now yelling, "No, wait, don't tell them our secret!" Well, it's out there. If it's sunny, you shouldn't have a hard time getting a seat, because on sunny days, the folks at Cosmo's take over the sidewalk and throw out a bunch of old plastic lawn furniture, thus expanding their overall seating from ten people to twenty-five or so. Yep, this is the place, a tiny little hovel of an establishment run by crazy people. Newspaper clippings and cartoons festoon the walls. In off hours, you might actually get a seat at the bar, which is, of course, the only seating. This place is rustic to say the least, rustic but loved. Cramped into the tiny service area are usually two staff members shouting orders and insults back and forth and interacting with the locals. Greetings can sound more like threats, but there is love back there in the question, "Where have you been? I haven't seen you in forever! I thought you died! Was that scrambled?"

Now, if all of this "Cosmmotion" and pushing doesn't float your boat, hang in there because you will eventually be served. They only have ten seats, so they are aimed at getting you fed and out of their hair as quickly as possible. The house specialty is the mishmash. It's a crazy mix of all things breakfast sort of lumped together. It's to die for. The base of all that is good there comes from the home fries. They take potatoes soaked in water all night and throw them on the grill with a diced onion and a right smart handful of margarine: yep, marg, not butter. It's margarine and comes from a big old pail under the counter, applied lovingly with a plasterer's trowel. They just mash the whole thing up there on the grill, and while cooking your eggs and sausages to order on the other side of the flat top, they brown those potatoes till they are just right.

This all sounds disgusting. It is, but it's good, real good. It's not the kind of meal that you should or could eat every day: it's heavy and greasy but godly. Nothing takes the edge off a hangover like Cosmo's.

If you're smart, you have booked your tour so that you have a couple days off to stay at your friend's place. Rent a Bixi bike and have a good time: go see some bands, get drunk, and fall in love. If you couldn't swing it and have to leave early in the morning after your gig, go load your gear out and swing by St-Viateur Bagel on your way out of town. Folks ignoring my advice and heading directly to Toronto after a show should keep in mind that expat Montrealers will pay a king's ransom for a bag of St-Viateur bagels.

Here's another tip for the TO band coming to Montreal: round up your expat Montreal friends in advance of your trip to Montreal and take orders. If you get enough of them together, you could cover your gas bill just from the markup you can charge on bagels and smoked meat.

The final note on Montreal eating is that the city has finally lifted their moratorium on street food and allowed food trucks. Google "Montreal Food Truck" and track them down. It's a veritable explosion of awesome food that up til now had been kept from us by the powers that be. It's weird because they are expensive, but the food is great, possibly some of the best food in town. My pick is Le Cheese Truck. Get that in yah, b'y.

The North Country

Back in the van, we begin now on the leg of the trip that is ideologically the most direct way to take on Canada. Jumping on the 15 northbound, grinding your way out of Montreal, via the Décarie Expressway, a short stint on the 40 brings you out the top through Laval. This road is almost always under construction, the traffic almost always stop-and-go, and it will make you wonder how anyone could ever love Montreal. Due to the fact that I have spared you this route until after you have now fallen in love with Montreal, it is now safe to see its crumbling concrete underbelly. It is also the only way to enter or exit to the north or west.

The 15 north gets a lot better once you get past Laval, our suburb of a million crazy people who for some ungodly reason have decided to call this sprawling, centreless region home. Put it in your mirror and things start getting better quickly.

The 15 begets the 117 and you are in cottage country, up around Mont-Tremblant, pretty quickly. A big ski area, filled with SUV people, put that behind you too and you still have a very long way to go to get up to Abitibi. The road meanders and there is not much out this way: a lot of trees, rocks, and fish on your eight-hour drive to Rouyn-Noranda.

Having taken a couple of nights off in Montreal, you are now all filled up on bagels, smoked meat, and dreams of girls with cool French names, so you want to get up to the north country on a Thursday. The towns up here are blue collar, so you're not going to do great guns on a Tuesday night. Seasons permitting, maybe come up and do some camping on the way. There is a whole lot of country up here, so take some in and cut that drive in half if need be.

Rouyn-Noranda, Quebec

I'm not even going to try and coach you on the pronunciation here. Get a local to walk you through it, or maybe try it onstage and see if the crowd helps you out. I don't think I have ever even come close to saying "Rouyn-Noranda" the way a local would. Rouyn ("*Rooeh*," there I tried) is a copper town. I mean it was built on the copper mines, and the entire area is awash in mines, pulp mills, and farms. The folks are hearty types, hard but enthusiastic and interesting people. With the help of some maps, bad directions, and your GPS you find the downtown core of this small industrial town. Located on Rue 8e is the Cabaret de la Derniere Chance. It sits mid-block on a very wide, not-so-tree-lined street, and on a cold, bright day, it sticks out a little, everything else on the block having a bit of a brownish grey hue to it, or maybe that is just me. The folks inside are welcoming, and they definitely seem to take their shows seriously. It is something that I noticed a lot when playing around Quebec: they have serious sound systems in a lot of these clubs, and if they don't, they seem to rent them at the drop of a hat. The soundman probably won't speak English, but he is more used to that than you are, so you will get by. French is very much the language in these parts. The rest of the towns I've mentioned in Quebec of course also speak mostly French, but there is certainly an ease to getting by, roughly translating back and forth, the folks giving you a lot more leeway in the southern and eastern regions. Up here they speak French. They aren't mean about it in the least, actually quite accommodating really, but they really just don't speak English. Suck it up and you will get by: it's fun.

Sound check quickly over, you will retire to the basement, or the green room. Depending on how badly they wanted to get you up here, or how bad your booking agent nattered at them, you may actually have a rider. They gave us a big old load of veggies, dip, and sandwich fixings, and, man, did that go over with us. Keep in mind, the big box in the corner that kind of looks like it could be one of those wine boxes from, say, a boutique cider mill does in fact contain very industrial cleaning products, so don't try drinking that, thinking, "Wow, look, they gave us eight litres of booze!" In our defence, it did have a very pleasing smell that didn't seem at all cleaning, product-esque.

Tucking into your veggies and sandwiches, you take in the room. As with all good green rooms, they have festooned the walls in previous show posters, and it does take a while to study them all. These walls represent why the Quebec scene is great and powerful. Scanning the posters, you realize all Quebec bands play everywhere in the province, not just along this thin corridor near the main roads that attract touring bands. The music scene reaches most parts of the province, and these poster-filled walls prove that. The good folks who live here in Rouyn-Noranda enjoy a year-round barrage of rock, indie, psycho, folk, singer-songwriter, and country. Considering that they are eight hours north and west of Montreal, I think this is a great feat, a feat that I'm ashamed does not repeat itself across Canada. The rest of Canada has much to learn about supporting culture.

One thing that keeps the town on the cultural map is the annual Festival de Musique Émergente, or the F.M.E. Every August, they invite all the bands that really are doing their work in the province, meaning the bands that are touring all around and are just starting to get noticed, and they bring them all up here on a weekend and get them drunk with a bunch of the music intelligentsia of Quebec, and boom! Six months later, you are suddenly having a real easy time of getting booked in clubs or written about in all the papers province-wide. After our appearance there, I myself turned up quoted in several articles the following year, and most of that was based on conversation I had sitting around the after, party bonfire. They weren't good quotes, because I was loaded, but, still, I was quite surprised how this festival really did help shoot us across the province.

Here's another tip: if you are from Quebec and manage to get into the F.M.E., they have magic beer fridges there. I've never seen anything like it. The fest puts all the musicians up, a ways out of town at a kids' camp. They give you dorms, and they really aren't that comfortable, but you will get by fine. They have a school bus to shuttle you back and forth from town, which is good because I never would have found the place on my own. So there you are, staying at a kids' camp, and you have your little bunk and communal bathrooms and such, and all is fine. Then Matt walks in and says, "Hey, there is a beer fridge over in the kitchen." I quickly make my way over there to get my share before the rest of the band takes it all, and lo and behold, even though Matt had been holding two beers, the fridge was full. I mean it was your usual fridge that you would see in any old kitchen, except that it was filled from top to bottom with Boréale. I've never been a Boréale drinker, but, man, that is a sight to see. Top to bottom, couldn't fit another bottle in it at all. So I took two beers and wandered off to explore the rest of the camp. It was nice, and about a half hour later, I came back to the kitchen and opened the fridge to find that my two beers had been replaced…weird. In all my years in a band, we have had many places that were very generous with beer, but I had never seen, one, a fridge completely filled with beer, unless it had a lock on it, and, two, one that was refilled so often as to look as though it had never been plundered. I must admit that I went home with my clothes in a plastic bag, and my luggage clinked when it was jostled.

The second tip, I have already mentioned: it's the fireside. You will finish your show downtown and will be all worn out from playing, and you will be talking with some real nice folks and thinking about heading back to their house for an after-party. Well, my tip would be to forgo this during the F.M.E. weekend and get your ass back to the campfire. There will be beer, there will be, of course, a fire, which is nice, stars above and all, and there will be some singing of songs that everyone will know the words to except you. But there will also be press. Try and keep your head about you because random conversations you will have will remarkably show up in newspapers across the province over the next couple months. No worries here, unless you are completely a douche. The undercover press at this fireside understand that you are post-show and having a good time, so they will be kind. It is really just a very informal, let's get to know each other, sort of affair, and will save you tons of time later.

Now back to a show at the Cabaret de la Derniere Chance. We played a Thursday night there in March, and this club gave us a real introduction to the folks from around this area. Unlike their brothers and sisters from the south and east of the province, they stand alone up there, cut off somewhat from the barrage of Americana, and Western Canada ideals. They have their own radio stations and TV and do a great job of supporting themselves culturally. Their language is strong and purposeful, thoughtful, and kind of on the rugged side. Before and after your set, they will listen to French music, music from Quebec. The Quebec scene is very powerful throughout the entire province, but it will shock you that outside of these northern regions they will play an inordinate amount of English music over the course of the night. Except not here in the Abitibi, where you will get an earful of Quebec *chanteur*, rap, and French indie rock. It's refreshing, really. At the bar I've worked at for the last ten years in Montreal, you would be hard pressed to hear any music that you would ever hear on the radio, my counterparts and I believing that you can hear that stuff anywhere, so why play it here? This stance really does make me feel akin to the folks of Rouyn-Noranda.

Amos, Quebec

Heading out of Rouyn, you take to the countryside. This is the homeland of Dylan Perron, our banjo/mandolin player. Dylan was our fourth mandolin player over the years, and this Northern Quebec country boy (as well as being a guitar god) served us as well as any who came before him. He also booked this leg of the tour, it being his stomping grounds. This part of the Abitibi region is farmland, and in early spring, it's brown out this way. We are in the North, not Polar Bear North, but North Country. It's probably just me, but I believe you can see the curve of the earth from up here.

It's pretty apparent that up here you work with either

cows, wood, or rocks. We saw quite a few mines, and certainly that big hole in the ground that we passed in Val-d'Or (roughly translated as Gold Valley) would start to explain why people find themselves up here. It's not the wild wilderness of Northern B.C., and it's not the once fertile farmland of Southern Ontario, so it must be the gold or copper or the wood that drew folks up this way.

Amos is a town that built on those realities. A town of of around 12,000 folks, it's relatively new: only established after 1900. It is kind of rare in these travels to find that you are pulling into a town in decline, a town that is less than 100 years old.

Amos has two main drags, one with the newer stores and the strip malls, and then the *main* drag, the confluence of the two being marked by a McDonald's.

We pulled up in front of Billard L'Ad Hoc, which is, yep, a pool hall. It kind of looks like a strip mall, maybe even a McDonald's Funland, but rougher around the edges. Hey, it is Friday night, and I've been going on about the good folks of Quebec showing up for shows, so let's see what happens.

Sound check went sweet, and here we are once again in a pool hall with $30,000 worth of PA. I love Quebec. After two or three hours of being barraged with heavy rock as a bumper soundtrack, we took the stage to a pretty good crowd. Dylan's friends all showed up, and a bunch of other people too. Now keep in mind we had never played up this way before. We were in a rock pool hall that holds, say, 200-odd folks. We had maybe seventy-five come out to welcome us. They danced, they catcalled, they bought us shots. Not a bad night for Northern Quebec.

La Sarre, Quebec

As I've stated before, I grew up in small-town Southern Ontario, a place called Cobourg. In my experience, when any two towns of reasonably similar size are close to each other, they are destined to be rivals. In Cobourg, we had Port Hope. Everybody in Cobourg thought everyone in Port Hope was an asshole, and a person of good standing in Port Hope would, of course, never date someone from Cobourg. Doing so, you would risk ridicule or even perhaps catch "the crabs." Later in life, I realized that this kind of rivalry extends throughout the country and throughout the world. Montreal hates Toronto, New York hates Los Angeles, and London hates Paris. I think, given the chance, the planet Earth would hate Alpha Centauri. Here in Northern Quebec, I was not surprised to find that when talking to folks at our Rouyn-Noranda show, everyone from there seemed to wince a bit when we mentioned we were playing La Sarre. I wrote this off as a regional tit-for-tat affair. Then we made our way up to Amos only to find that everyone there seemed to have a hatred for La Sarre as well, describing them as mean-spirited and maybe a little dumb.

Filling up on gas Saturday afternoon in some random hamlet, I believe the counter person seemed to feel bad for us when I mentioned we were heading to La Sarre.

Needless to say, we entered town with some trepidation. It was slushy outside, and a spring snow blanketing the region overnight had made things a little browner and a little greyer than the day before. There was no stage in the Bistro La Maîtresse, so we put our gear against the back wall and headed out to Mikes for dinner.

Although I have said that Quebec is not big on chains, this is not exactly true. They love *some* chains: Nickels, Belle Province, Dairy Queen, and Canadian Tire dot almost every town. And, of course, there's Mikes. They just don't like "come from away" chains. Canadian Tire is not from Quebec, but it has been around long enough to have dug its way into their hearts. Even McDonald's got its ass handed to it in Quebec many times over, and it's only in the last few years that it has gained ground. But Mikes is omnipresent in large, and small-town Quebec, serving a weird, watered-down menu that leans towards Italian. They do one thing bang on, and that is serving mostly bland food to the masses. Here in Quebec, they come out for blandness. In some towns, Mikes actually takes on a central cultural role, hosting live music, serving okay wine, and in some towns actually being the place to be. On several occasions, I've heard the question, "*Vas-tu chez Mike, ce soir?*"

Here in the regionally disdained town of La Sarre, Quebec, Mike's is bistro-style, and we loaded up on non-regional food. I think I had the Caesar salad, there was pasta, and there was a wine list. I did not have any wine. It was pretty expensive, but, alas, on this slushy Saturday late afternoon, I think we got the finest cuisine that this Northern Quebec town was going to offer.

Back at the bar, we found that the soundman had arrived and was assembling the stage and setting up the massive PA for the evening. The sound set up and check seemed to take hours, so we hung around with great trepidation as the locals started to make their way into the club. They arrived early because they were broadcasting a Habs game and the Trioscouleurs were well into the playoffs. We resigned ourselves to the fact that if we were to have a supportive crowd tonight, it would hinge on the outcome of the game.

I remember the game went into overtime, and by the end, the bar was packed. I sat in the basement smoking cigarettes and drinking coffee, not being a fan of hockey. I could follow what was happening from the groans, moans, and cheers telegraphing the process of this historic round of sportsmanship. In the end, the Montreal Canadians won and we took the stage.

We've had scads of openers for shows over the years. Some good, some bad, and some amazing. The amazing openers really give you something because you have to work to keep the crowd with you. Elliott Brood's show is the toughest to follow because they are the best, but they always inspired us to elevate our show. Bad openers aren't that much easier because you have to bring the crowd back from boredom.

The usual was a well-matched band that played well and got the crowd into seeing a show and then we would sweep in and take it up a notch. As an opener, following the Habs in off-season turned out to be a very notable experience. The folks in the room, totally happy about the game, were already half drunk and now just waiting to celebrate. Here in this town that had filled us with trepidation, we had a slam-dunk of a show. The sound was kind of all over the map, and it was obvious that the crowd understood not a word that I had uttered all night, in French or English. There was no recognition at all when switching from one to the other, but they just rocked out. We played loud, they jumped up and down, pumped their fists, applauded, and at the end demanded encores.

We finished the night truly satisfied with La Sarre. Thank you, folks. The rest of the north has done you wrong. La Sarre being only miles from the Ontario border, we leave Quebec with a bang-up show and bid the province goodbye for two months.

Ontario

Northern Ontario

Winding our way out of *La Belle Province*, Route 388 becomes the 101. Stick with that for a little while and you will pick up the Trans-Canada somewhere around Black River-Matheson. At that point, you will realize two things, the first being that you are now only eleven hours from Thunder Bay, which is the middle of Canada. The second thing you will notice for the first time ever when scanning the map is that you are directly north of North Bay. Wow, Quebec makes its way west quite a bit, eh?

The cool part about all this is that to drive from Montreal to Thunder Bay in one shot takes about twenty-two hours, following logging trucks that are following heavily laden and poorly driven RVs pulling wobbly boat trailers. In season, twenty-two hours is more like twenty-seven. So here you are approaching halfway across Canada, and you have now realized why I sent you out west by way of the Abitibi region. You just rocked three small towns that otherwise you would never have played and gained a ton of respect in Quebec for making the effort. Here is the King Kamehameha reason for this detour: you did not foolishly try to drive across Northern Ontario in one shot. Northern Ontario is death: it's long, it's boring, and it's not all that pretty. It's trees, rocks, roadkill, and grey-coloured lakes that would make you to question why anybody, ever, bought a Group of Seven painting...ever!

Don't worry; if you keep at this game long enough and make several trips back and forth across Canada, you'll see it in its entirety. Believe me, some fine day you will be sitting in Winnipeg on a Sunday morning, and Eddy Blake, who will eventually be your bass player for at least one western tour (it's a small music scene in Canada and he's good), will say, "Hey, why don't we just drive all the way to Montreal in one shot?"

You are enlightened, you are knowledgeable, you don't even smell too bad, having just grabbed your first shower in a week courtesy of some nice Winnipeg suburbanites, and yet, right there and right then, it will seem like a great idea. Even though I have warned you, you will be talked into it by your band, and you will do it. Thirty-seven hours, four tanks of gas, thirty packs of cigarettes, and, yes, two snowstorms later, you arrive in Montreal. It will then take you the better part of a week to get over one of the worst drives, nay, one of the worst experiences of your life. Not if but when you foolishly take this trip, you will be able to look at a mother in the throes of childbirth, crowning no less, look directly into her eyes and say, without even a hint of a lie, "It's not so bad, dear." Well, don't actually do that, because you have already made the first mistake, which is driving across Northern Ontario in one shot.

Highway 11, the Trans-Canada, is what my buddy Jimmy called it ten years ago when we started thinking about touring.

Jimmy says, "Well, coming out of Thunder Bay and heading east, you got two choices: Highway 17 and Highway 11. The truckers take the high road 'cause there are less hills, less traffic, and less everything." Years later, I found that Jimmy was right on all accounts. The mileage difference between the two routes is negligible, and there are certainly fewer hills, this being the original route for the transcontinental railway and fewer hills means faster trains. All of these towns along here were originally railroad towns, mostly inhabited by French-speaking logger types and railroad workers. But Jimmy was right about fewer RVs too. The tourists just don't make it up here, so the locals, some hunters, and trucks have the run of this road. I'm not terribly sure 'cause I haven't looked it up, but getting a ways north of Lake Superior, generally I have found less bad weather, too.

The one thing Jimmy did not mention was less light. In winter anyways, it does get noticeably less light than the low road, with the sun going down far earlier than you are used to.

Apart from the quality of the light, especially at night in the summer, and the flying saucer in Moonbeam, Ontario, I find it hard to grasp any particular events from this drive. Jimmy is right: there is very little up here to see, just a long, rough two-lane that spirits you through towns you've heard of but have never seen before, towns I have now forgotten. Cochrane, Kapuskasing, and Hearst. You'll find these are the towns you drive through without seeing anything worth delaying your progress, so you stop at the west end of town on the side of the road to piss and have a smoke.

Today's tip: the north is filled with tress, a lot of them,

even here on Highway 11. Standing beside the van readying yourself for a piss, dig your heel into the gravel and make a bit of a hole. While smoking, piss in the indent, making a little lake of it. That is your ashtray. Smokey the Bear says, "Only you can prevent forest fires."

Van Smoking: to smoke or not to smoke

This band has always been some sort of a haven for smokers, going back to our origins in the backyard of 650 Vinet in Little Burgundy, sitting around the big, round, green table plotting the overthrow of the music scene. We drank Wildcat, we smoked, and once in a blue moon we would play some music. I don't think we ever hit 100 percent smokers in the band; there was almost always a holdout. But, as the years went by, members came and went, folks quit and then restarted, and we sometimes had a majority, and sometimes a minority, of smokers in the band.

Smoking is bad…especially for a musician. It's going to slow you down, it's going to eat up your per diem, and it's going to put you out behind a club in the freezing rain, which is not generally where you should be when you have pneumonia and you are just about ready to go onstage and hack through a set. Smoking is bad.

Even at times when the band has been two smokers to four non-smokers, for some reason, the two smokers were actually allowed to smoke in the van. I can't believe we got away with it. We had tours where we smoked in the van and tours where we didn't. Sometimes we would talk about it before the trip and decide, hey, let's not smoke in the van. I'd usually vote no smoking if I had been trying to quit, and yes smoking if I was in full denial. When we voted no, we didn't smoke. After the first couple of hours, I really didn't miss it at all. Those tours everybody was actually much happier, especially the smokers because it was cheaper and we got farther into the tour before we got sick. You will always eventually get sick with six folks in the van, sharing mics, sharing beers, and meeting tons of people. The band cold — it will get you before the tour is over.

We've had smoking tours, too. Our first trip to the West Coast, driving our old van we lovingly called "Howard the Truck," a 1988 GMC custom: no back windows, no air-conditioning, bad heater, no snow tires, busted electric window roller up and down thingies, wiring hanging out from under the dash like so much multicoloured spaghetti....

We were taking off for a month-long tour, and it was winter. Kev, banjo player number two...Kev was the dude, always smiling, even when he was throttling someone. Man, I miss Kev.... Anyhow, so Kev takes a collection from the smokers in the van and runs down to Kahnawake and loads up on rez smokes.

He shows up the day we left with six bags of raunchy, cheap, old Putter's: long, rectangular ziploc bags each containing 200 smokes. Kevin throws them up on the dash, where they stayed, open, and everyone just reached up and grabbed one whenever they felt like it. It was like being locked in a losing poker game you can't extract yourself from. I don't think there was ever a single moment of that month we were away that there wasn't at least one smoke burning in the ashtray.

That winter tour of open bags of smokes was the grossest thing I can remember. Man, it was a dark pit of hell in that van. I reeked, I think my guitar reeked, Filly reeked, Kevin reeked, Matty reeked, Eddy reeked, Gus reeked, towns we drove through reeked, girlfriends we called on the phone somehow reeked after talking to us. It was after that that we decided to not smoke while touring in the winter, what with the windows all done up and the window windy thingies broken.

In the twenty-seven years I've smoked, I have tried to quit twelve time,s but touring is the hardest to do without smoking. Waiting is what the music industry is all about, grand chunks of time waiting for sound check or empty miles to burn. If this sounds like your problem, too, the best you can do is to at least ban smoking in the van. Don't make your girlfriend stink just because you called her on the phone. Smoking is bad.

Longlac, Ontario

Longlac, Ontario, is a sprawling, low-to-the-ground affair where we stopped at a roadhouse and had burgers. Post-food, the band dispersed to walk around and get the road jimmies out of their legs after a day on the 11. They kind of scattered, and it took us an hour to get everybody back in the van. Sometimes it goes like that: it's spontaneous, nobody votes on it, nobody mentions his or her intention to wander off; it just happens. A half-hour burger stop stretches into close to a two-hour sojourn towards the end of the day, in a desolate town that just really doesn't offer that much to do except to stare at a lake and swat midges and blackflies.

The meandering band members reclaimed and reinstalled in the van, we point west again and head for Thunder Bay and a night's sleep at the Apollo.

Nipigon, Ontario

The convergence of the north and south lines of the Trans-Canada takes place here where the 11 and the 17 become Trans-Canada proper. It also becomes the Terry Fox Courage Highway right around here. Terry Fox, the amputee with cancer who tried to run across Canada, is the only Canadian hero I can think of who has been turned into a pictogram. Him and Anne of Green Gables, but she was fictitious. Terry's pictogram is common around Nipigon, bearing the bold outline of a runner with a pole for a leg. It's a sad fact made sadder when you realize this is where his journey ended.

Nipigon's other claim to fame is its two battling truck stops. It's a sorry battle, this being a main road, Canada's mainest road, the only east-west thoroughfare in this part of the country, and those two battling truck stops always seem to be closed, the loser being the traveller in need. Everyone arrives here needing fuel, but we seemed to arrive at 11:05 p.m., and both stations close at eleven on the dot.

We have arrived in Thunder Bay way too many times on fumes, having missed the Nipigon fuel stops by just minutes. The trip across Highway 17 in general is what forced us to upscale our touring vehicle. Our old van, Howard, was a pig on fuel, and to boot had a very small fuel tank. We used to get only 300 kilometres from its eighty-litre fuel tank. This is not the biggest problem when rolling around Southern Ontario: you play gigs, and you put huge amounts of gas in the van; it's how it works. But head west and you will find frequently after nine p.m. that gas stations that are open at night are generally farther than 300 kilometres apart. The biggest reason for buying our newer van, Oscar Peterson, a 2006 Ford

E350, besides having windows in the back for the band to look out, a stereo, and air conditioning, was its 120-litre tank. We were able to get an average of 740 kilometres to a tank of fuel, thus being able to travel the expanse of Northern Ontario and all of Saskatchewan at night on one tank of fuel. These two regions are the most desolate places on earth after nine p.m. Driving Howard, on a few occasions, we had to put up for the night shy of our travel destination due to a low fuel tank and no services.

The scariest experience of my life was arriving in Wawa, Ontario, in a snowstorm in Howard. Having drifted across the top of Lake Superior in a major snowstorm at night, we found an open gas station and bought gas. The tank when filled registered 79.4 litres of fuel to fill it. As mentioned, Howard had an eighty-litre tank. That was a white-knuckled ride.

Thunder Bay, Ontario

Rolling into Thunder Bay, it's night. It's always night when pulling into Thunder Bay. We have never pulled into this town in daylight, even in the summer when the sun sets after 10:30 p.m. in the north. Thunder Bay, formerly the cities of Fort William and Port Arthur, is not the actual geographic centre of Canada, that distinction going to an area just east of Winnipeg. But when traveling across Canada from St. John's, this is the emotional centre of Canada. Here, there is no high road and there is no low road, there is just the Trans-Canada, running ten hours east to Sault Ste. Marie or nine hours west to the Peg. This is pretty much the only place to find a show in the nineteen-hour drive between the two.

Thunder Bay. It's the midpoint of any tour of Canada: you're halfway there, and halfway from home.

Surprisingly, Thunder Bay has a population in excess of 100,000 people, and one would think this would be far big enough to host a myriad of cultural events. Well, not quite, it really is a big, old, sleepy, low-lying small town. But due to its geographic location, it is an absolute certainty for a stop on any music tour. All bands must stop here because it's just too far to continue your drive if you overshoot it. I don't think the folks of Thunder Bay actually realize that they get more touring acts through their town than Montreal does. I don't get the feeling they know that it could stop happening. I don't know if they know it keeps happening because of the crown jewel of their nightlife scene.

We pull into the back of the Apollo, located at 239 Red River Road. The Apollo is my home away from home. We have stayed in her third-floor apartment, which is a converted office space boasting eight bedrooms and two bathrooms, more times than any other place in Canada. I have my own room: fourth door on the left toward the back. My room has no door and a double bunk. The upper has no mattress, so that is where I throw my bag, and I sleep on the bottom. The lack of a door makes the room unattractive to everyone else, and it's good to have your own room when on the road. It's even better when it's "your" room. Filly's room is across the hall. She gets her own room too, and hers has a door. She's a girl and always a good trooper when traversing the country with a bunch of smelly boys, but whenever possible, she gets her own room. She deserves it: most places she has to put up with boys farting and snoring. We routinely take our days off at the Apollo and always leave feeling somewhat rejuvenated.

The Apollo dates back years, and I have heard many, many stories about its origins and history. Originally a Greek restaurant owned and run by Tina and her husband, it later turned into a restaurant and music venue.

Not everyone in Thunder Bay loves the Apollo. It seems as though a previous manager was ousted, and that rubbed some locals the wrong way, and there is still bad feeling about it these years later. Thunder Bay is actually a pretty small town, and I know how small-town bar wars can become quite mean, and it would seem that this town and this bar typify this.

To the credit of owners Tina and Sheila, they have dug in and over the years spent most of their energy trying to win the war by being kind to musicians. This tactic has made great strides in the past few years, attracting band after band. First, the bar attracted, the Lakehead University students, and now, slowly but surely, the locals show up on a regular basis.

We load in late on a Sunday night. Fighting bad Northern Ontario cellphone reception, thirty minutes out of town, we managed to make contact with Alex at the bar. Alex is a man of mystery, a Toronto boy who arrived on the doorstep of the Apollo many years back, a man on the run from something, a man who ended up here when he was out of gas, or his bus ticket ran out or something like that. He took up residence on the third floor and started doing sound for the bar. He's quiet but nice, and a damn good soundman. Alex is one of those guys who, years from now, will be acknowledged for his deep understanding of the Canadian music scene. He has done sound for tons of bands over the years. If you are on the road in Canada, you stop in Thunder Bay, and if you stop in Thunder Bay, at least the first time, you will play the Apollo. The second time you might play one of the other clubs, but probably the third time you will be back at the Apollo. So that means Alex has met and done sound for everybody, and he's heard all the inside on every band, every bar, and every song that has been written that is not played on the radio. He knows who gets along and who doesn't, which band is into drugs and which is into beer. He hears the bitches and the fights and the parties. He is discreet, he has the lowdown, and he says nothing. He knows more than any Toronto hipster bartender, more than any Montreal promoter, and he should be pulling a paycheque from Sony as an A&R man. He might actually be quietly doing intel for some major record company, but treat him right, he is a saint. Alex, write a book, damn it, and tell all, make millions!

Alex comes downstairs and unlocks the bar and takes up a seat at the bar while we load our gear onto the stage. We talk for a little, maybe there are beers bought, and we pass the time of day swapping stories and finding out who has been through this month. We decompress after the long drive, catching up a bit on the comings and goings, and retire to the third floor and a night's sleep. Not just a night's sleep, but we get to sleep in, no alarm, wake up whenever we wake up.

The third floor is a sprawling affair of maybe 2,000 square feet, its bedrooms filled with bunk beds, and spare mattresses. It has two bathrooms, yet usually only one is functional at any given time. Morphed from fifties-era office space, it reminds me of a youth hostel. It is in fact large enough to host Alex's bedroom and many bands at once, and it has.

One trip we played the Apollo with Washboard Hank, who is truly my favourite man of Canadian music. I love Hank with his hard-drinking, hard-playing, slap-on-the-back, straight-shooting, no-shit demeanour. We played the show with Hank and his boys, them coming back east from Winnipeg and us heading out west coming from the Sault. It was a raucous show, probably our biggest at the Apollo. That night, we shared accoms with another band, whose name I have forgotten. They had also been heading east when their van's transmission broke down in Nipigon. They had it dragged down to the Canadian Tire there, and Sheila borrowed a car and drove up to Nipigon and brought them back to the bar so they had a place to stay for the couple of days it took to fix the van and rebook the shows they were going to miss. And herein lies the true success of the Apollo. Due to a scheduling problem, that band wasn't even playing at the Apollo that week. Sheila is just cool, and the club has built its name from one end of Canada to the other as being the nicest goddamn folks ever. They take care of you. The bands come back 'cause they offer a refuge on the road, food, drink, and a show, and, in some extreme cases, a ride from Nipigon.

We have been offered many a gig in the other bars in town, and had huge offers and huge pressure from our agents over the years to play elsewhere. But, I like Sheila and Tina and Alex, and they have saved us thousands of dollars over the years, on accoms, food, and beer. They are our friends and an example I mention when I'm asked how to make touring work. It is rarely about who pays the most money and more about who can save you the most money that makes a return trip possible. They do what they can and it works for them.

Tina is Sheila's mom. Tina is my mom. Tina is everybody's mom. With all due respect, I believe she is a little over seventy, and she is routinely there from open to close. The Apollo was once one of her two or three Greek restaurants. Tina is Greek. Tina smokes. Tina talks quietly and watches. And Tina cooks. The day of the show, Tina sets one of the tables and the starts bringing out food. It is an extravaganza of food. There will be two salads, a soup, and then the other stuff comes out. There are chicken wings and fries and onion rings, there is some meat dish, maybe pork, there is rice, and there are pierogies. Now this is the start of pierogi country. By the time you get across the Prairies, you will tire of pierogies, but I'm here to tell you, Tina makes great pierogies. Well fed, you make your way back upstairs to nap before your show. Disclaimer: Tina has been getting on over the past few years, so one may not expect this same level of service that we in fact had enjoyed years ago. If you don't get fed, go find some mid-Ontario Chinese food.

The show will always be a worry. Downtown Thunder Bay can be very quiet, and this is a Monday night. We hit the stage at nine-thirty, and by the third song, a throng of folks comes piling in.

We always play a full-on, thunderous show here because they have the best PA system in all of Canada. Located on either side of the stage is a wall of passive JBLs about fourteen feet tall. The PA built for this bar is from another era: it's a wall of rock built for the likes of Kim Mitchell in a club that has become more a folk club over the years. I love it, but I know Matt is wincing while reading this. Matt Watson, our number one electric guitar god and founding member, always seemed to find the dead spot on the stage, the spot where the sound just doesn't seem to mix. He always had a problem with it at the Apollo.

We plunge into our set, and the crowd starts to yell and dance. It's a big room and could probably hold 200 folks. On this Monday night, we have sixty, but the layout of the room works well, and the folks are all up at the front. A crew of students from Lakehead University, some forestry workers, and a few townies thrown in make a boisterous yet some how intimate crowd, everyone taking part in song set-ups, yelling back answers to the questions I would routinely ask, like, "Has anyone in the room fornicated today?" Thunder Bay folks were always a great bunch to play for.

It's a weeknight, so we close the bar early and hang with Shelia, a true character. Sheila is wonderful, and Sheila loves old music, and we dig into her vinyl collection for a one a.m. dance party interspersed with conversations about the comings and goings of the Canadian music circuit. There is beer, and when there is not beer because it sold out to an unexpectedly large crowd, we plunder the off liquors still available. I have gotten drunk on Blue Curaçao and Tia Maria on a few occasions after the beer ran out. That's a rough hangover but never regretted. The Apollo is the only place on earth where I have willingly participated in a Blue Shark-cocktail, vinyl, all-eighties dance party.

With blue tongues, we load the van the morning after the show, once again playing the game of Tetris that ensures all the gear is in the van. We walk the stage, checking for any forgotten gear, and when satisfied all is in the van, we close the back doors and head for breakfast.

Today's band tip: always load gear in the same way every day so you will know if anything is missing. Over the years, our band has developed jobs for each person. We called them captains: merch captain, driver captain, accoms captain, and that sort of thing. The load-in captain is the first one out of the van and goes inside to see where and when we load in. He also arranges overnight storage of gear and subsequent morning pickup. His other job is usually loading the van. Now, everyone should be involved in the actual walking the gear in and out of the club, but the most important is the one who plays the Tetris in the van. In the case of our six-piece band with a stand-up bass, our gear will only fit in the van if it goes in a very specific way. We built a deck in the back storage compartment just below window level, and it was always the goal to get all the band's gear under that deck. If the gear was under there, then it would be a lot more difficult to steal. Even with all our stuff, on every tour we managed to get it all under there with the exception of, say, Flipper's 4x10 bass cab, which rode on top of that deck. This still left enough room up top for one band member to sleep beside it on long drives.

The best part about that underdeck was that it was so precisely arranged and packed so tight that if the doors closed easily, you knew something was still onstage. I remember being the van packer on one tour, and twice I was able to ascertain that a small gig bag was missing due to the fact that the doors closed without my having to lean on them just a little bit. The stage was searched, and the small camera bag containing tuners and cables was located. The tip again: always have one person load the van, have that person load the van the same way every time, and you will not leave gear behind. We lost a banjo back in the early days; it was a spare, and nobody even knew where it had been left. That was the incident that led to this rule. After that, the only thing we ever lost was in fact that small camera bag filled with Gus's gear. It was Toronto, and everybody wanted to party, so we ignored our rules and he lost a couple of hundred bucks in pedals and cords, left, I think, on the stage of the Horseshoe Tavern. Sad but not a bad record for ten years of road shows.

Breakfast!

Parking the loaded van directly in front of Thunder Bay Restaurant, we file into the diner, a quirky throwback to bygone years. Road signs, taxi metres, and various ephemeral memorabilia is strewn on the walls, but the place looks more like a junk shop than a kitsch family restaurant. The place is small, it's weird, it's old, and so is Denise, the owner. As we shuffled around and chose seats, a yell from the kitchen suggested we get our own coffee. This is early morning for us, eleven a.m., and as soon as we are finished breakfast, we are heading for Winnipeg. Coffee is a godsend.

On her way from the kitchen, Denise trades jokes with the regulars. She stops at our table and kind of looks us up and down, summing us up as out-of-towners. On our first visit, she immediately guessed that we were a band. Apparently, regulars grab their own silverware and coffee before sitting down. The fare of this restaurant is definitely breakfast, although they have burgers and poutine too.

It took me a couple of trips to Thunder Bay before I actually got around to trying the town's number one best delicacy, the Finnish pancake. It just never sound like something

I was going to like because I imagined something involving dried herring. And then I tried it.

It was a surprise to me when it arrived with a side of sausage. It's not a pancake at all; it's a crepe. Okay, let's back up here: there are pancakes, those thin, fluffy breakfast cakes that come with maple syrup. Then there are crepes, those thin, really flat deals that you wrap around ham and fruit. Then there is the problem that in Quebec they call pancakes "crepes," and they also call crepes, well, "crepes" too. The only rule being that diners serve pancakes that they call "crepes," and bistros and creperies serve crepes. Cool…got it. Well here in Thunder Bay, I got a crepe, it's thinner, it's eggier, it's a wee bit greasier and it hits me that the Finnish pancake is what I grew up calling a *palačinka* (pronounced *polachinky*).

My Grandmother Vlcheck is Czech, from a town just outside of Prague that has probably been in six different countries over the last 100 years. She made these flat, greasy, pockmarked beauties for us when we were kids. You smothered them in jelly or cinnamon sugar, and rolled them up. I ate tons of them. Grandma Vlcheck taught my mom how to make them, she taught my sister, and I realize I must get the recipe so I can teach my daughter someday. Man, I like Finnish pancakes, or *palačinka*, and I can't believe it took me several trips through town before I tried them.

Denise returns with our food, a pretty quick order considering she is working the grill and the floor by herself. She distributes the orders, and we get to work. This post — Blue Shark hangover cure works well, the coffee goes down like oxygen, and we actually start to talk to each other for the first time since load out. We talk about the stuff all over the walls, we talk about the vinyl dance party, and we talk about the show. Matt confirms he thinks the sound is shit, and everybody else disagrees. We work out the plan for the day, and we prepare for the 695 km drive to Winnipeg.

Denise returns, and we settle up for the meal. There is a twenty-five cent surcharge for leftovers, which goes to charity. I like this place, and we always eat here at least once every time we are in town.

A footnote: at time of press, there were rumours Thunder Bay Restaurant may be closing. If indeed it is not to be found, please get your Finnish pancake fix at the Hoito. Its less fun, but the food is great.

Westward

Heading west out of town, you are faced with the decision again: high or low road? In this case, the role reverses and the 17 goes north and the 11 goes south. The 11 is the tourist road, snaking its way towards the Lake of the Woods. This part of the country is a big old chunk of land where I would say there is more water than land, really. Mostly just a couple of thousand lakes, all scattered around. It's where the tourists go, so naturally we don't, and we make a beeline for the 17 and take in some of the most boring bit of Canada you will ever see. The 17 is a stretch of mostly flat bog, and the towns you will run through are generally gas stops, and LCBOs.

A lot of the trek follows the CN rail line, so there is that to look at, but it gets old quick. It's just hours of rough brush country, and you start getting mesmerized by the old telephone poles that run alongside the tracks. They are those ones that have dozens of wires on them and those badminton, birdie-shaped glass insulators everyone in the world has bought at a junk shop at least once in their life. Once they would have carried telegraph signals, but I have no idea what they are used for now. Train signaling? Or is that underground?

And when did telegraphs stop? Can you still send a telegraph? If so, why? Can you send a text to a telegraph agent, and have them send it? I want to do that.

Bored out of your mind, the telegraph poles already making you more bored than you were, but fear not, there is excitement afoot. Somewhere between Ignace and Dryden, the time zone changes from Eastern Standard to Central Standard Time. For the third time in this trip, you get to set your watch back. This is also where your cellphone will switch back one hour. Now, if this doesn't seem exciting to you, then you haven't been driving across Northern Ontario for the better part of a week.

You are freaking out bored: there is no radio reception up here, and you are by now tired of fighting over CDs and playlists. You have heard just too much rockabilly, or psychobilly, or clown music, and, yes, you will of course want to see your cellphone flip back an hour. You don't think you would, but you will.

Now, with all that going on, you, the good reader, just had a question answered. You were reading about breakfast in Thunder Bay, and I mentioned you had 695 kilometres to drive today, and the smart ones in the room thought, "They started breakfast at eleven, so maybe back in the van by noon. With an eighty-kilometre speed limit, they are never going to make sound check at seven p.m. Seven hours is nowhere near enough time to get there."

Well, now you know, you actually have eight hours to get there. If you are the tour manager, or the driver, or, say, the "Mom" in the band and are in charge of scheduling, you know that all five-piece, or more, bands lose one hour for every five hours driven due to pee breaks, gas breaks, and very quick, grab-and-go food stops. Folks who aren't driving think it takes one hour to go 100 kilometres, but with the exception of driving across the Prairies, this just isn't true. The driver knows hills, corners, and small towns, even in a good van, can knock that down considerably. Here is today's tip: it is always difficult to get folks in the van. Nobody wants to be in the big, smelly van. It's better to be hanging around a coffee shop or getting stickers or knick-knacks at a tourist shop. Simply standing around smoking is far superior to riding in a van. It is easier to get kittens into a box than to get musicians back into a van.

If you are in charge of driving or scheduling, don't tell the band about the time change. They always forget, and you who have been sweating the time on this trip will get a little breathing room. Act surprised when you see the small sign on the side of the 17 that tells you to set your clocks back.

This handy-dandy time zone change has just saved you from arriving late to your gig. This will, in fact, repeat again a couple of times as you move west. Yay! More on traveling east later: it hurts.

Dryden, Ontario

Getting up past Wabigoon Lake—no, not "Woebegone," this is Stuart McLean country not Garrison Keillor—you find yourself running into the town of Dryden. Immediately roll all the windows up. You might find you even have to turn off the air conditioning, and you drive through town as fast as you can, risking life and limb trying to get to the other side of town and past the paper mill before you need to take a breath. Ah, mill towns, we do bash them, 'cause they stink.

Kenora, Ontario

Burning out of Dryden in winter, things get spooky up here. The area has had a lot of forest fires over the years, and you can drive for kilometres and see the devastation, although in the summer, the devastation is much greener. There are long, low fields covered in a whole whack of greenery. All those plants that had been lying dormant for years waiting for sunshine explode when given the chance. All that low-lying vegetation, relieved by the few naked trees here and there that did not get burned down. Winter or summer, it is really a place to experience.

Getting into Kenora, you have a chance to get to know the local law enforcement community. If you are in a band in Canada, and you own a van, and you have ever played a show anywhere, you have been pulled over in Kenora. Late one night, after a gig in Peterborough, we found ourselves being pulled over in Kenora. If you haven't been pulled over in Kenora, that means you fly east to west and rent at the other end. When figuring out expenses for your trip out west, you will compare the merits of flying versus driving, but plane tickets are expensive and car rentals in Calgary are steep. Then you have the four days driving across, the gas, the food, and the accoms. It's funny that after ignoring your own time, you

— 195 —

come to realize that flying a six-piece band out west versus driving is remarkably close in cost. That is until you realized that you have missed one hidden expense: the Kenora traffic ticket. They will get you speeding, or making a wrong turn, or having a headlight out or something like that. It's a given. Now, before you go thinking that the local law is just beating up on bands, they are not. They are profiling you, but it's not just bands they are after.

As you drive from one end of the country to the other, you will see other bands. You can spot them a mile away. They are driving a two- to ten-year-old Ford or Chev window van, in some cases hauling a trailer, an orange trailer with the name U-Haul painted over it. There will be feet on the dash and bored non-tourist-looking people lazing around inside it, with nobody looking too interested in their surroundings. There is always a fedora on the dash. This is the modern tour van.

As an industry, we have come a long way. Gone are the completely-held-together-with-baling-wire pieces of crap that used to be tour vehicles. The days when you toured in your dad's donated Delta 88, with enough leg room for all, squeezing your amps into the trunk or trailer and driving that bitch into the ground are gone. With the price of gas these days and the cost of repairs and maintenance, most bands that are serious about touring have been forced to buy second-hand rental trucks and make them their own. They are big but efficient, expensive but really the cheapest way to get a whole band from A to B.

So, as I've said, band vans are super easy to spot, and spot them they do. The cops flock to band vans like flies on road kill, but they have a secondary motive. They know that a heck of a lot of dope moves from B.C. to Quebec by way of the Trans-Canada. That is what they are on the look out for. Routine traffic stops of larger-than-usual passenger or panel vans have nabbed them more than their fair share of hockey bags full of dope. Unfortunately, bands get lumped in with those guys. But it never hurts to pull over a band van: they know as well as we do that if they pull them over, and they feel like it they can get you on something. The average band always has something to hide: seat belts, poor maintenance, a cracked windshield, or a little dope stuck down the back of someone's pants. They know that if they pull you over, then they get to take a look around your van for a hockey bag full of weed (although why would we be taking weed west at this point?), and when they don't find anything, you will happily accept your ticket for 15 kph over the speed limit and be on your way, no bitching and with a big sigh of relief, and they move on to their next prey.

Natural borders

Most borders that designate countries, or regions of countries, come by way of political battles and war. The battle over the Manitoba-Ontario border was a long-fought war, the boundary changing a few times over this country's history. It was settled in 1884, finally, when all had to recognize the folly of the argument. The Man-Ont provincial border is just not an argument, it's nature's way of saying, hey, put a line here!

You have been driving across Northern Ontario for a week, playing shows, stopping for meals, and scanning for radio to find none. It is a *Flintstones* episode rolling in your mind. Two-lane road, oh, hey, look, there is a grey, angry-looking lake to your right as we go up a hill that has a curve at the top of it. Get over that hill and come down the other side to find a grey, angry looking lake, the two-lane running up yet another hill, and at the top, it curves and produces more of the same, *ad infinitum*, the increasing intensity of this fact growing more repetitive with each hill. The names of the ugly lakes are labeled on small, green signs: Jackfish Lake, Little Lake, Hue Lake, Jackfish Lake, Smiths Lake, Jackfish Lake, Momma Lake, Daddy Lake, Baby Lake, and, of course, once again, Jackfish Lake. The monotony is incredible: you actually pray for snowstorms just to break the never-ending vista. You wind and wind your way through all of this, never getting above 90 kph, and at one point, you see on the horizon, after a full afternoon of anticipating it: the world's most natural border.

On the Ontario side, it is construction, with blasted Canadian Shield rock strewn everywhere, dust rising from the sides of the road. There is a dead deer on the side of the greyish brown road, with bluebottle flies laying eggs in the eye sockets of the carcass. You almost hit it while trying to veer out of the way of an oncoming logging truck, but then you make it to Manitoba. There is a big welcome sign, and, like in *The Flintstones*, at some point there will be a change of scene, and here it is. The road changes immediately, going completely straight. Rocks flatten out to become fields of flat, lush grass, the road widens to nine straight, flat lanes with a 160 kph speed limit, and standing on the side of the road is the Premier of Manitoba, Greg Selinger, stopping motorists to shake hands and say, "Welcome to Manitoba. You've made it." He hands you a welcome gift: a crisp, new, unsoiled gift certificate redeemable for a free pack of smokes at any 7-Eleven. You have made it to the promised land. You are through Ontario, it is good, it is orgasmic, and with your new-found will to live, you set your cruise control for the first time in four days, adjust your seat, turn the wheel once, and only slightly, about forty-five minutes in, you veer just a bit north, and fifteen minutes after that you are in Winnipeg.

Manitoba

Winnipeg, Manitoba

It's big, it's historic, it's shaped like a big donut lying in the middle of a really big field, and this town will move you and eventually leave you wondering why folks live here. I don't mean, "Why Do Folks Live *Here?*" but in the grand sense, why do folks live *anywhere*?

Spending some time here, you will meet nice folks, you will have good times, and you will probably see bar fights, and great shows, but at some point you will ask yourself, "Why do these folks live here?" Winnipeg raises the big questions, like "Could I be one of these folks and move here?" and "Why do *they* live here?"

Some towns you will just dismiss, and some towns it's a given. You might not like Toronto, but it is a given that folks live there. You won't ask yourself why they live there, or should you, they just do and you don't. It's a given. Winnipeg will have you wondering. You probably won't ever move here because you'll chicken out, but you will think about it. Hmmm....

You pull up in front of the bi-named Times Change(d) High and Lonesome Club, a derelict-looking old building on a derelict-looking old downtown street, just blocks from the famed Portage and Main. You are late due to a truck accident back in Ignace. You find the door locked, and you will be searching your clipboard for a contact phone number. The club doesn't seem to be open during the day, and they seem to show up only after finding out that there is a band playing tonight, the staff seemingly finding out only as they receive your phone call. If you are lucky, you are that band making that phone call.

Winnipeg hosts a couple of show bars, some venues, and a café gig or two, but if you are playing anything down the road of roots music, the Times Change(d) is the show for you. We got real lucky a couple of years ago, when Matt Watson noticed that a band called the D.Rangers were mounting an eastern tour, and based on Matt's say-so, we finagled them into having us host their Montreal show of that tour. Skip forward a couple of years on our first trip out west, and the D.Rangers returned the favour to us, opening for us at our debut in their hometown. Not only their hometown but also their home venue. They even opened for us. Wow, this band could easily fill this place up any night of the week, and they were very cool and took the opening spot and served us up to their hard- won audience. We hit it off with Winnipeg right off the bat, and the Times Change(d) became our only Winnipeg stop on a western tour for the rest of our years, with the exception of the Winnipeg Folk Festival, which I am sure we got due to our showings at this club. The venue's owner even took the bold and friendly step of opening up on a Tuesday, a night they are usually closed, all to accommodate our tour. Nice folks! We owe them some good shows.

The club is old and has a high ceiling. I love clubs that have high ceilings because they make a smaller place bigger and give you some room to move with the sound. We always had fun there. The place has a clubhouse feel, and it actually is a club. You have to join in order to drink there, which is one of those weird liquor law deals, but in the long run, it probably has served the place well. It has a very friendly feel, and everybody is real close to each other, or so it would seem. The PA is tricky, but there are always regular folks around who have played here, so they will help with sorting your sound when you get lost.

We play a raucous show to a raucous bunch, people hooting in all the right places, dancing, responding to the banter, and even laughing when called upon. They are a warm bunch, especially when it is minus 35 outside.

The show over, I hobble off the stage. Almost every time we played there I was injured in some way. I think the first time we ever played there I was sporting forty-three new stitches, but that of course is a story for Regina and not here.

The best thing about the High and Lonesome Club, other than a rack of bathrobes that you are encouraged to don post-show, is that it is obviously a place where you are encouraged to let your hair down, and they do. The music goes great, and the regular crowd is awesome, but the greatest part of the night is yet to happen. The patient folks will drink some beer post show, and just a little before closing, it unfolds. A tradition I actually heard about from Dan Livingstone, another touring musician. He told me about the Great Chicken Toss.

In the years between his telling of the story and my making my way to the Peg, I had actually forgot where the Chicken Toss had been held. Here I was, one a.m. after a show, my leg all bandaged up from the tour, smoking 'cause it was still allowed inside back then, when I witnessed the Chicken Toss. And then it hit me.... Oh hey, this is the place Dan was talking about.

All competitors throw $5 in the bucket, and then they take the bucket and put it in the middle of the floor on a well-worn *x*. The participants line up behind the fowl line located in the doorway to the hall that goes back to the bathroom, and without crossing the line, you arc a rubber chicken way up into the air and try and land it in the five-gallon bucket located about twenty feet across the floor. It sounds easy, but it is not. The first-timers take a bath on this every time, with the advantage going to the club's regulars without exception. Rubber chickens don't fly predictably straight like a lawn dart, the bucket isn't all that easy to see in the closing- time dim lighting, and the true winners of the competition are folks who have honed their skills. After a long round-robin game of three pitches each, each round knocking out the poorer player, and in most cases the drunker player, the game comes to an end, and the winner, in this case the bartender, takes the spoils, a bucket with about $60 worth of $5 bills in it. Yay! Chicken Toss!

The Flying J

Stopping on the west side of Winnipeg, you fill up for gas at the Flying J, one of those truck stops that I wish had been more common in Canada during the years I drove truck. It's a big monster of a place catering to trucks. Big parking lot, a big gas bar, and it hosts a restaurant, a convenience/truck store, showers, laundry, and I think someplace where you can hang out if you are a truck driver, a lounge of sorts. They have Internet, but you have to pay for it.

The restaurant is predictable, with a buffet, which is pretty expensive but all you can eat. The food is bland but only because we are in Canada. I have eaten in quite a few Flying Js over the years in more southern climes, and as with most starchy, fatty foods, the farther south you go the better it is. Here, just on the west side of Winnipeg, the food is bland and only a memory of southern food. The menu is mostly the same, but they just don't know how to make a brisket up here. This is strange 'cause they probably get all their food from the same place as the other restaurants in the chain, but they just f. it up in the Canadian stores.

The band took one trip through the southern U.S. on our way to SXSW in Austin, Texas, and we ate at a couple of truck stops and some Denny's. At first, the band was scared by the food, but later, they started to get into it and started to understand "my people" and their food. Once you get south and start eating these big, satisfying meals, you start to understand that there is a big difference between crappy fast food and large, satisfying homelike meals. It is not the diner stuff that is making everybody fat, it's the low nutritional value, completely unsatisfying fast food that has Americans getting fatter and fatter.

A couple of years ago, my wife and I took a trip across the U.S. The only rule was we were to eat no fast food, and at no franchises. So we lived on Mom and Pop diners and local restaurants. I'm not saying I was somehow the picture of health at the end of trip, but after six weeks in a car, I lost weight eating biscuits and gravy, chicken fried steak, tacos, grits, and BBQ. The thing was that all this food was satisfying, and I didn't eat snacks. It was a religious experience.

The trouble is that over the last thirty years, most small places have taken down their menus and started serving fast food. They bland it down, and they reduced the nutrition, not so much that customers won't come back but just enough to get them to eat more and more.

Having sampled the Flying J in Winnipeg twice, we wrote it off as being expensive and bland. It's a good place to fuel up and get coffee for your trip, the last stop on your way out of town.

The Yellowhead

Loaded up on fuel and coffee, you head west on the 1. After a couple of stoplights, it becomes the highway, and what a highway! This is easy country: it's straight, it's flat, and it has a 110 kph speed limit. If you have a good van, you just set the cruise on 113 and give'er west. On the long traverse to Saskatoon, you will wonder whether to take Highway 16, which is called the Yellowhead Highway, or go by way of Regina and run up to the Toon by way of Highway 11. Here is the secret of the Yellowhead: *Don't take it.*

This question, or should I say argument, comes up every time. The 16 is the most direct route and arguably gives you a better view of Saskatchewan than you are going to see from the Trans-Canada. Google Maps says it is shorter and quicker, but it isn't. You get up past Yorkton, and it really is a slow piece of highway, with a ton of trucks and stoplights and small towns to deal with. As well, if it is winter, you will have high winds and snow. I remember on at least one occasion trying to make Saskatoon at night and literally busting snowdrifts as high as the hood of our van.

My call is stay on the more boring Trans-Canada, set your cruise at 113 kph, and just go. You will get there quicker, and you will see enough of the Prairies by the time you reach Saskatoon.

Brandon, Manitoba

Tooling out across Canada's big-sky country, the kilometres racking up at a remarkable rate, the road is mostly straight, there is not much traffic, and you burn along enjoying the day. The great part about traveling out here is you don't need to pay attention to the weather reports. It's just not necessary: look in the direction you are heading, and you can see the weather you are heading for. It usually takes a couple of hours to reach the storm clouds you see on the horizon, and you will run through weather fairly quickly. Once on the other side of it, the clouds recede behind you, and since most weather seems to go with the prevailing winds, meaning most weather is heading east, the open flat fields offer absolutely nothing to slow it down.

Brandon, Manitoba, looms on the horizon after a couple of hours, and here is the tip of the day: Always play Winnipeg on your way west. The many times we have done the western swings, we have almost always worked it out so that we play Winnipeg on the front end of the trip. Brandon is why. If you are heading west from Thunder Bay and trying to make time, say deadheading to Calgary or Edmonton, Winnipeg is only nine and a half hours out of Thunder Bay, so you will probably not stop there for the night. If you are deadheading, you will probably want to get at least twelve hours of that drive out of the way, and that will leave you in Brandon. Travelling across Canada, there are towns that everyone stops in just because you get there at the end of the day. Heading west through Canada, Thunder Bay is one of those towns, and Brandon is too. They have a bunch of crappy motels, and they know that there is nowhere else to stop unless you push on to Regina, which is more than four hours up the road. Between seven-thirty and nine p.m., every single night of the week, every motel room in town fills up, as the westward travelers get this far and decide there is just nothing after here. They stop, and the feeding frenzy for accoms begins.

Brandon is a small, completely asleep sort of Prairie town and really does not attract tourism at all. Folks just stop here to sleep for the night and eat shitty food at its truck stops. The town itself is quite a few miles south of the main highway, and on many occasions, we have travelled downtown only to find little to occupy us while there. Sorry, Brandon, but you are boring, and because of your distance between two points, you are a begrudging must-stop. The worst part is that you have to book your room before nine p.m. or get frozen out. This actually leaves you too much time to enjoy the town and be let down by its lack of things to enjoy.

We actually played Brandon one time. We got booked into the Lady of the Lake, which is this restaurant just on the north side of Brandon proper. It's a weird place because two-thirds of the building is a medium- to high-end furniture store, and the last bit is café/bistro affair. It was one of only two furniture store gigs ever, the second being the Thrift Store in Guelph. They have a stage, and the food they give the bands is really good—kind of high-end for a furniture store. But the crowd was very sparse, and since we were playing for tips, all was bleak. The worst part of the evening happened in our second set when four cool kids wandered in having, I'm sure, heard that there was an out-of-town band knocking it down at the weird furniture store up in the strip mall part of town. These were early twenties kids decked out in snowboard/skater wear and sunglasses. They sat down right up front, in a room that could have held 100-odd folks but this night holding fifteen, listened to two of our songs and got up and left. I almost stopped playing, my head buzzing with, "What? Like you have to go see something else going on? Come on, we are the coolest thing that could possibly be going on tonight. Where could you possibly be going?"

This went on in my head, but I held my tongue, and I did not embarrass myself or my bandmates. From the audience, I guess this might have gone unnoticed, and we probably looked professional as the cool kids left. Our egos bruised, we carried on to finish our set, and the thirteen people left were grateful for our hiking all the way across the country to come play for them, but we were defeated 'cause the cool kids dissed us.

It seems petty, but, yes, getting dissed by small-town cool kids really was the nail in the coffin for us playing Brandon again. That, and I don't think we were ever asked back. I do remember playing a good show. Oh well. We shall chalk it up as Brandon sucks.

Here is another tip when stuck in Brandon. There is this motel whose name I can't remember, but it's one of the first ones you will see upon entering town on the Trans-Canada. Their sign said, "Our rooms are so clean our mothers are proud." Here's the tip: they aren't. The room actually made me throw up in my mouth a little bit, it was so gross. Man, their mother must be a real pig.

Food-wise, you will eat at one of its three truck stops. It will be uneventful, unless you are travelling with Dylan Perron, as he will go on a two-day tirade about canned vegetables.

In your travels, you will stop in Brandon. I hope my bracing you for a letdown will go a long way towards your not hating it as much as I have. The many times we were forced by weather, night, or empty gas tanks to stop there goes a long way to explain my annoyance with the town. Brandon is unavoidable, so try and make the best of it.

To the folks who live there: sorry. I'm sure you are a great little town, and it's not your fault that geographically you are just placed on a part of the road where people are forced to stop, thus making it harder to endear yourself to them.

Saskatchewan

Regina, Saskatchewan

Sitting at home, having not toured at all during the period I am writing this book, at the advanced age of forty-seven, I am tired after a year of being sick and worn out. On a hot day in August on the *terrasse* at a local café, I take stock of my post-Steel Workers career. Other than the prattling in my head about this era I lived through, I'm left with the scars of the last ten years. The most recent scar is a knee injury cum fourteen-inch surgery scar I have named "Bizzy." I have many visible remnants of my history to delve from. All my scars have names, and pre-band history they are as follows: My forehead is marked by a hole that I call "Tricycle." My first memory of life is riding around in the driveway of our suburban Ohio home. My daughter is now two years old, and this brings back with remarkable clarity how unstable the tricycle is. How come nobody invented the quadcycle? I remember driving around in a circle trying to pick up this bit of red rock, circling around it, this little rock sharp on one end, this rock a flaw on the otherwise pristinely kept, sixties suburban concrete drive. I bend over, and the rock rushes forward toward my forehead as gravity wrestles to win over balance and I end up with the sharp end of the rock in my to-date flawless face.

Many scars made their marks on me over the years, countless bicycle and car accidents leaving my shins marred, and a motorcycle left me with a eighteen-inch scar above my belt line, witness to being impaled on a tree at the age of eighteen. I call this one "Hawk," after the 1980 Honda Hawk I was driving at the time.

In my twenties, these scars started to fade somewhat, replaced less frequently than before. As an adult, you do fewer stupid things in life that leave you slashed up. That is, until you start to tour with an indie band.

The scars that I acquired during my stint as an indie musician are as follows: There are the constant sores I've acquired on my forearms, old scars kept alive by years of leaning on van window sills or arm rests; these I refer to as the "Sills." My right shin holds "Wakefield," a scar on top of a scar, from a bar fight in front of our van parked awaiting load out at the Black Sheep Tavern. A scar on a scar makes for poor healing, and it took months to regrow a semblance of tissue.

To continue the "tour du Gern," I am reminded of my superfluous bladder scar, "Surge," or maybe "Serge," an eight-inch surgery scar from where they had to remove a 2,000 cc growth of extra bladder from my innards. This happened at the beginning of the band's travels. The subsequent kidney stones took place after that, leaving no noticeable scars but creating havoc on the road, and I'm sure leaving countless internal scars. The most notable of the publicly seen scarring is on my left shin, a six-inch triangle of tissue resembling cellophane, darkened with age and subsequent abuse, simply know as "Regina."

We only ever played Regina once, and it was on our first trip west. We were on a knockdown, drag-out three-week tour that had us playing twenty-six dates in thirty days. This was our first trip, and we didn't know what we were doing when we booked it, so we just ran hard for thirty days, arriving home beaten and bruised and broke. I have no idea why we never seemed to ever play Regina again. It seemed nice, and we had some fans there, but the gigs just never came up, I guess. The one thing I know about playing there was that most of the clubs that have bands in from out of town are located out of the downtown area, and that meant that everybody gets up and goes home at midnight, 'cause that is when the last bus comes through that part of town. Early starts seemed to be the idea.

We had a great local opener, Kory Istace. He was enthusiastic and gave us a great welcome to town. Our show ended relatively early, just after twelve-thirty, as the management had figured the folks streamed out at about 12:10, and we finished our show to a mostly empty room. The few folks who had stayed cheered us on and after the show plied us with many pitchers of beer. I passed on the beer since I was the designated driver for the night, and it was my charge to get us back to the as-yet-to-be-decided-upon accoms for the evening. A bunch of beer was drunk, and we started to load out, and planned to start searching for a place to crash for the night. I was carrying a couple of guitars back to the back room where there was a loading dock, and on my way through the door, I caught my shin on the bottom peg of Eddy Blake's bass.

Now for folks not in the know, a lot of stand-up basses have this big, heavy, sharp spike at the end of them. I think the sharp ones are for the more symphonic level of basses. They are supposed to go into a block of wood on the floor and then the bass just doesn't move around a lot, which allows for greater control and technique. These types of spikes are not usually found on the bottom of a rock and roll bass, 'cause the guys tend to really throw those things around a lot. Well, Eddy, being from a symphonic background, had one of these posts on the bottom of his bass. I caught it with my shin, where it stuck, and me, the bass, and two guitars took a ten-foot stumble across that loading dock, a feat witnessed by Kevin McNealy that left him howling with laughter, howling until he saw my shin, which was splayed open like a flayed trout.

As fortune would have it, one of our biggest fans in Regina was a young doctor who happened to be still sitting at the front-row table drinking beer. As he assessed my injury, which would obviously need stitches, the band loaded the van and we headed out for the emergency room. Now, if you are in Saskatchewan on a Friday morning at two a.m., and you need medical attention, you can expect to be waiting in the ER for a while. That is unless you are in a band and your biggest fan in town is a doctor. On the arm of a doctor, whose name I won't mention, I breezed past two glassings and a broken arm, all three products of late-night bar fights, and I was on the table getting stitched up. It must be said that the guy doing the stitching was, of course, not the doctor whom we had been drinking with all night but in fact the doctor on call. It took forty-three stitches to close the wound, and I swear we were only in the hospital a half an hour. That was brilliant, and the doc did a bang-up job. It looked real good until all the stitches pulled out on the way home due to the fact that I have a disease called Ehlers-Danlos Syndrome, which is a connective tissue disorder that affects the stretchiness of the skin and causes very poor healing in general. Also, I didn't take care of it very well, being on the road with a band.

So here I am, disgorged from the Regina General at three a.m., and the band pulls up in Howard the Truck to announce that every hotel room in Regina is booked due to a skating competition going on in town and that we are heading for Winnipeg, *now*.

The idea was that we would do the eight-hour overnight drive and save the hotel fees, book in early in the Peg, and, as the D.Rangers quoted, "Check in real early, get two nights for one."

Twenty minutes later, we are careening down the Trans-Canada in a snowstorm, with 40 kph crosswinds, and I am reminded that I was to be the designated driver that night. I will not mention who was driving, but he was quite drunk, and on my request, fearing death and another trip to the ER, we pulled over and I took the wheel. Coffee in the cup holder, my leg slung up on the dash, and a smoke in one hand, I drove all night through a snowstorm, and we arrived to an ice-covered Winnipeg early morning.

I'm sure the members of the United Steel Workers at the time remember having to drag my old, banged-up ass across the country that winter, but I must say that I remember that night and that drive as one of the most heroic drives of my career. I am reminded of that trip every time I look at my left shin and the scar I have named Regina.

The big hill

Rolling north from Regina is a long stretch through farm-land consisting of brown grass. Both summer and winter finds this region always seemingly needing either more or less water, both conditions leaving the land brown. The highway is quick, and as you cross the countryside, you notice something. The back of your throat has a weird itch to it, and you feel a pressure on the inside of your neck's innards. You will, even after reading this, write it off as a cold coming on, or that you smoked and drank too much last night. Well, I'm not telling you that you didn't drink and smoke too much last night, 'cause you probably did, but that is not what you are feeling. For the last month or so, you have been driving up hill. It is really not that noticeable, but the entire country does have a considerable grade to it starting at sea level on the East Coast and ramping up fairly gradually as you drive west. The folks from the high west are immune to what you are now experiencing: altitude sickness.

Yep, you are driving along on the Prairies, which to most folks are the flattest chunk of land they have ever seen, and guess what? Even though there isn't a hill in sight, you are suddenly at 480 metres above sea level. It has been building for the last couple of days, and you probably didn't even notice that the amps got heavier on the last two load outs, and drinking two beers gets you as drunk as drinking four beers back east.

As you go higher, the air gets thinner, and thus your body thickens your blood so as to absorb more oxygen, thus keeping you alive. Your heart works harder to pump the engorged blood and makes life a little harder physically. The only cure for altitude sickness is to go higher for a while and then get lower the way the guys climbing Mount Everest do it. Flying out west seems to be the best plan, the plane getting real high, but of course pressurized, even then to a higher altitude than you will be when you land. We have found that altitude isn't nearly as affecting if you fly. Unfortunately, if you fly, you don't have your van with you, and you will have missed all the cool stuff in between. When driving, the altitude rises very gradually over a long trip, and you never get the chance to go higher and then return to a lower level. The people in your band who will be most affected will be the singers and the aged. The vocal cords, thin strips of tissue stretched across your airway, will get engorged with blood. Then the thin strips coming in contact with each other will cause you to feel uncomfortable and hoarse without any noticeable cause. Because of this, you will push your voice and probably do some damage with the cords all banging into each other. Injury aside, the biggest problem I have with this is that the rest of the band for some strange reason insist that altitude sickness is a myth and will hassle you about being a wuss. The problem is they feel it too but don't have to show it 'cause they aren't about ready to lose their musical instrument for a week or two in mid-tour. Yep, be prepared to have singing be a real problem or at least a much greater problem than it usually is.

With this in mind, I have tailored this part of the trip to help get the vocalists and the aged through to the coast.

As I said, it will probably start somewhere around Saskatoon. If you don't do vocal warm-ups, start now. Go easy, maybe some humming in your higher register, some do re me scales. The farther you go west and up, the more intense your regime may become. So far, you shouldn't need the vocal remedies yet. That will probably come later. If you don't know what they are, then call another vocalist. We all have our own slew of cures from warm water with lemon, good for a "slight tickle," to the "I can't even talk and have to do a live recorded broadcast today," which will require the nuclear bomb effort of Neo-Laryngobis. It's a suppository: really, you put it in your bum, and then you can sing again. You can't sing well, or in any of the keys or ranges you usually can, but with that in your backyard, you will squeak out the show you have no choice but to play. In between the lemons and the bum-bomb are a slew of meds that every well-travelled singer knows. We trade these meds between us as we pass each other on the road, handing off trade secrets that won't make you well but will get you through. My favourite remedy is Sapino's lozenges, which were introduced to me by the Burning Hell's Jill Staveley a few years back while laid up in a hostel in Utrecht, Holland. They are pills filled with tree sap. Take one on your day off, or better, post-show the night before your day off. The sap will coat your vocal cords, causing you to be very froggy, so go easy on the talking. The day after that, do a thirty-minute warm-up to clear the mucus off your cords, and you will find that your voice is magically restored, depending on how badly you f. it up before you have the chance to try to fix it.

I know from years of travel that for the singer it really is the worst feeling in the world to be travelling across the land and feeling your instrument going away with every show. A deep sorrow that takes over as you sit in the back of the van alone and terrified that it is all your fault that the band had to cancel its tour. Fear not, you are not a bad person, this is not your fault, and it happens to most everybody. If you are careful, you can get through it when it happens. Hopefully, the route I have chosen will lessen this effect. The idea is that you will go from Saskatoon at 480m/sl to Edmonton 650m/sl then Jasper 1,100m/sl. Jasper is high, probably the highest point on the trip so far, and just as you feel you can't take it anymore, I will plunge you back down into the interior of B.C. at 800m/sl and give you a break for a few days, the lesser altitude helping to restore you. After that, we will get you to the coast and sea level, where hopefully you can have a day or two off and get your voice back.

Saskatoon, Saskatchewan (The Toon)

I like Saskatoon. It's my favourite city in Saskatchewan. Well, there are only the two, so let's just state here that I think Regina is fine, but I've seemingly managed to spend a lot more time in the Toon over the years.

To be honest, the biggest reason we have played Saskatoon more than Regina is Lydia's Pub. We have had a bittersweet sort of relationship with Lydia's over the years due to some disputes about money, mostly a disagreement arising over receiving bills at the end of the night listing twelve comped beers at $5.75 apiece.

Let's look at this. Now, *comped beer*: "*comp*" is short for "complimentary," and "*beer*" is long, or at least normal length, for "beer." Put the two together and you have free beer. Lydia's, like almost everywhere else on the planet, gives the band two comp beers per band member. After the band has drank their two comp beers each, the bar is really cool and actually charges staff price on the rest of your beer, which would be like $4. Cool, except at the end of the night when you find out that your twelve free beers are, first, being deducted from your door and, second, being deducted at full price.

When I started out to write this book, I really was trying to avoid calling folks out. It's not fair to go slagging folks off, because it's a one-sided affair, and to be honest, they may have changed this policy since last we were there, but, dude, this had to be mentioned. Free beer at full price! Yay!

With this recurring issue, which is known now as the "Ongoing Comped Beer Affair of Northern Saskatchewan," you would think that maybe we would think about playing somewhere else. The thing is, there are two reasons why we kept playing Lydia's. The first and foremost reason was their soundman, Ian Dearborn. Ian is the dude, a very credible soundman indeed, voted most likely to become the seventh Steel Worker if ever we were to have gotten successful enough to hire a travelling soundman. Ian is mid- to late thirties, an ex-truck driver who is laid back, insightful, and has a pretty decent pair of ears. He makes us sound good in a room that, when he is not there, we do not sound good in. Wrestling the sound out of our band has never been easy for anyone. We had a lot of strings onstage, big hollow guitars plugged through amps, and a massive amount of stage sound. To be honest, most soundmen found us to be a pain in the ass. We did our best to try and minimize the pain for them over the years, but we really weren't easy to do sound for. Ian, you were great and made us sound great. Thank you, sorry we never got you out on the road with us.

The second reason for always playing Lydia's, even though they charged us for comped beer (look at me still harping), was that they offer free accoms. Located above the bar, just up a fire escape right offstage, are the infamous Lydia's accoms. They are just four rooms above the bar, two of which are stuffed with beds. I'd say nine beds spread out over two rooms. Then there is the living room, which really is just big enough to hold an end table and a loveseat, which I'm sure has seen a fair amount of love over the years…eww, ick.

The final room is the Jägermeister bathroom. I don't know why it became the Jägermeister bathroom, but that it is. The bathroom is small: toilet, sink, and shower. The walls are painted black and red, the floor is black and red, the sink is black and red, even the toilet is black and red. I mean, they painted the toilet black and red. Yes, they painted the toilet. I didn't even know you could paint a toilet, but they did. So the whole room is black and red, and they have these great big old Jägermeister logos all over the walls and doors and, yes, the toilet. WTF, yo?

I guess it is like, "This poop has been sponsored by Jäger," or "This vomiting session has been brought to you by the good folks at Jägermeister. Please regurgitate responsibly." I've never been sure if the folks who did this to an unsuspecting bathroom thought it was cool, or ironic. Still wondering. How do you get paint to stick to porcelain?

Actually, we don't stay at Lydia's because we like the Jägerroom, it's 'cause the Jägerroom is free of charge. It's the one thing that does not show up on your post-show bill at the end of the night. Once again, a word to bar owners everywhere. See how much you can get away with when offering free accoms? Mind you, your soul will still ache if you do in fact charge for comp beer.

Gig finished, throat sore, you make your way down to the 7-Eleven confectionary. Out west, they call them confectionary stores. Let's part this up. On the East Coast, they are, I think, convenience stores. Quebec calls them depanneurs, Ontario convenience stores, and at some point they start referring to them as a confectionery. So here we are, and the notable thing about here is that this is where the 7-Eleven transforms. Back east, they are just sort of stores that sell coffee, cigarettes, bread maybe, lotto, and some slushies. But the farther out west you get, the better their hot snacks get. The hot snacks are not evident in Quebec at all; Ontario does have the dogs, but usually not much else. Well, here in Saskatoon, they are just starting to get good. There are three different types of dogs and chimichangas. We are not quite in the land of all-you-can-eat melted cheese, but we are getting close. You load up on cough drops and pick up a hot dog and head back to the Jägerroom to eat and have a shower. Okay, eat, then have a shower and a night's sleep.

If the lack of nutrients in the 7-Eleven bacon cheddar dog left you hungry from the night before, a great place to get some morning grub similar to breakfast would be Schnitzel Meister at the Market Mall Food Court 2325 Preston Ave. Yep, you have found German fast food. They have schnitzel, and they have spaetzle noodles. Get them. German fast food is awesome, and when in Saskatoon, it is far cheaper than flying to Germany just to get spaetzle. This fast food environment was the first I've ever seen to offer flattened breaded meat and a side of gooey, starchy noodles. The first in Canada, anyhow. In Germany, this fare can be found in gas stations on the Autobahn as well as just about any mall food court.

Schnitzel Meister is not nearly as good as any random versions of this medium cuisine to be found in the fatherland, but it will go a long ways towards making you feel heavy. Not so heavy, however, as to decline a "German Euro Dance Party" right there in the middle of a mall in Saskatoon.

Highway 16 and The Lloyd, Alberta/Saskatchewan

Leaving Saskatoon, you head out Highway 16. Yes, for this part of the trip you can take the Yellowhead. It will be slow, but it is only a six-hour drive up the road. It's flat and grey; well, it is on a grey day. I've never run this leg of the trip when it wasn't grey. I'm sure on a beautiful spring day it would be sunny. I've just never seen it that way, although I'm sure it's nice that way. So with a 200 kph side wind buffeting your van's midsection, you plunge forth across the Yellowhead Highway trying to make time 'cause the German food slowed you down.

You will pass through North Battleford, but unless you forgot to get gas in the Toon, sail right on by this Prairie enclave with your eyes set on the horizon. Grey skies in the distance will have you anticipating weather and the chance to strike another province off your trip as you pull into the sprawling fortress of Lloydminster. Lloyd, as the locals call it, as well as being the birthplace of our number three and previously mentioned bass player Eddy Blake, has always been a difficult place for me. It is a border town, split down the middle by the Alberta-Saskatchewan border, a town that always has me wondering whether to refer to it as Lloydminster, Saskatchewan or Lloydminster, Alberta.

I believe I have taken this subject up with a few Lloyd residents over the years, and the consensus seems to be that the town's location affords the residents the luxury of identifying with either province. It has been explained to me that when trying to get a free beer out of a Calgary bartender, you mention you grew up in Lloydminster, Alberta. The bartender, being an Albertan, will see you as a friendly, almost brotherly, compatriot. In the rest of Canada, however, you say you are from Lloydminster, Saskatchewan, so people don't immediately think you want to privatize healthcare.

Either way, about halfway through this sprawling town, right near a KFC, I think, you will cross the Saskatchewan-Alberta border. There is a traffic light there, and this may cause you problems. Now, when crossing a border, be it provincial, national, or even, say, a time zone, some drivers will honk their horn. Hell, we all do it. We all have, and on this trip, you have now gotten to do it several times. Well, Lloyd may rob you of this. Unless you happen to be travelling at night, there will be traffic as you pass across this easy-to-miss provincial border. If things line up with the light, a small beep that will help you sleep better tonight may just be written off by a guy in a 4x4 with those damn chrome bull testicles hanging from his trailer hitch as a "hey, the light changed and you should put your foot on it" gesture. Keep in mind, if the car in front of you is a cop maybe just bang on the dash and shout, "Yay! Alberta!"

Oh, and you are also on Mountain Standard Time now, and depending on the time of year, you may have just gained another hour. Keep in mind that Saskatchewan is mostly in the Central Time Zone, along with Manitoba and Northwestern Ontario. However, Saskatchewan does not observe a time change (back or forward by one hour in the fall and spring) *except* in the city of Lloydminster, which observes Daylight Saving Time but is also in the Mountain Time Zone. I'm sure none of what I just said makes sense to you, 'cause it did not to me either. This leads to today's travel tip: when leaving Saskatchewan, wait till you are one hour west of Lloydminster, and then pull over at a gas station and ask them what time it is now. You don't live here, so there is no point in trying to figure out how they keep time from day to day. After stopping and asking what time it is, you will then, and only then, find out if you are late for your gig.

Alberta

Edmonton, Alberta

The $100 City. To date, we have played Edmonton six times and have made, all told, $600 for our efforts. Due to some issues the town has with promotion of out-of-town travelling bands, this town could easily be struck off the Canadian touring circuit. This is unfortunate, because I love Edmonton, and it is my favourite town in the west. Yes, that's right, my favourite town west of Thunder Bay, Ontario, is in fact Edmonton. This is the gateway to the north, to the tar sands and mining camps. Edmonton is a staging area for everything heading north to plunder Canada's vast riches. Yes, my favourite town. To spend a night on Whyte Avenue, summer or winter, is to love this town's nightlife.

Edmonton is a college town, and the epicentre for lefties in Alberta and Saskatchewan. If Calgary is the engine of the province, then Edmonton is the luxurious back seat where all the fun happens.

Unfortunately, we have never made any money playing this town. We have played the Black Dog, and the Pawn Shop, the university cafeteria, and the Haven Social Club, all to decent crowds, and made no money. Decent crowds with the exception of the Haven Social, which holds the standard that is the high and low of the United Steel Workers' career. July first, we played Calgary's Canada Day celebration in Fluor Rope Park. It was our biggest stage show of all time. We were scheded to play the bumper set to the fireworks. That meant doing a half-hour set, then breaking for thirty minutes while they set off fireworks behind us. A big display, the kind of show the big end of the town shows up for. And then we had the job of following the fireworks and getting the crowd back, which by all accounts we did. Keep in mind this was a free show, and the overwhelming majority of the folks had no idea who we were, but we had a rocking set and an amazing time playing in front of somewhere between 10,000 and 15,000 folks. It was great and we had fun.

The next day, we were very quickly transported back to the real world, a three-and-a-half hour drive north to Edmonton to play in front of twenty-eight people at the Haven Social Club. Please don't get me wrong: the Haven is a new place and is way out on the outskirts of town. They are a great place and getting better. As for our show, you try and pull folks into a club on a sunny day after Canada Day weekend to sit in a basement and watch a band. We were very happy to have twenty-eight people show up. This, of course, is touring Canada as an indie band.

Edmonton as a whole has always been this town to us— it always seemed like we were there on the wrong day, or the wrong time of the year.

I think our most remarkable show in Edmonton was possibly the most mismatched show we have ever played anywhere. It was a Saturday early evening opener at the Pawn Shop, opening for Hey Ocean! We were out west touring, and we were trying hard to find a gig in Edmonton. Flipper, our fourth bass player, had some friends in Edmonton, and we had had some fun if not lucrative shows there, so we really wanted to go back. We pushed our agent to get us on a bill, any bill. The promoter in town kind of owed us because the last time out we had put 180 folks in the Pawn Shop, and for some reason, there was only $100 for us at the end of the night. So we pushed him, and he did his best and got us a lunchtime set in the cafeteria of the university. We played it, it was lame, and we made $100 as agreed upon. The carrot was that we would have another gig that night, an opening spot, which would pay another $100. We showed up at the Pawn Shop, a second-floor place on Whyte Avenue, all dark and at this point very hot, being early summer. The place packed out, and we dutifully arrived to play our twenty-five-minute opener. Now, I'm not going to slag Hey Ocean!, because they are a perfectly fine band. In fact, we actually opened for them again two years later in Saint John. That wasn't as bad 'cause it was an outdoor show, and in fact both of us were opening for Bedouin Soundclash anyhow. No, I have no problem with Hey Ocean! They are just not in our scene, meaning they are successful.

We only had a twenty-five-minute set, so we got together before we went on and decided that we only had twenty-five minutes to play, so let's just lay it out full throttle, no song set-ups, no slow tunes, just rip through the fast songs and get as many of them out as we can. Play fast and hope the crowd would buy some of our merch.

It didn't really work. We hit the stage, getting up before Spiral Beach and Hey Ocean! who have a mean average age of about twenty. We looked like a bunch of old farts, with the exception of Filly, whose timeless beauty would normally carry her through any crowd, even with us old codgers on stage. So we, or more to the point, I, limped up onstage for our second show of the day, and amps set on eleven, we launched into all our fastest tunes, these tunes made faster over the tour by having played them many times in a row. This happens on the road, songs get faster. Well, at this point, they were real fast, and I think the soundman had a thing about scaring the teenyboppers and had us maxed out in the mains. It was somewhere into the second song that I managed to spy out into the crowd to see 200-odd eighteen-year-olds, dressed in seafoam-coloured polo shirts, sitting motionless, in awe, if not downright scared, staring back at this loud monstrous show that was pouring off the stage. It was fun. I think we really shook them up. Certainly a little too much 'cause we sold almost no merch that night.

On a side note, I must say that Spiral Beach was awesome. They took our lead and rocked it out of the ballpark. Hey Ocean! brought the mood down a bit for their set, and the crowd was glad. They certainly seemed as though they were waiting through our set to a point in the evening to have a nice time, and we weren't it.

Thanks Spiral, and thanks Ocean! We didn't steal your crowd by any means, but we had fun and, of course, made $100.

Highway 16

Up early, having stayed on the floor of some post-war tract house just blocks off of Whyte Avenue, we reload the van and hit the highway again for the five-hour drive to Jasper. At this point of the trip, you are now definitely in high country and getting real tired. If you did in fact play Thunder Bay, Ontario, last Monday, by tonight you will have done six nights in a row and travelled 2,370 kilometres and gained almost 700 metres in altitude. Please keep in mind that other than the harrowing drive across Northern Ontario, this is the hardest stretch of the trip. You have crossed three provincial borders and two time zones. If you are ever going to feel like quitting the music business, this is definitely one of the times it will be in the forefront of your mind. Breathe deeply: once you get Jasper out of the way, things are going to get better.

My plan for this leg of trip is getting you over to the peak of the mountains, getting you high, say, 1,700 metres, and then plunging you back down to what will then seem like luxurious levels of 600 to 800 metres for some rest. Fear not, there is sleeping in your future and some nice scenery too, if you like that sort of thing.

Jasper, Alberta

Entering Jasper is a mostly uneventful experience. The most striking thing about the town is its size, less than 5,000 permanent residents. Jasper is a tourist town and looks like it with sort of a Wild West theme running through its architecture. It is not the fake looking streetscape of Banff: it seems a little more organic than that — but it definitely has the feel that you may see a guy in a coonskin cap walking through town in an unironic sort of way. Mostly the sidewalks are crowded with the extreme sports types decked out in Gore-Tex and wool caps, the caps hiding monster sets of extreme dreads, "dude."

The touristy-looking streetscape is definitely softened somewhat by the rail yard that takes up the entire forefront of the town. Jasper is where the shorter trains coming up from the West Coast are doubled up to make one long train for the big trip across the Prairies. For the rail enthusiast, of which I am one, a lovely afternoon can be had watching the comings and goings of the trains. From a bench on the sidewalk of Connaught Drive, you can sip a coffee and smoke half a pack of cigarettes while watching them hook and unhook trains and get them underway for their trips east and west. This does mean it's hard to get in or out-of-town while the trains are coming in or out of the station. A quick trip to the south side of the track could leave one stranded for fifteen minutes while the big, lumbering hulks traverse the level crossing on their way to somewhere else.

Loading in to our gig at the Downstream Lounge, we set up for the night's show. This bar looks a little bit too much like a restaurant, but we found that it does function quite well as a venue. We only played there once, but lots of local tourist industry workers were hungry for some out-of-town music and our show was a great success. The town's small size definitely worked for this: word of mouth gets around town pretty fast when something is going to happen, and folks seem to come out with very little PR or even advance notice.

Today's travel tip involves gear. We found the Downstream to be lacking in mics, stands, and XLRs, those pesky things once referred to as mic cords. They may have remedied that situation by now, but all good road managers should call ahead and make sure they have the gear there. Using the odds and ends we normally travel with, we were able to patch together enough gear to make it work. On that note, I would advise all bands to regularly travel with some backup gear. I always had a couple of old kicker Shure 58s and a couple of beat-up XLRs stuffed into my guitar case. If you are the type to worry about that sort of thing, maybe always bring your own 58 with you to every gig. Using your own mic will cut down on the infamous band cold, and not sharing mics and spit with the touring bands at large will help you avoid succumbing to the ill health of others. Ninety percent of Canadian venues use Shure 58s as vocal mics onstage. Bringing your own 58 will go a long way towards not pissing off the soundman who regularly uses these mics and in general EQs his room to the sound of this standard microphone. Being up with the standard always helps, and the standard is the SM58. There are better mics, mics that can make you sound better, give you better gain, look cooler. But the 58 is the standard, and once you get used to it, you will figure out how to make yourself always sound good on it. They are only about $150 brand new, last forever, and take a shit-kicking. Start your touring career by buying a new one and fall in love with it.

Shure commercial over, let's get back to Jasper. Jasper's size also goes a long way to making you feel at home. On our one trip through town, we opted to take a day off here, and by the time we had finished breakfast the day after our show, it seemed as though everybody in town knew us. Even the folks who had worked the night before and had missed our show had picked us out walking down the street and said hello and please come back. Wow, it really was a great place to have a Sunday afternoon off.

Let's revisit you feeling like crap. So here you are on the verge of crossing into B.C. You are almost over the great hump that is topographically and culturally the end of the Great Canadian Hill, and the feeling of accomplishment is what is holding you together. If you did not think of it the day before, please right now go find a health food store and buy some Sapino's. That's the tree sap stuff. You are going to have a day or two off, get that stuff in you and let it start working. If you were smart, you took your first dose last night as soon as you got finished your set. If you did, you will find that you can barely talk. If this is the case, it means you probably did do some damage to your vocal cords last week. It's probably unavoidable, especially if you are the kind of singer that sings in the same register as you speak. Here is another tip for the new vocalist: if you are really not decided on how you want to sound singing for the rest of your career, start trying to teach yourself to sing in a register that is different from your speaking voice. Sing higher or sing lower. If you do perfect this, you will be spared a lot of grief later. Singing with my speaking voice is what I'm all about and has really caused me problems when flying or playing in high altitude. It has always been the aftershow part that really does in my cords. Smoking, drinking, and excitedly yelling about how great the show went is the real culprit here, but unless you are going to immediately leave the stage and hide in the van, it is inevitable that you are going to be rough at these altitudes. Well, life on the road is a balance. You are there to play, and sell merch, and have people get to know you, so try and balance that out with drinking, partying, getting laid, and getting the job done. All bands eventually find their balance when it comes to getting the job done and partaking of the beauty and the fun that is touring, that beauty that helps you swallow the fact that you could be at home making a lot of money doing anything else, and spending time with your loved ones. Take the Sapino's, and don't try to sing for a couple of days.

To all bands: please let your vocalist rest a bit during this leg of the trip. Let them have more vocals in the monitors, and go easy on them. There is still a long way to go, and once you have conquered the mountains, you will find that your vocalists should get over it, and everybody will get stronger for the push home. As well, keep in mind that this is probably your first tour, and you are learning. It won't always be like this. You will get good at this business and learn how to get through all of this and be strong. Till then, hang on and good luck.

Safety tip: when in Jasper, you will see elk, great big elk, and they will be eating out of a garbage can. They are like twenty-eight feet tall. I shouldn't have to say this, but here goes. Give them a wide berth or they will gore you and stamp on your guts. This will probably hurt the tour in the long run. If you see one, snap a quick telephoto of them and go the other way. They are wild animals, and so are the bears, and cougars, and snakes and ducks, and, who knows, mongooses or some such. Don't feed them and don't try and commune with them. Leave them be, even if you are drunk. You want to be the band that makes headlines 'cause you are awesome performers with great songs; you don't want to be that band that makes the headlines cause your drummer was eaten by a badger. They say all press is good press, but they are wrong. Losing members to wild animals makes you look foolish on the world stage. If this does happen to you, try and make it look like the drummer OD'd on meth. On the world stage, OD'ing is cool, even if he OD'd and was then eaten by a badger, although if you make it look like he was eaten by your band, that could work too. See, there are options to dealing with press and wildlife.

Icefields Parkway

Heading out of Jasper with a full tank of gas, massive paper cups of Starbucks house blend in the cup holders, and a gravelly throat, you are set on some scenery, and today you will see it. I have used the term "if you like that sort of thing" in the past, and that is because I do in fact like to look at the mountains and wildlife just like every one else, but, find myself not as enthusiastic as most when it comes to the Rocky Mountains. I am an easterner, and it is at this point in the trip that my fear of the West Coast starts to take hold.

Back east, sliding down an ice-covered highway in, say, the Pocono Mountains in a fully loaded tractor-trailer, I can say, "I think the mountains are pretty, and, hey, look, a deer," as my trailer wheels break traction and she starts coming around. The scenery out east is at one with humanity. The nature lovers can still at this point find some possibly untouched nature and build a nice cabin on a lake and get on with life. Here in the Rockies, all things nature are grand, very grand, very tall, very cold, very windy, and pretty much just very extreme, dude. I can, in fact, appreciate that grandeur but not have not the enthusiasm for it. I think in general it leaves me feeling too small and insignificant, a feeling that my 6'2" frame is not used to. As well, it seems to me that most people who live out here feel that way too, and as far as I'm concerned, the folks who live out here kind of have a death wish, mixed with an ever-present feeling that everything they do is ruining the landscape. I think they are guilt-ridden by their own existence and have lost the healthy ability to be scared.

The reverse is true back east. Those Victorian towns of Ontario play out on a quasi-natural basis, giving way to countryside that is at first farmland, then fields, then forests, and then wilderness. In the west, you are in a town and then, boom, you are being attacked by nature. If you build even a modest home, it seems as though you have offended God, or at least the gods.

Add to it the fact that simply stopping to change a flat tire you run the risk of being run down by a bighorn sheep. Yep, the whole nature thing out here bothers me a little bit, and the way it seems to bother the average citizen bothers me a little bit more, not to the point of not enjoying my time out here, or making friends, but it does get me to thinking about smoking a big fattie and letting myself "chill, dude." Smoking a fattie is definitely something I haven't done since I was in my early twenties, and with most things I did in my twenties, I get weird about repeating them. To reiterate, you don't have to hate the west, but I kind of do 'cause I'm a scaredy-cat for nature and I don't hold truck with smoking weed just to get through my day.

All that aside, you are tooling down Icefields Parkway, and

it's a bright day. Well, one would assume it is, 'cause if it's snowing, you should still be holed up in Jasper. Braving the Parkway in bad weather is not advised, and being as you have a couple of days to kill, better to kill them in Jasper than to kill yourself trying to make Golden in a snowstorm.

Getting a little ways down the road, you are really starting to get into the mountains here. The mostly two-lane road winds all up through some pretty impressive mountains. Keep an eye peeled and you will probably see some bear, elk, and bighorn sheep. The hills will get higher and higher, and if your GPS unit has an altimeter setting, you are watching it climb. I was unable to find the data online but I do believe you will hit at least 1,700m/sl as you thread your way down through Jasper National Park, Lake Louise, and Banff National Park. There are a couple of great places to get out and take pictures and have a pee in this pristine natural environment. You will see some glaciers. Make note of them so ten years from now you will be able to tell your children, "Hey, there used to be a glacier there." Yep, they are going away fast, but at this point you, should still be able to see what is left of them. Take a picture, and if you last ten years at this game, you will be able to take another one on some far-off trip and be able to compare how fast the glaciers are going away. Please remember when posing for cameras outside in front of the vista to wear something nice and comb your hair maybe; this picture could someday make headlines. CANADIAN INDIE BAND PROVES THAT THE GLACIERS HAVE RECEDED.... DRUMMER GORED BY SHEEP!

All this whiling up and down very steep hills will make your already sore ears pop, and your throat even sorer, but, hell, you aren't playing tonight and the scenery is awesome, so enjoy. Ending your journey on the Parkway at the point where you hit Highway 1, you turn west. "Wait a minute!" the band shouts. "Banff is that way!" You continue on your way toward Golden comfortable in the fact that you are not going to play Banff, or Canmore, on this trip. Prepare yourself for the fight 'cause if you have more than three people in your band, it is a sure thing that at least one of them spent two years working as a busboy in Banff when he was nineteen years old and didn't feel like going to university. That member of your band will be all pissed about not playing Banff, thus not being able to relive his younger days.

Notes on Banff, Alberta

So here is the deal on Banff. Imagine you are just starting your career as a band, say, you've had three rehearsals and now know five songs, you have worked out your rhythm section, and are now working on really cool backup harmonies. Stop the rehearsal now and go find a computer and look up the Rose and Crown in Banff, Alberta. Send them an email mentioning you would like to book a show there, say, sometime in May about three years from now.

To my knowledge, the Rose and Crown is pretty much the only cool place to play in Banff, but the downside is that they seem to book three years in advance. I think we did five western tours over the years, and even starting our bookings eight months in advance, we were unable to secure a gig there. Add to it that Banff is a tourist town that looks like the backlot of a cheap Hollywood movie. It's all shiny and fake-looking, kind of like a mall without a roof, the entire population of the town speaks with an Australian accent, and all the people on the street are Chinese. The town is surrounded by a ring of beautiful mountains that in this setting gives you the feeling you are looking at a green-screen effect. This is an expensive town, and it's crowded, and if you don't have a gig there, do everything in your power to give it a miss. As well, it is 1,400m/sl so your vocalists are still not having fun.

Notes on Canmore, Alberta

Canmore is a bad place for you. If you thought Banff was too pretty and fake, well, hell, maybe Canmore will float your boat. It is definitely the poorer brother to Banff. It is a true mountain town, although still a tourist destination. Canmore does have that element of fakeness, but at the same time there is really a town here.

The immediate problem with Canmore is that about a third of the folks you will run into out here are townies, born here and not in Australia. They've lived here for years, some even their whole lives, and they are working folk. They are rough around the edges from too many brushes with people who are just passing through. Let's think about the dance folk who just didn't get along with Baby at Kellerman's Resort in the movie *Dirty Dancing*. It's just like that. Even though you are a touring band, you are the rich upstart who wants to be cool, and the blue-collar townies will treat you like a rich doctor's daughter. Really, as a touring band, you will be lumped in with the tourist, a part-timer, and you are.

Unless you are an AC/DC cover band, their response to you will range from disinterested to outright anger. Now, in all situations, just like the movie, townies will eventually come around to liking you eventually. Given enough time to shine, you can wear them down. Buy them a few beers and have a couple of conversations and over time become friends. But you are not Jennifer Grey, and you are in a band, so you do not have that kind of time. My advice is do not try. Give this town a miss

Added to the lacklustre welcome you will get, Canmore always seems to be the symbolic turning point in all tours. Our band almost broke up every time we played there. Be it the altitude sickness, the bad sound, the drunkenness exacerbated by altitude, holed up in the accoms of the Canmore Hotel, we drank, fought, pissed in the sink, had nightmares, and were injured spiritually. We didn't break up there, but we almost did, many times.

Our best show ever in Canmore was our last show there back in 2011. We had booked the Drake. I had at that point in the band's history decided to not book Canmore anymore, but we were lured in one more time with a large guarantee. I think it was $800 plus hotel rooms. For a travelling band, this is nothing to sneeze at, so we took the booking. We arrived and did sound check. The altitude here is somewhere around 1,400 m, so we were feeling it, but we got through the set-up and had some time off to chill out before the show.

We took the stage at eleven p.m. and ran through the first part of our first set as people filed through. They were the townies, and they stood at the back of the room talking loudly, waiting for us to start playing real music, music that sounded more like AC/DC. We did not, but at the point in the night when it seemed like they were going to start getting ugly with us, a big crew of folks came in and hit the dance floor and started hooting and hollering and cheering us on. It was great. We finished the show to mass applause, thinking we had finally found our peeps here in this beleaguered town. Having a couple of beers after the show, we found out that the night's festivities were a result of the fact that we had not managed to book Jasper. Ironically, we had missed Jasper because Canmore had offered us the big guarantee. The folks who arrived in time to save our night were a very large crew from Jasper who had made the four-and-a-half hour drive down to Canmore to see us. Word to the wise: never book Canmore over Jasper. But if you do, book an off night, a Tuesday or something, because the Townies are drunker and meaner on weekends.

Highway 1 (Death Road)

Once again on the Trans-Canada, I hope you notice that I have spared you much of the Highway 1 experience. Running you up through Jasper and avoiding Banff and Canmore has cut a significant part of one of the worst pieces of scary highway down to a minimum. This highway is scary due to one fact and one fact alone: the traffic, which is made up of two types of vehicles, heavily loaded tractor-trailers and heavily loaded RVs driven by inexperienced drivers. Spend just an hour on this highway and you are likely to see a mighty dust-up between the two. Tourists and professional drivers trying to meet impossible deadlines come to blows on this stretch of the Trans-Canada.

This danger is at its height during tourist season, but come winter, the RVs are replaced by bad weather, so snow and big hills and trucks make for an even showing when it comes to road closures due to traffic accidents. There is a lot of awesome scenery out here, but please, if you are the driver, do not be distracted to the point of forgetting the seriousness of this drive. It's beautiful out here, but it can be deadly.

Coming into Kicking Horse Pass, a piece of topography named for another historic traffic accident, you will be plunged down "The Big Hill." This hill was called that by the work crews of the CPR because it's the biggest and most unruly hill in the entire Canadian rail network. The Trans-Canada you are driving on right now was actually built in 1962 based on the original CPR main line. This hill will give you goosebumps when thinking of how they managed to run trains down it. Some of them even made it to the bottom still remaining on the track. I say some because a lot didn't, and if you look down into the deep crevices, you will still see the rusted hulks of locomotives that mark the graves of many.

To solve the dangerous problem of runaway trains, in 1909, the CPR built the spiral tunnels. There is a big sign on the side of the road as you head west pointing to a lay-by where you can pull over and read all about the tunnel. If you are lucky, you will get to see a train go in the tunnel and then emerge way up top of itself. Usually, you will be able to still see the end of the train going into the tunnel as you see the head of the train emerge from the corkscrew. The tunnels were built in order to decrease the grade that the trains had to traverse. It worked and cut the grade in half. It is an amazing feat of engineering to witness, and with the frequency of trains on this mainline, there is a better than average chance you will get to see a train use it.

Jumping back on the highway, you are still running full

tilt downhill to Field, B.C. Don't forget to honk as you cross into British Columbia, and once again set your clock back, and pat yourself on the back too. You have now been through ten provinces, and you are seasoned. By the time you start getting down around Golden, you should start looking for someplace to spend the night. If you are the type of band that travels with camping gear, feel free to get out a B.C. travel guide and find someplace to camp, weather permitting. We usually travelled with camp gear, just the bare bones that would get you through a night's stay in the woods. This tactic must be balanced by how much room the camp gear will take up versus how much band gear, luggage, and comfort you want. I know on many occasions we hauled camping gear from one end of the country to the other to only use it once or twice. The ultimate thing about camping for a band is the rare chance to get your own room, or in this case, a tent. After months on the road, a small layer of nylon may be the privacy one would need to have just a little "me time." Alas, sometimes band gear will get in the way, and you will be forced to stay in motels.

Here's a tip that Matt came up with. When crossing borders, whether state, provincial, or national, you will generally find a welcome centre. In a lot of these, you can sometimes find motel flyers, sometimes with coupons for camping or motels that can save you some money. This is more common in the U.S., but we have found it also useful touring Canada and Europe.

British Columbia

Golden, B.C.

Having given up on the idea of camping because I have now filled you with the belief that a Sasquatch will eat you, and adding the fact that sleeping on the ground is for children and tree planters, feel free to be less naturalistic and check into Mary's in Golden. Mary's is a rustic sort of affair. We have found the floors to be damp but mostly the non-smoking rooms are odour free. The big point to Mary's is that it's located very conveniently in the centre of town. Having a couple of days off in a small mountain town, it is good to be right near where the small amount of action is, thus allowing the band to come and go of their own free will, and not needing rides or to be organized in any way. It's free time to wander, eat when you want to eat, and do whatever the hell you want to do, without having to think of your bandmates. The motel option might seem expensive, but it is worth it to give everybody a break at this point in the trip. A quick look online will probably prove Mary's to be the cheapest in town either way. One thing you might try is getting in touch with the venue, probably the Rockwater, and see if they have a deal with old

Mary. Maybe you can get a reduction on your hotel stay if you work it right.

A couple of days off in a small town. You have explored all that is Golden, eaten some nice diner food, and got drunk in some of its bars. The day of the show, you are now well rested, and since you are now on lower ground, say, 800 metres, it is time for the vocalist to start doing some warm-ups and clearing all the build up of Sapino's off their vocal cords. Do about a half hour of me..me..me's and some do.. re…me's, and you will find as you cough up that pine-tasting phlegm you will have some semblance of a voice to work with tonight. Unless you truly f. up your voice, you will now be very surprised and relieved to find out that your vocal career is not over. Keep in mind that you still have a bit of work to do to make sure your voice gets strong again. If you do all this right, you are going to find that in the back third of this trip your voice has actually gotten stronger. The voice is in fact a muscle, and using it every night under the right circumstances, it will build to be strong.

You will find when touring, at least when all things are level, that somewhere around the six-week mark, your voice will start to improve. That, of course, only applies when not having to deal with the gradual grade that is heading west in Canada. But now that you have conquered the Continental Divide, it is all downhill from here. After this section of the tour, you will start heading down to sea level, eventually landing in Vancouver, spend a week out that way, and when coming back this way, which will be a much quicker trip to the maximum height, you will find that the altitude doesn't affect you nearly as much.

After climbing the hill on the way back, you will spend the rest of your trip gradually decreasing every day, so that, and the fact that you will be stronger, is what is going to get you through the back third of the trip.

I have always found that all tours can be split into threes. The front end, the middle, and the back. The front third is when everybody is full of energy, excited, and full of hope but unrehearsed, not tight, and kind of just getting their legs under them. The middle is the sweet spot: the band is tight, the shows are seemingly effortless (at least in comparison), and most of the fights have gotten to a truce state. Everybody is resigned to being on the road. The back third is the way home. That is when everybody starts to conceive of being at home and not having to play shows every night. They start thinking about being in their own beds and not loading the van every day. Fights restart, as anticipation resumes. The shows can become robotic at this point, you finding it possible to play an entire show without having to even think about it. Mind you, when this starts happening, you will also find that without having to concern yourself with remembering the songs, you can actually take the show to another level per-formance-wise. The angst of returning home gives you a lot more energy onstage. It's weird but very cool to experience when it happens.

The fun thing about this three-part tour phenomenon is that it seems to apply to any string of out-of-town shows ranging from three shows to six months on the road. Even the three-nighters after a while will start to fit this formula. This is the argument for long tours: the middle third, the "sweet spot," will be longer and more fulfilling.

Back at the Rockwater in Golden, it's all business. We've had some real great shows there towards the end of our career. In fact, the entire B.C. interior has really come on to be the biggest reason for us to play the west. The folks of Golden are partiers. There are a lot of townies here, and they seem to mix a bit more with the recently arrived. Golden is not the tourist mecca that Banff is, or, to a lesser extent, Canmore. The town is a mountain town, and the folk here work in forestry, as well as the tourist trade. They do wear those wool caps, and some have rad dreads, but in this part of the west, they are a little less extreme, dude. Not completely, but certainly less. They are a little more like country folks out here. Country folks are usually cool to be around. Mind you, one of the biggest off-duty pursuits for the younger folks around this part of the world is getting high on hallucinogens, so that does come into play here. Shrooms are big out this way. If you are playing a show, fully expect your audience to be tripping balls, yo.

Right, the Rockwater. We've played this club a couple of times. The load in is easy, and the folks there have always treated us well. I remember our most notable show there happened to land on my birthday. One of the folks from town had been following our tour through the interior and had picked up on the fact that it was my birthday, and just before we went on, he presented me with a bottle of Jameson. It was sweet. We never really reached the point in our career that we expected folks to be following our tours closely enough to know when our birthdays were, so it was kind of stalker-y, but cool nonetheless.

We had had a pretty grueling sound check. I think the soundman was new to the game, and once again, we can easily be a very difficult band to do sound for, and that night we sounded bad. To get through it, we played hard, we jumped up and down, we slammed through a set, and screamed at the audience and generally ignored our microphones 'cause they really didn't seem to be doing that much anyways. Other than it hurting, we had fun. Sometimes bad sound just goes that way, and you learn over time to just work with it. Mind you, sometimes it hurts and sucks.

So here we are, tearing through a set, and the crowd of 100 folks are jumping up and down pumping their collective fists, singing (well maybe not along with us, but singing), and there is this really high dude moshing right in front of me. He is jumping up and down and knocking into folks and running into the stage and on three occasions knocked over my mic stand. You get used to that sort of thing, and you keep going even when you can taste blood in your mouth from the mesh of the microphone having been bashed into your gums a bunch of times. We finish the set after about an hour and forty-five minutes, and I crawl off the stage and on to the rear patio of the bar to have a smoke.

This dude follows me out and bums a smoke off me. I'm sweating and still panting, and it's maybe minus two outside, steam rising off my sweaty shoulders. We start talking about the show and generally passing the time of day the way awkward smokers will, and the guy looks at me and says, "So what are you doing in town?" I look him straight in the eye as the memories of him go through my head: him rocking out right in front of me, yelling *dude* at me, knocking over my mic stand three times. I am dripping with sweat, and still waiting for my heart rate to return to normal, and without a blink, I say, "Ah, we are here to do some skiing."

I must say that when it comes to crowds in Golden, they are a lot of fun, and the shows are fun. But, really, your great show and the audience are kind of two different parties going on in the same room, and finding that out can be a bit of a reality check. It was a great birthday for me: I went back to Mary's and had a couple of birthday shots with Matt. Matt and I always had some secret whiskey here and there after shows.

Revelstoke, B.C.

I'm not sure why, maybe the name Revelstoke just hit me wrong over the years, but I think I thought about it as a mining town filled with wilderness types, the rough-and-tumble sorts that would be more interested in wildlife, and skinning a bear, than listening to alt-country. So for many years as we traversed Canada, we managed to give the town a miss. I was wrong. We had a great show there due to a woman who decided to bring us to town. This goes back to what I was mentioning earlier about believer clubs. Sometimes you don't even need the club part to become one.

In Revelstoke, our believer was named Amy. Amy had seen us out this way before and really liked our stuff, so she worked it out with the Big Eddy Pub just up the road from her house and offered us a gig. I believe she just contacted our agent and made an offer. She set a cover with the Big Eddy and met our rider requirements. Wow, to be honest, I think this show was the first time anybody actually met our entire rider.

At the time, our rider was as follows: a place to stay for

six people, six packs of smokes, seventy-two beers, two bottles of wine (one red and one white), throat lozenges, six towels, some nine-volt batteries, and a bottle of Jameson, oh, and some food. For those not in the know, a rider is what the band requests to have made available to them for the show. Riders are intended to make sure that the band is at sound check at a set time instead of running around some town they don't know looking for batteries and things. Riders are unheard of to the younger band, playing club shows where riders usually amount to two beer tickets. It is not till you get to playing larger shows that these come into play. Even on our latest tour, most of our gigs were riderless affairs. That did go along way toward being an even more special surprise when we actually got one. That said, we almost never got our full rider, ever. Jameson and smokes always seemed to be a sticking point with most venues. But here we are in Revelstoke B.C., and, hey, we got our full rider. Yay! We were very excited.

Now the big part about the Big Eddy show came out of a festival we had done three years before called Little Fest. It was somewhere up in the Slocan Valley, east of Nelson. These guys heard about us on our first western trip and had been bugging us for a couple of years to come out and do their festival. Now Little Fest is that: it's a small festival, maybe 800 folks show up for it. It's way up a back road, and it's real down-homey. The B.C. interior is filled with these small festivals, and they are very worth playing.

It took a couple of years for them to get us booked. They would get in touch with us every year, but they just didn't have enough money to make it possible for us to get out there. It is really expensive to get six folks to the other side of the country and then get them to the middle of a valley. But finally, this one year the stars aligned and brought us to Slocan Valley. We just happened to have scored a gig in Fort Macleod, Alberta. That had a good enough guarantee to make it possible for us to tour all the way out there. So we hung around out there till the following week, playing some shows around Alberta and B.C. The fest went pretty well, we had a lot of fun, and we got to open for the Agnostic Mountain Gospel Choir. The weekend was really laid back, and other than swallowing a big bug in the middle of a big dramatic vocal part and almost throwing up onstage, things went off without a hitch.

It wasn't until the following year that we found out how important that show was for us. It seems that this small festival that didn't have a lot of money, and it didn't seem like there were that many folks at it, is what sewed up the B.C. interior for us. The following year swinging through B.C., we found out that those folks who went to that show were the fervent show-going types, and they had decided that they really wanted to see us again. Suddenly, every show we played within 150 miles of Slocan Valley were full if not sold out. That one $1,000 show a year before packed out Golden, Revelstoke, Canmore, and Coleman. It was one of the best weeks of touring we ever had.

Revelstoke was certainly one of those nights. The Big Eddy is a roadhouse sort of place. They act like a restaurant during the day and have bands in now and again when things warrant it. We showed up on Wing Night, and they have good wings. Wing Night ended at nine or so, and then they kicked everybody out, or at least made them buy tickets for the show. It was sold out by 9:30. They apparently had to turn away a bunch of folks who had driven up from all over the valley. Yep, you get a name for yourself out there and folks travel to come see you, just like the folks from Jasper who drove down to Canmore to cheer us on. Man, that is a good feeling to sell out. Very sorry to the folks who drove up and didn't make it in.

We had a great show and some great wings, and a bunch of rider beer, and with a ride supplied by the bar, we made our way back to Amy's house for the night. I remember driving around Revelstoke that night before the gig, having the true mountain experience: snowdrifts fourteen feet high, and cold. We slept in Amy's basement, and the next morning they made us breakfast. Man, being taken care of goes a long way to making it worthwhile. I know Amy risked a bit to bring us out there. If the bar hadn't sold out, there is a good chance she might have been on the hook there, but it went very well, so I think she covered all the costs. I think she asked us back again not that long after, but we never made it back west.

Once again, the "If you build it they will come" thing plays out here. If you live in a town that doesn't see a lot of shows, it can be possible to get bands you like to come there. You just have to find a place to do it, put up the money, dicker with some agent in a far-off land about riders, and then get everyone to show up. It is possible and becoming a fairly common event on the Canadian music scene.

Kelowna, B.C.

Kelowna is the Toronto of the B.C. Interior, the big town that all other towns in the Okanagan Valley seem to have a hate-on for. The locals of Nelson, Vernon, Salmon Arm, and Revelstoke all seem to write the place off as a den of thieves, not a proper town. A town located on Okanagan Lake, some-where down around the middle of the valley.

The valley, which I must say I like, runs from Vernon in the north to way down south to Osoyoos and peters out around the Crowsnest Highway. This is Interior B.C., or as the kids call it, South Central Interior B.C. It's right between the Big Hills you come over leaving Alberta and the not-quite-so Big Hills that backdrop Vancouver. This is high plateau country, farmland, and there is the lake which is home to a sea monster, Ogopogo or some such thing. The hills are the homeland of Big Foot, the Sasquatch, too, so it's a picturesque yet monster-ridden environment. The lake is beautiful and come summer is completely filled from one end to the other with boats and other boat-like watercraft. I mean really filled — you can almost not see the water at all for all this water-borne enthusiasm.

I talked at length of my fear and loathing of the west, but here in the valley, I get my break from all that. Maybe it's the decreased level of altitude, but this part of the world reminds me of Central Ontario, maybe even Peterborough. Not that Peterborough is all that great, but familiar nonetheless. The farms and the winding roads, the lakes and the small towns, seem to leave me at ease. Certainly the architecture is similar, as well as a lot of the topography, if you manage not to notice all the hills in the background.

The folks are laid-back country types or small-town sorts, not really the hey, dude crowd. They are not extreme in any way and seem to love living in towns that they can, when they want, leave and go get all up into the mountains and see some scenery but not in a Mountain Dew commercial sort of way.

There is still a bit of a dependence on drugs out here, it being the centre of marijuana cultivation for probably all of North America, so it does have a slight hippy tinge to it. This, of course, is where they invented the grow op, the small suburban home filled to the top with grow lights and hydroponics. That aside, I guess the people could be described as beer, drinking farmer types that happen to grow a lot of weed. I can dig that. I like the South Central Interior. I like the valley a lot.

Kelowna, in the Okanagan language, means "grizzly bear." Just thought you should know that, since it's a far cry cooler name than Antigonish, which you earlier found out means "where bear go to remove bark from trees." I guess the indigenous folks out this way are a little more cut and dried than their counterparts back east. Or maybe the Okanagan people just thought Kelowna was going to be a little more of a cut-and-dried place.

With a population of almost 100,000 people, Kelowna is easily the biggest town around. It has the tallest building anywhere between Vancouver and Calgary, coming in at twenty-six stories, and a floating bridge that connects it to West Kelowna. The entire town's population of one tenth of a million people work in the tourist trade, excluding of course the folks who work in the grow ops, but then again, that could be considered service industry too. So every single one of them spends their entire life in subservience to tourists. Whether West Coast, Prairie, or U.S. tourists, this town abounds with things for the folks with nothing better to do than to arrive and expect to be waited on by the local folks. This and some heavy-duty traffic that would shock major centres like Calgary have left the locals sort of fair to middling in their disposition. They seem to be happy enough to be there, with big well-worked smiles. They are nice folk, happy to help, but looking as though they could use a big joint or some fine wine. Both of which are abundant here. The high plateau region offers a couple of renowned wineries and, as already mentioned, a heck of a lot of lived-in-looking houses that are filled with weed.

This is where the great Canadian weed trek starts, the trek that ends in Northern Ontario with you getting a routine traffic stop. Maybe try and avoid the whole thing and import wine instead.

We booked Kelowna twice in our travels, and the first place was the Minstrel Cafe. It is a great little restauranty sort of place. We had a cool crowd, and the food was real good. We had some friends show up here, my mom and a weird mix of folks I knew from high school, since this is where the kids of my generation headed after school, as well as some fellow travelers and fans that had been seasonally working out this way. Say what you want about Kelowna, but it is the big town in an area that abounds with things to do. The Minstrel offered up a weird night of a very homey crowd. A lot of these folks had never seen our band before. They were just folks who had been hearing about us over the years, and we had finally made it out to where they were. I remember it being a nice experience.

I also remember blowing up their PA system. It was a system that I guess had worked for them on their usual folk gig nights, duo shows and the odd soloist passing through hawking their quieter sort of tunes to crowds of wine drinkers and pasta eaters. But if I remember, this six-channel PA being plugged into what looked like stereo speakers really didn't hold up to us. I'm talking smoking speakers here. But the owners of the club didn't say anything to us about it; in fact, they enjoyed the show. And one could hope that they now have a newer and better PA system now that we gave them no choice but to upgrade.

Our only other brush with Kelowna came towards the end of our career when we had booked the Cush Tavern. It was in the middle of a big run of one-nighters, all strung night after night. We were heading for our gig after a pretty grueling schedule and got a text from our agent telling us that the gig in Kelowna had been canceled. We pulled into town to find that, in fact, yes, the club had lost its liquor license briefly and had canceled the show, but were going to honour their contract. They put us up in a hotel and paid us the guarantee of, say, maybe $800. Now I know that everyone out there wants to hear me say that we were really bummed out about not playing the gig. But, man, after six straight nights of playing, we found out we not only had the night off, but we had a place to stay and got paid. For that one night off, I am forever happy when I hear the name Kelowna. We got paid! I went out for dinner with my mom and got paid!

Nelson, B.C.

Nelson, hmmm…Nelson is a small-arts-and-culture-based community. It's a pretty town that took a big downturn in the eighties, but what town didn't? They lost their mill, and they opened a mall. Wow, there is a book right there: why did every town in Canada open a mall in the eighties when we all knew what would happen next, and it did. The downtown died.

So here is why I like Nelson, I mean really like Nelson. Their response was truly inspired. Most towns in the eighties did step one: they beautified. Reading about Nelson, I found out that meant removing a lot of aluminum siding from their downtown storefronts, exposing some remarkable architecture, brick nineteenth-century Victorian commercial buildings. Step one was to bring in the tourists, which is what happened. The folks streamed in to see this beautiful tourist town, and it is. But step two was to make this town a cultural haven, thus insuring that the folks did not just become a bunch of smiling yobs hoping the U.S. dollar didn't take a nosedive. They poured their resources into creating art space, theatres, galleries, venues, coffee shops, and the like. A real big local economy movement sprang forth, there being public spaces for the locals to meet each other and support each other's endeavours and ideas, and to cap it all off, they grew an inordinate amount of weed. This helped infuse the local economy with money to get them through the tough spots.

Now why didn't this happen everywhere else in Canada? No, not the weed part but the local cultural space part. I personally watched my own hometown shrivel up into a pretty and culturally vacant community over the late eighties and nineties, but they are only now starting to deal with these issues.

Driving down Baker Street in Nelson does fill me with a bit of awe, taking in the prettiness, yet there seems to be a substance to the town. The downtown core being ringed with mountains, beauty abounds. This mountain town of ex-loggers and ex-American draft dodgers was beautiful enough to have Steve Martin choose it for the setting of his 1986 classic love story *Roxanne*, a fine movie that shows off the charm of this "could be any mountain town U.S.A."

It is also the town where you will see mountain folk wandering the streets, all decked out in coonskin caps, and ponchos, and old, worn knapsacks. These folks coming into town to get supplies. I'm not making fun here, these are not ironic folks playing a part. They actually live a ways out of town up in the hills, off the grid. They grow their own food, living off the land, and routinely come into town to trade their wares and buy provisions. It's an old-school way of life for these "homeless-looking" folks. One trip down the main drag and I spotted three people fitting this description. I'm sure in other places out this way they would be written off as the rummies, or even crack addicts, but these folks were wearing not just cast-off clothing but clothing that looked as though they had made it themselves. There are quite a lot of folks out here that live that way, and the locals seem to find it not that out of the ordinary, they themselves seemingly a little closer to nature than most places I've been. The people of Nelson just seem a bit more real than most folks I've come into contact with, a little bit closer to what is around them. Is it being surrounded by nature? Is it the isolation of this mountain town? Or is it their efforts to keep culture alive and keep their kids from the constant want of moving away, offering a life out here in the pines?

The Royal on Baker is a nineteenth-century hotel, rejuvenated in later times and served us up a great packed-house, Sunday-night show. With the help of some honest and true support from the local radio station, we packed an end-of-weekend show there. The room itself was a little too modern for the building and definitely had way too many speakers for its own good. But it did bring in a whooping and hollering crowd that made us feel at home. This venue, which we only played once, boasted a pretty impressive lineup of shows for a town of 10,000 souls. Proving that if you have a place to play, and folks are made used to you offering a non-stop sched of talent, you can fill a room often. It takes work, but the Royal as well as the town itself seems to have done its work.

With rooms booked in the local chain motel, it was Nelson that started the three a.m. mid-street boot toss. This is a nice town to toss your boot at three a.m. I think the boot toss was a tie between Dylan and Steve, but with an honorable mention on behalf of Gus and Filly. I left the scene early, not wanting to injure myself, and spent a lovely thirty minutes wandering the downtown core. Nothing like the silent night on the main drag of a small town, post-bar, post-show, checking out the architecture, pausing to watch the traffic lights change, keeping an eye out for the local cops, and hiding that squirreled-away beer in your pocket just so, that balance between concealment and getting a soaker. At last, home was the Best Western and a good night's sleep.

Morning found me eating at a diner on the main drag that if I remember correctly was a Chinese restaurant/diner. Breakfast was good.

The Crowsnest Pass (the high low road)

Bidding the fair town of Nelson *adieu*, you make your way south on the 3A. If you started your tour in February, you should be in full-on spring mode. The rush of spring weather rolls in through the cracked open window, fresh air filling the van and disgorging old cigarette smoke and body odour. Spring has sprung, and you are revitalized, I hope. The trees, rocks, and fish you will see on this route, the 3A, are quite idyllic. But put that aside because you have miles to book today. Google maps has your trip at nine and a half hours, but it is still early springtime, so leave room for a monster snowstorm as you get into the mountains, especially if you are getting a late start and will be conquering some of this trip in the dark.

You travel south through Castlegar, and upon reaching Highway 3, the Crowsnest Pass Highway, it is time to ponder. Sitting at this intersection, you will decide whether to turn right toward Vancouver and backtrack down the pass or head home. It was always my argument over the years that this entire western B.C., or the coast part of the Canadian tour, is optional. It is an argument I lost every time. My side, after having played Vancouver several times, was why do we take all this time out of our tour to drive down and play a town whose music scene is in a shambles due to years upon years of condo development, a scheme I am desperate to not see happen in my home-town of Montreal? Vancouver is a long haul, and if you are not taking in the Island, it just costs a buttload of money to get there and a couple of days out of your life just to play the railway club, get a parking ticket, then pay through the nose for parking and have cyclists give you the finger as you try to load into the club across a bike lane.

I always lost that argument. The band would scream, "It's Vancouver, the place that was the scene back in the eighties and early nineties. It was the biggest scene in Canada before the big collapse!" The folks in the van with you have friends there, and you have decided to book the Island, so you then turn right and head west toward Van, backtracking across Highway 3. It must be said that if you wanted, you could have booked Nelson on the way back up through, but as this tour has laid out, I was really looking for someplace nice to play on a Saturday night and a nice place to have the Sunday off, so Nelson was it. Now you are doing that band thing by backtracking about two hours through the pass.

Now you're on the Crowsnest Pass Highway. The downside is that on this stretch you will not actually go through the Crowsnest Pass. It's the other way, but have no fear; you will on the way home. What is in store for you today is one awesome drive up through some pretty serious mountains. If the snow holds off, it will be a nice day. Once again, I have taken you by way of Nelson and the Crowsnest Pass so as to give you a chance to not drive the Trans-Canada. The 3 is a great piece of road, beautiful, challenging, and very little traffic. Due to the very large hills, the truck traffic avoids this route, and it would seem that so do a lot of the tourist trade. The big, heavy, underpowered RVs just don't get up this way. So life is good on the road out here as you traverse the high country and towns like Grand Forks and Osoyoos. Past those rolling hills of wine country around Osoyoos, the hills get real high. Check your altimeter because you will probably get up around 1,700 m today, which should now not be a big problem for the vocalist, and maybe your ears have finally gotten used to all the ups and downs of mountain travel. As well, check the map. You are almost in the U.S.A. many times across this winding mountain path of a highway. Please choose any diversions carefully to avoid driving into Washington State and some U.S. border guards who might be pumped at the chance to look through your bass player's underwear. It's not to difficult to stay on the well-marked main road, but I have heard stories of folks accidentally wandering into U.S. territory.

Keep an eye out for wildlife: bighorn sheep, bears, cougars, and Sasquatches abound on the roadsides. Today's travel tip: if you happen to get a picture of Big Foot, maybe don't tell anybody 'cause it will overshadow your tour.

Several hours of driving later, you will descend these mountains in a maze of switchbacks and seemingly sheer drops, and watching the altimeter drop down to almost zero, you will find yourself in Hope, B.C. Maybe look around and think about staying the night because the motels here are a lot cheaper than you will find in Van. Your Vancouver show should be booked for, say, a Tuesday or Wednesday. I've never seen it worth giving Van a Friday night. Unless you have a real kick-ass promoter or your band is super hot right now, a Wednesday night should fit the bill. Save up your weekend for the Island; you will need it to fill a club out there.

After a week and a half rolling through the mountains, the land you are now traversing on Highway 1 will seem remarkably flat. It's not an illusion, nope, it's level out here. Green fields of flat-ass farmland is what you are going to see for the next two hours as you make your way to the big city. The towns of Rosedale, Chilliwack, and Abbotsford will roll by you, finally coming alive after a lifetime of hearing about them on the CBC. These mostly nice towns are great places to get gas. We found that the gas stop just off the highway in

Chilliwack had a great Mac N' Cheese to Go cup. Mixed with a day-old sandwich, it really fit the mid-afternoon lunch requirement. But like all other travelers of this region, you will ignore most of this in an effort to get to town.

Vancouver, B.C.

Now, I've often taken the piss out of Van. It is well known that I don't do well on the West Coast, but before folks all start getting too mad at me for dissing their big city of the west, I must say it's not that I hate it here, it's just that this place puts me on edge. Maybe it's recovering from the altitude, maybe it's 'cause this is where you turn around and face the long drive home, or maybe it's just the vibe. Vibe-wise, it's probably a perfectly good vibe for the folks who live out here, and once in it, I'm sure things are great, but, man, it is a different vibe here.

To understand the vibe of which I speak, let's look at Canada from coast to coast. You start out east in Newfoundland. Everybody there is sort of yelling at each other, a lot of the time saying some pretty nasty stuff very fast. There are fist fights, shouting matches, and love. They are all grouped together, locked in a struggle of wills, sitting real close together in bars and family get-togethers. It's loud but nice, like a wedding. It's exciting. You traverse west and things calm down some, Quebec and Ontario having a real similar feel, but folks start sitting farther apart, they talk slower, and there is a little less yelling and a little less love. This continues as you drive farther west. The Prairies seem to be very social: it's all about the community, yet nobody talks about politics or anything that controversial all that much. Not wanting to have a fight with the neighbours, they are polite yet cautious on the flat land. Then you crest the hills, and you are on the coast. The vibe west of the hill seems to be an unspoken "nice to see you, glad you made it out here, but leave me alone please, don't you know I moved all the way out here to get away from you!"

Don't get me wrong: they are polite, easily the politest people I have ever met in the world. West Coast folks make Belgians seem crass and argumentative. But there always seems to be this unspoken angst to folks here on the coast. I'm from back east, and I'm speaking it. I feel free to do so because I don't think, outside of West Coast talk radio, anybody will ever call me on it. They will be mad but will probably not say so. In their eyes, I am just an easterner who doesn't get it. I don't expect the westerners to be super happy about me saying this, but they will not say much about it and will individually ignore my thoughts on their culture, which will culminate in absolute quiet mixed with some angry outbursts at a book launch in Abbotsford some day.

It took me a long time to really put my finger on it, but after many trips west, I think I have gotten to the heart of the matter. It's the beauty out here. To stand in Vancouver and see this truly amazing city, all lit up with its twentieth-century architecture glass and retro-fitted, earthquake-proof structures, is to be in awe. It really is a nice-looking, modern city, with lovely high-rises, big natural parks, bridges, highways, bike paths, and pleasant citizenry. But it's the backdrop of the pristine mountains that throws you off. The mountains are beautiful, and so is Vancouver. Standing there, you start to get the vibe. Wow, we built this big, beautiful, modern city and, man, is it ruining the view. It is a new city, and most of the towns out here are new. Back east, there are all those old, down-at-the-heel post-industrial towns of red brick Victorian factories that been there forever. The steeples from the colonial churches even blend into their surroundings and the backdrop, the softer backdrop of the softer terrain. The terrain is older there, the mountains are older, more worn down, less threatening, safer-looking. The Rockies, the western mountains, are beautiful and aggressive-looking.

Nothing man built on the coast blends in with the remarkable and stunning beauty of the West Coast. Even remarkably beautiful architecture is somehow at odds. I think this makes everybody a little upset about being human. Everywhere they look they see how they have marred nature and have not added to their surroundings in a cohesive way. Simply living and the things you need to thrive, housing, commerce, and highways, have this way of looking as though you are screwing up this awesome vista. I have talked with many Vancouverites over the years, and I always ask them what they like about living in Vancouver. Nobody answers Gastown, or living on East Hastings is great, or I love Chinatown, or the food is cool, or my neighbors are outstanding. Nope, every one of them says, "It's great here. In fifteen minutes I can get in my car and be in the middle of nowhere, all by myself." I then interject with my back-east wit, "So…the thing you like about Vancouver is, not being here. Why don't you just go wherever 'there' is and find something to do to make a living?"

My tip is: when touring Western Canada, specifically the coast, don't be a dick like me. It will go a long way towards helping you have a good time. Enjoy Gastown, East Hastings,

Chinatown, and meet some folks, smoke a fatty, and get into the vibe. Don't worry if you start feeling edgy at any moment—you are a fifteen-minute car ride from somewhere you can be all by yourself.

Loading into Pat's Pub, located on the ground floor of the Patricia Hotel, East Hastings, Vancouver. It's not like I'm going to have to tell you to keep a spotter by the van. It will become apparent to you as you get out of the van and are immediately accosted by a street person, who is now offering you some of their vodka, that this is really not a safe place to leave the van loaded with all your gear. Send someone in to work out the load in and someone to go to the front desk to get the accoms worked out. Then, when they get back, load in. But always leave someone with the van while it is loaded with gear and baggage. Pay for the parking in the lot next to the club and leave your empty van here. It is as good as anywhere in the neighbourhood, and at least you can check up on it now and again.

You think I'm making light of a beleaguered part of Vancouver here, but I'm not. It's a rough part of town, and I am not exaggerating at all. It's not the Wild West, there aren't bullets flying around you, it's just a heck of a lot of street folks, all hustling to stay alive and get through their day-to-day existence. It can be a quite interesting place to spend a day or so, but don't leave your shit lying around, 'cause it will get gone quick.

East Hastings is the epicentre of the West Coast of Canada's homeless ills. It's a melting pot for all of Western Canada, if not all of Canada. It's where folks come who are near to ending up on the street. See, back home, it gets real cold come winter, and it really is tough to keep from freezing to death. So built into this whole countrywide problem for Vancouver and the West Coast is that this is probably the only place in Canada where the winters don't get cold enough to kill you outright. Now, that sounds great, except not freezing is not the same as living, and though this does bring some of the biggest problems to the coast, they get multiplied by the fact that the folks out here can get by on the streets, which means it is harder to get them back into the system and maybe get them off the streets.

The centre of this big problem is Vancouver's East Hastings. All can be seen here, all can be bought and paid for, and anything can happen.

The load in finished, and the baggage delivered to your rooms, you make your way downstairs and set up for sound check. It should go pretty well. In my experience, the club has some pretty bad gear, i.e., Behringer mics and Peavey monitors. But the couple of times we played there, the soundman was great and got this sound system to sound good. Pack up your instruments and take them upstairs and hit the streets for dinner.

I think the club gives a meal deal to the musicians, but I'm saying give that a miss 'cause you are just blocks away from Chinatown. Yep, bounding out the front door, hang a right and keep trucking on down the block till you get to Main. Hang a left, and you are in Chinatown, just a few short blocks away. Arriving at the corner of Pender, you can go right or left. I have not found a favourite restaurant there to date but find that just wandering up and down the street you should find some good grub. You are on the coast, and Van's

Chinatown is historic and old.

I believe the first time we made it down there we all piled into this cafeteria-looking place. It seemed easiest, what with six people all trying to eat quickly and cheaply. There was a thirty-foot-long steam table behind a sneeze guard and a bunch of folks behind it who didn't speak English but were very used to dishing out what ever you pointed at. I settled on some fantastic noodle dish. I have no idea what it was called, some sort of chow mein, but I remember it being cheap and good. Kevin, on the other hand, pointed to a tray of something mushy-looking and asked what it was. The answer was incomprehensible, but he's the bravest of all of us, so he just said, "Why not?"

Once we sat down, we worked out that Kevin had ordered tripe. It's rubbery and smells pretty funky, so the rest of us kind of backed away, leaving Kevin to plow through it like a good sport.

Back in the rundown yet clean rooms of the Patricia Hotel, you start trying to watch TV in hopes of chilling out a bit before the show. Unfortunately, your mindless TV enjoyment will be constantly interrupted by more interesting things to be seen out the window. From the fifth floor, we sat on the window ledge and in half an hour witnessed at least four arrests, a brawl, twenty-three drug deals, countless deals for sex, and an all-together camaraderie we have never seen before. Matt said, "This is better than the Discovery Channel."

Dressing for the show, please make sure to wear some light clothing because the stage is hot. We start up our show after an amazing warm-up set by the Pine Family. Years later, Hank Pine reminded me that he and I met that night. The Pine Family was a little more laid back than Hank's later act, Hank Pine and Lily Fawn. Yet the Family did do a nice job of getting the folks going. Due to some good work by our promoter, Fireball Productions, the place was pretty packed, and this on a Wednesday night. We took to the stage and knocked a very friendly crowd into East Coast — reminiscent dance maniacs. But it occurred to me during the third song, "Man, this stage is hot!"

When I realized the temperature was about 40C, I figured it was just the lights in an absentminded, one-show-after-another sort of way: stage lights can do that. But then I realized that there really wasn't anything in the way of lighting onstage, just a dreary blue light that was either malfunctioning or had been accidentally turned down. There we were in mostly gloom, and yet it was hot as f. up there, a "pits of hell" sort of heat. Later in the set, when we did the song "Meaner Than You," I put down my guitar and went onto the floor to physically bother the audience. Usually, I writhed on the biggest guy I could find, and in this case, I think it was *Corner Gas*'s Lorne Cardinal. The writhing complete, I made my way back on stage to find that, yes, it was easily 15C hotter on stage. At the end of the song, I went back to retrieve my guitar that was leaning against a curtain covering the back wall of the stage. That's when I found out that the entire ground floor of the building's heating system was located behind that curtain, and located only onstage. To all would-be bar designers, I'm just going to put this out there: don't locate the heating, or for that matter cooling, system anywhere near the stage.

Many pitchers of beer later, you slink upstairs and take a shower and collapse in a creaky bed. You have conquered Vancouver and are happy you went to all the trouble to come out here. The Van audiences are worth it.

Waking the next morning, the first stop is to check the van, and with crossed fingers you find it as left. All the worry was for naught. Loading up your van, you take to the streets, which leads to today's travel tip: never trust the green light. Vancouver has one of the most dangerous exceptions to the Highway Traffic Act known to Canadian drivers. In Montreal, you can't turn right on red. It's a thing that is unique to Montreal, and there are signs on the highway as you enter town telling you this. You can miss those signs, and they are in French, so you might not completely understand the signs while speeding by them at 100 kph. It's no real biggie, based on the fact that you are only going to turn right if it is safe to do so. And if you happen to turn right on a red and a cop sees you, there is a good chance he will let it pass as long as you have an out-of-province plate, and even if he pulls you over, it would seem that you have a good chance of not getting a ticket for it, just a lecture on Montreal's unique traffic laws. The law is designed to lower intersection traffic accidents. It works, and I actually like not having to try and merge with cross traffic. If the light is red, just sit back and wait for it to change. Nobody will honk at you for sitting at a red light.

Well, Vancouver has its own unique law about traffic lights too, except it seems to me like the most dangerous law ever. Those flashing green lights that you are going to see while tearing down the major thoroughfares of downtown Van are not flashing to tell you that you have the right of way to opposing traffic. Nope, they don't mean that at all. Everywhere in Canada, when you see a flashing green light, it means that the folks coming the other way are going to stop because they have a red light and you have the right of way. In fact, if you have a flashing green light, it means that everyone else has a red light, so feel free to turn anyway you would like. Knowing this, you pull in front of the oncoming traffic with full confidence that the folks in the other direction are probably going to stop. But in Vancouver, a flashing light means that that light is going to stay green, or at least continue to flash green, until some driver or pedestrian in the perpendicular direction trips a switch, thus sending the light to a solid green and then on to yellow and then red. *What the fuck, yo!!* How would anybody not born in Vancouver know that? Wow, I remember it took us at least two near misses to find that out. Once again, wow! So the tip for today is: if you see a flashing green light in Vancouver: STOP, get out of your van, wave down a passing cop, and ask him what you should do now! What the hell, man!!!! This almost killed everyone involved!!!! And I don't even care why you do it this way, where can I buy new underwear? I just shat myself, you son of a....

When being released from a Vancouver police detention cell, please remember to take with you the B.C. traffic law exception pamphlet the lovely policeman gave you after you calmed down and stopped yelling obscenities at him and every other person you saw in an official uniform.

Just to be clear, in Vancouver, a flashing green light means go for everybody, and a solid green light means go for everybody too. Just thought I'd clear that up for you.

Get me to a ferry! And bring a blanket.

The Coast! (Look! Water! We made it!)

Spending time cruising the Internet, trying to make sense of the BC Ferries website, you are daunted and impressed by the BCFS's massive job, which is to supply car ferry service to what seems like hundreds of islands off the coast of B.C. Yep, they have a big job: there are a bunch of islands, and people live on most of them. These people are the people who I think got tired of living in Vancouver, and got tired of being only a fifteen-minute drive to some other place they wanted to be. For this, I nod my head and think, "Good on you, folks. You are making it work, hustling out there in the near wilderness, making a life for yourselves in a place where you want to be, and leaving the ills of city life behind you."

What makes all this possible is the British Columbia Ferry Services Inc. The BCFS is a provincial crown corporation, also subsidized by the Federal government, and is the only thing that manages to link the mainland to the bevy of communities that lurk on, near, or around Vancouver Island and up the coast. Vancouver Island is the big one on the map, located right across the Georgia Strait from Vancouver. Located on that island are the two big towns Nanaimo—yes, the bars were named after it—and Victoria. There are a bunch of other towns located on the big island and some possible gigs all over the place, but Nanaimo and Victoria are the for sure places to get a gig. I would head for Nanaimo first, maybe push for a Thursday-night gig, thus leaving you a Friday and Saturday to book the other towns. This part of the trip is going to be hard financially, starting with the ferry ride.

A quick run-down on the schedule will find that it is going to take near to $140 to take the ferry over, so you are going to have to eat that. One cost-saving measure passed on by West Coast bands to us was bring a blanket with you and throw it over two of your bandmates while pulling up to the ticket booth. If you are six folks, say you are four folks. The local bands swear it works. The United Steel Workers where chicken, so when asked how many folks there were in the van, I said six. The ticket agent, not even looking up or out the window of his booth on this grey, all-too-common, misty coastal day, just said, "One hundred and forty dollars," and fished around with the change trying to find my hand as he went out of his way to not look up or at me. Man, we thought, that would have been easy to hide some folks in the back of the van. They must check our tickets later. Well, they didn't, and we felt sad later when, as it turned out, the locals had been right and that nobody seemed to care how much we paid to get on the boat. I'm not advising you to commit a crime here, 'cause you never know, and nobody wants to miss their gig, cause you got hung up at the ferry terminal, but it is worth mentioning that your warm-up band in Vancouver or Nelson will coach you on this cost-saving measure. Also, be prepared to feel somewhat ripped off by the BCFS when after paying your full fare nobody cares whether you did or not.

The deck plate hitting the dock at the Horseshoe Bay ferry terminal, you will pull your van into the hold of the ship. It's a smaller ship than those on the Newfoundland run, a fact that will have you questioning your measuring skills as you remember the height clearance of your van. Pulling into the upper deck, I was assuredly worried that somehow my math was going to be wrong and that our van in no way, shape, or form could be under seven feet, the height clearance for the upper deck. But the boarding crew urged me on, with the van's roof riding just two inches under the roof of the upper bay. Man, that was tight, but the boarding crew is used to it, getting all those SUVs coming and going day and night. Here is a quick note: it might actually be a good idea, right now while you are in the planning stages of your trip, to run outside with a good tape measure and measure the dimensions of your band's van. It will come in handy for booking ferry passage, and is always good when entering a parking garage to know exactly just how high you are. Maybe write those dimensions on a sticker and fasten it to the dashboard of your van so one of your absentminded bandmates doesn't try to use the 6'8" drive-through at the Tim Hortons. Knowing your dimensions is always a good idea.

Sliding into your berth on deck, the band disgorges and takes to the passenger decks. There is a cafeteria and room to move. This slow-moving boat will take in some beauty, especially if it is that one day of the year when the weather is nice on the Georgia Strait. If the weather is its usual grey, rainy self, then keep happy in the knowledge that your boat probably won't run into high seas or pack ice. We are still in what would be known as inland water, with Vancouver Island being an amazing buffer to the wilds of the Pacific Ocean. For this, the ferries are more of the inland water type, lower, longer, and not the grandiose ocean-going affairs of the Gulf of Saint Lawrence, but it's a nice trip just the same. If the weather is good, maybe take your lunch out on deck and enjoy the trip, or if it is rainy, bring your travel Scrabble with you from the van. The trip takes a little less than two hours.

Nanaimo, B.C.

Arriving in Nanaimo, you plunk down on dry land again at Departure Bay and immediately head for the venue. The town of Nanaimo is a sprawling hulk of an old mining town that has been overrun by modern, low-to-the-ground housing and strip malls. This town of 80,000 people owes its history to coal mining and forestry, and, in modern times, paper and the ferry terminal you are now leaving. You wind your way to the downtown area and go in search of the Cambie.

Nanaimo is a two-venue town: the Cambie and the Queen's. We have played both of them with very little success. This from a town that had us tracking our first album on the local college station for years in advance of our arrival. First shot was the Queen's. Everybody we knew who knew the scene out there said we were to play the Queen's, and after we played it, everybody in the know agreed that we should have played the Cambie. It's like this with struggling two-venue towns, when you bomb out of one place, everybody involved will agree that you should have played the other place. Then, upon returning playing the other, all can agree that the first place certainly should have been your bar.

All this in, let's go to the Cambie. It's got accoms right upstairs and is located right on the main drag of downtown. If the show doesn't go well, then at least you had a place to stay. Disgorging from the van, I guess you engorge the Cambie with the band's presence in the late afternoon. Immediately upon entering the bar and making yourself known, the bartender runs out from behind the bar and says, "Is your van parked out front? You should unload your van right now.

Don't leave it on the street with gear in it." You turn on your heels and go back out to the van to find more than a few seedy-looking types, yes, hovering near your ride. If you are smart, you start unloading right away, once again leaving a spotter with the van at all times until it is completely empty of all gear and baggage and even things that look like baggage.

I feel it is necessary to mention this, cause when touring Vancouver Island with its idyllic beauty, it can be a bit of a mind-f. once you realize that the folks who moved out here on this island got to leave the big city behind but unfortunately did not leave all its ills in Vancouver. It was the single biggest thing I noticed out here. There were lots of places that reminded me of driving around the East Coast of Canada with the small towns and the picturesque post card scenery, but there, you can rest a little knowing that the downtown rules of security do not apply. Well, here on the Island they do. A lot of the island can seem quite rural, but the mild winter weather also brings a lot of the homeless, and drug issues, to most of these quaint towns. It's not a stabfest, and you aren't going to get mugged probably, but there are a lot of street folks out here and a lot of drugs, which is sort of the perfect kind of scenario for someone to rip off your gear, or at least the stereo in your van, which is weird 'cause who buys used car stereos anymore?

We load into the Cambie, and the staff seem nice and get us checked into the accoms upstairs. It's a little rough around the edges, but more than adequate for the travelling band. There's a room with a bunch of bunks and a bathroom that we converted to a small restaurant affair. We referred to it as the "Shit and Shuck Café." Chris Reid, banjo number three, is a great fan of seafood, and upon passing a roadside stand for oysters, he picked up a big bag of them. The accoms being rudimentary, the shellfish were deposited on ice in the bathroom sink. This may have gone a ways in masking the overall smell of the otherwise typical band accom by leaving a fishy smell that soon took over the room.

The "Shit and Shuck" installed and the band's bags stowed, we went back downstairs to find out when sound check was to be held. We were informed that the soundman had decided not to do a sound check and that "doing it on the fly would be fine." Never wanting to do more work than was necessary, we took it that the soundman was, of course, competent and we headed out to get some food.

Located just up the block at 1 Commercial St. is Pirate Chips. It was time to see if the West Coast could upstage the east on fish and chips. The Pirate was very promising. It's a small place: the kind of place I would think of if someone mentioned they were going to pop down to the chippie. The place looks as though it has some history to it, and upon entering, the smell of frying fish and potatoes did in fact transport me back to my youth. The food held up to this, offering the nicest fries I have had in quite some time. Not overcooked, sort of blonde in colour, and just a little mushy. Unfortunately, both times we were in Nanaimo this little fish and chip shop seemed to be running low on actual fish. I did manage to get some fish in me, but when I ordered, the counter person gave me a look as she said all they had left was pollock and then waited to see if I was going to cancel my order. Both times I mucked in and got the pollock. It was fine, nicely battered and tender inside, but I must admit it was a little less of an experience than, say, cod from back east, and made even less so by the counter person prefacing that this was all that was left and wondering if I still wanted to eat it. But, overall, it held up as being in the top five fish and chips I'd had on this run across the country.

Bellies filled with spuds and battered pollock, we tramped back to the Cambie just in time to meet up with our co-headlining band for the night's show, Hot Panda out of Edmonton. Nice bunch of guys whom Felicity met up with online as we were booking this leg of our tour. We were trying to shore up the Island leg of the tour, and Hot Panda had the slot we wanted in Victoria and we had the Cambie gig they wanted locked down in Nanaimo, so we joined forces on both gigs and decided to split the money from both gigs. They had just loaded in. Being from the west, they knew well enough not to leave gear in the their van either.

We went back inside to see if the soundman had made an appearance yet, and he had not, so we all hung around getting to know each other a bit. This lasted for a couple of hours while we still awaited the arrival of the soundman. At about 9:45, he showed up, drunk if I remember. I believe he mentioned that it was his birthday, so "sorry I was late." I think we worked out that Hot Panda would go first and we would follow. They set up their gear in about ten minutes. The Panda is a poppy, indie act, the usual drums, bass, and electric gear and whatnot. Road act folks like them manage to get amps and a drum kit together pretty fast. And then we all sat around for 40 minutes while the drunken soundman tried to get three mics to work. The show started around 11:30, and by the third song, we knew we were going to have a lousy night onstage. The sound was not only awful but also sporadic in nature, often cutting out altogether. Hot Panda mucked through their set quickly to a handful of angry "just dropped by to see who is playing and get stupid drunk on beer specials and Jäger" sort of crowd. Finishing their set, Panda was totally nice about the whole affair and got their gear out of the way fast.

The soundman, who at this point was still drinking, came up to me and asked in a wobbly way why the first band was removing their drum kit. It was at that point that I mentioned we didn't play with drums and needed a whole slew of lines to plug our mostly acoustic instruments into the system. I remember taking to the stage about an hour later to an almost empty room and spending an hour on stage listening to feedback and screaming into mics that didn't work. I think after about ten songs we just gave up and lumped offstage. We then got drunk and went to bed. Showing up down in the bar the next day to get paid, we found out that between the two bands, we made $38 for playing the night before. That $38 we sheepishly split with Hot Panda, and we told them thanks for coming out, and we will see you in Victoria on Saturday.

I guess in retrospect we should have played the Queen's.

Courtenay, B.C.

Licking our wounds, we headed north up to the Comox Valley to squeeze in a Friday night at Joe's Garage in Courtenay, B.C. I feel I must mention again that we have not played extensively on the Island, so Joe's was a godsend. There are rumours from the Vancouver- and Vancouver Island-based bands that there are a lot of great places to play out here. But I believe it really does take someone from the Island to figure out the ins and outs of playing here, knowing where everything is, which ferries take you to which island, and what night you can make any money out of that gig. My advice to anybody coming out this way is to try and find a friend that lives there to figure out your shows for you. With that in mind, we arrived at Joe's Garage on a rainy Friday night. Joe's is a little café cum bistro/music store and sometimes venue. We had a lovely show at Joe's, and the food was great, as we played to a small crowd and then ate a really good meal. The only other memorable part was that Gus needed some guitar strings. Gus usually did because he's a hard player and goes through his fair share of them. I remember being surprised that located in the corner of the café was a little music store sort of kiosk. I remember thinking that it didn't really fit too well with the bistro vibe but that cafés and bars could probably do well to have a rudimentary music store set up as a bit of a side business. Done right, offering strings, patch cords, and the occasional mic could not only bring in some dough from the travelling bands but also attract townsfolk into your establishment who would then find out who was going to be playing this weekend.

Bounding back down the Inland Island Highway (the kids refer to it as the I.I.H.), winding through some damn nice scenery and a heck of a lot of traffic, the next day was spent running as fast as we could towards Victoria. I do believe that on this trip and the ones before it we were actually robbed of seeing the Pacific Ocean. We never got to run out onto a beach and dunk a cold foot in the water. Strangely, it is only now that I realize that. You would think going coast to coast there would be that push in your mind, one foot in the At-lantic and then, months later, one foot in the Pacific to close things out. But you have to realize that the trip you take as a band is not the trip that the average backpacker is taking. We are not counting countries and reading plaques about historical things, and it's not tours of art galleries we are doing here. We are here to play shows and interact with folks who live here or have also travelled here. We are here to see what the scene is in this part of the world. Over the years, we did take in some of the sights and see some historic finery but usually only when there was a lot of spare time to kill and money to burn, which didn't really come up that often. At this time, I guess I must admit to not feeling robbed at all. The folks who backpack everywhere have not seen any of the things we have seen and I guess we have seen, half of what they did.

With that in mind, we didn't even have the thought of not seeing the ocean in our minds as we sped toward our next destination, Victoria, B.C.

Victoria, B.C. (Canada's Florida)

It seems weird, upon entering Victoria, to find after driving from one end of Canada to the other that you have arrived in Protestant Southern Ontario. Nope, check the map. You didn't. You are still on the West Coast. Vic is a larger version of, say, Guelph, a place that will seem almost like England, but it's Canada. The "City of Gardens," as it is called, will shock you back into the realization that Canada was in fact a dominion that was bestowed its nationhood by the Queen of England. Well, of course we all knew this growing up in Canada. Someone of my age can still remember the teatotaling fish chipperie that was Canada not so long ago, back when people bandy about terms like "shuttlecocks" and "rather."

Okay, not "rather," but they said "shuttlecocks" way too much. It's a birdie, damn you! This just west of the U.K.'ness that Paul Gross has made an entire acting career of extolling. That Mid-Atlantic accent is more prevalent here on the Pacific coast than anywhere else in Canada, although ornamented by the word "dude" from time to time.

Admittedly, I realize only now that since arriving in Montreal twenty-odd years ago, and having spent ten years travelling Canada, I have seen that image of Victorian Canada erode. Canada as a whole seems to have come into its own as a nation, yay! Not sure if that is all us, or that England itself has become less recognizable in my time, but, true, we seem to play less darts, eat fewer pickled eggs, and spend less time in pubs and more time in bars, and the effect of the Legion as a culture mooring point has diminished some. It was not until arriving in Victoria that I realized that this receding glacier of culture had begun to let loose its grasp. Perhaps it was Conrad Black getting jailed for, say, the last ten years. This post-Britishness is not and has never been an in-your-face sort of thing — it's subtle, the accent out here is weirdly British, and Victoria is a beautiful representation of the Canada of a bygone era.

British Columbia's provincial capital seems incongruous with the overall feel of B.C. or even of Vancouver Island as a whole. B.C. has a lot of different types of folks and cultures ranging from quiet stately white folks through hippies, indigenous cultures, mountain people, fishermen, beachcombers, and back to stately white folk, but it is not till you arrive in Victoria, a town of vegetarian, earthy non-smokers that you are reminded of Canada's not-so-distant forefathers. This does make me wonder why it is that capitals don't often actually reflect the areas they represent? Who in Canada actually thinks Ottawa represents the average Canadian experience? Or Quebec City the province of Quebec? Old Vic is right up there with most capitals: incongruous but nice.

Here I've gone and given you the idea that Victoria is filled with pie-eating, dart-throwing lawn bowlers. Well, it might be, but for the most part, you are going to see some nice folks hanging around independently operated cafés. They do jobs like woodworking and other crafts, making things out of wrought iron or trinkets to be sold on the boardwalk down by the harbour. Or they work in forestry or as modern-day versions of stevedores. It's kind of a touristy sort of town, but its inhabitants are far more grounded than first impressions let on. They will talk your ear off about how f.'t up Victoria is on a political level. The average citizen seems a little miffed by the stateliness and stolidness of their local government, and like most other touristy towns, when prodded, the locals have a healthy chip on their shoulders when it comes to tourists and the prettiness of their town.

I like Victoria. I find it relaxing, pretty, and the folks are enthusiastic and less laid back than I've been getting used to since driving west of Winnipeg.

Logan's is located right beside, actually, in the same building as, the neighborhood liquor store, with the store giving this part of the street a little bit more action than some of the other blocks. It also makes it possible to find parking directly in front of the bar. A good turnover of parked cars coming and going to the booze store actually frees up those sought-after spots in front of the load in door quite frequently. Hang back double-parked and usually with in a couple of minutes you can score the spot right in front of the load in doors. Nothing like an easy load in to help the day seem better.

Logan's is the venue you are looking forward to, and upon arriving late afternoon, you walk in to find Carolyn Mark hosting a folk jam in the front room of the bar. Joining her is Lonesome Larry Whittaker, a long time ex-member of the USWM, our third and final drummer, and a good friend who made the move west years ago. Great shows in faraway places are always made better by running into friends. We load in, and get a couple of beers, order some food at a discount, and sit down with Larry and get caught up.

Now, for the folks who don't have ex-members in Victoria, here is today's travel tip: getting to know the locals is going to save this leg of your trip. Hotels in Victoria are quite expensive, it being a tourist town. So it is very important that the single members, the attractive people in the band, do their best to really put it out there now for the good of the team. It is up to the skinny, young members of the band to hook up with some cool-looking, sweater-wearing, earthy girl with hairy armpits to score with, thus getting the band free accoms. You just spent $250 on ferry passage, $150 on gas, $150 on food, $100 on smokes, and played two shows that brought in, say, $135 in merch and door, and tonight's show is going to pay probably $300 or less. This requires the "players" in the band to step up and score some quick accoms for you guys to kill a couple of days and make up some of the deficit the band is now in. If you are in a band like we were, where pretty much all of the band members were in relationships, married or other, it might be said that searching Facebook for some long-lost high school buddies who happened to have migrated here years ago could work as well. This is go time; this is when bands get dirty in a moral sense; and fortunately, you just spent months eating bad food, hawking wares, and fighting with each other, so you are on the right level now to start taking advantage of other people. It's fight or flight time, and right now the band is hurting. Do you want to hitch home, or do you want to do what it takes? What we are talking about here is maybe pushing yourselves out of the shell you have found yourself in after months of shows and pushing yourself to shake some hands and give prospective fans the chance to hang with some now-seasoned road musicians. As long as nobody throws up on anybody's couch, all will be a fair trade. You decided to do the Island, so this is what it takes.

We, of course, were lucky, and Larry was there for us. His large apartment, which put up half the band, was a godsend, but that aside, it was good to see Larry again. At the time, we needed a couch and some floor, but months into the tour, the chance to talk shit with an old friend was far more important. Touching base with a non-stranger felt good.

Hot Panda arrived to the bar just after us and installed their gear backstage. Sound check went well, thank Christ! We really were feeling like a bunch of punters from the show we put on when last we met these guys, and sound check alone went a long way towards making us feel like we belonged onstage. At this point in the tour, folks are pretty worn out, and a bad show can really put a zap on a band, especially if you have a bad show in front of another band, even if in fact the bad show was not your fault. A proper sound check did go along way towards making us ready for the night's gig.

We were in the opener slot at Logan's that night. It was our second time out in Victoria and our second kick at the can on this stage. Our set went well in front of about 100 people. We tore through a one-hour set, and not wanting to overplay our set time, and always worried we were going to make the closer wait needlessly to get on with their night, we finished our set and immediately started packing up. The crowd would hear nothing of it and banged, yelled, and jeered for five minutes until we did an encore after checking with the guys from Hot Panda, 'cause in most cases, doing an encore as an opener is kind of a dick move. Panda seemed to be cool with it, so we took to the stage and did a quick two-song closer. The folks loved us, and like a bunch of scared high school students, we were back on top of our game having resurrected our self-esteem. Thanks, Vic, for cheering us on and making the $300 we split that night with our stage mates go down a little easier. The folks loved us, and although we were now broke, we had a couple of days off after a good show. Having a couple of days off after a bad show can be scary, everybody having too much time to feel bad and question why they are out here. People start thinking about quitting, and giving up. Vic spared us that, and we were to head east for the first time in months feeling redeemed, as well as heading in a homeward direction.

The holy grail of food awaited us after the show that night. Here we were as far west as we get on the grand Canadian tour. The entire trip, the convenience store experience gradually got better with each and every late night, and now, here on Vancouver Island, we found the late-night nirvana of unlimited melted cheese. It's the age-old story: who hasn't been there? Heading back to Larry's, it's late, and there don't seem to be any real restaurants open, and the local guy suggests the 7-Eleven. Larry is not the junk food type, and I think he really just wanted to get home, so he directed us to the store in a "let's get moving" sort of way. It's three a.m., and we are buzzing from a triumphant show, half-drunk, and then here comes the worst of all guilty pleasure. On the East Coast, you have Irving's double cheeseburger in the convenient, double plastic, microwavable bag that goes pop! In Quebec, there is Ashton's or the like, Toronto has street meat, and after that, you find yourself succumbing to the 7-Eleven dog. Here in Victoria, standing at the mustard-smeared hot treat counter of 7-Eleven, I was left with the drunken, soon-to-be-guilty decision of just how much hot, unlimited, melted cheese to put on my Fatboy bacon dog. Yep, just press a button and all the steaming, plastic, synthetic, non-dairy cheese spread you can stomach is yours, at no extra charge. The dream is realized, the promise fulfilled: a big, greasy dog with bacon inside, covered in yellow, salty slime. I put way too much on, this being my first foray into unlimited cheese. I'm sure the locals have made their peace with it and use it as a topping and not a dip. There is no greater prize in the three a.m., "I'm going to regret this later" food treasure hunt than the three a.m.Fatboybacondogwithextracheese! Dig in!

The next day, you feel bad; I mean, your soul hurts as you look in the mirror, cheese sauce still slightly crusted to the corners of your mouth. Your stomach aches, and you have diarrhea. But still, this is the cornerstone of a complete night of debauchery and late-night glory food.

Sorry, Victoria, I'm sure you have great restaurants. I'm

sure the height of haute cuisine can be attained in your city, but, yes, I talked about unlimited fake cheese. Sorry about calling you a bunch of Limeys too. Hey, look over there! That is a beautiful garden! We are out of here....

The Ferry (return)

I remember the ferry casting its lines and plodding east out of the harbour on a beautiful sunny day. You have installed yourself outside on one of the upper decks. You have had a couple of pretty decent spring days so far, being as you are on the West Coast and the weather will run to moderately warm. But here on the top deck of a boat as it weaves between islands, it's somewhere around April 2nd. If in fact you have followed this book to the letter and left on February 3rd or 4th, today is the first day of spring. Well, I know the first day of spring is March 20th, and there is no real way for me to predict that April 2nd is going to be the first really awesome sunny day of the year for you. In fact, with the glaciers rolling back, that could well take place on February 2nd soon. With that in mind, in my head I remember the first beautiful day of the year happening as we heaved-ho out of Victoria, and as I sat on the top deck of that boat, it was nice, real nice. It wasn't just warm, it was that first day with the jacket off. Not big-time hot, but that first day. The day the girls all wear short skirts and no leggings, bare shoulders. If you were in Montreal, the terraces would be full and the streets thronged with beautiful people flirting. Yes, in my mind, that was that day, as we headed east on our way home, sun shining, gorgeous scenery passing us by.

Herein lies yet another reason for leaving on your trip in

February. For us, that beautiful day, the first beautiful day as we headed west repeated itself seven times on our way home. Yes, on April 2nd it was the first warm day somewhere on the Georgia Strait, yet back east it was still snowing on the Prairies, and certainly back in Ontario and Quebec. But it takes a good chunk of time to cover that distance, especially because you have shows to play all the way home. And that one year, we nailed it. We got the first nice day in Victoria, and then the first nice day in Calgary, then again in Lethbridge, Thunder Bay, and I remember pulling into Toronto, which had been getting kicked by reasonably heavy snow only the week before, and, yes, there we were in Toronto, thirteen days after Victoria's first nice day, and Toronto was beautiful and alive.

I cannot even come close to guaranteeing that this is going to happen to you, but I know if you debark for your tour on November 2nd, you will probably not have this miracle happen to you. February 2nd is the Magic Date.

Killing time

So here you are, heading homeward. It's Sunday or Monday, and your next show is not until Thursday probably. Now maybe one of your bandmates got lucky, maybe not. Holed up in a basement or in the back of the van, you guys are mostly broke. Not real broke: you had shows, a slew of them, but all of that is going towards paying down the fool who fronted this tour by offering up his $10,000-limit Visa card. If you did, in fact, play all these shows and diligently sold merch at every show, you are, in fact, getting close to breaking even on the tour. We always found if we were going to break even, it usually happened somewhere around Lethbridge. By there, we had usually covered all the expenses of gas, accoms, and per diems, thus leaving us with all of the return trip through Ontario to actually go home with some money. As for the issue of how to make money on the road, I will speak to that soon. For now, here, just after the turnaround show, you are still broke but probably not that bad… as long as somebody has been counting the beans.

Once again, you are in the back of the van or in a basement, so you are stealing somebody's Internet. Well, let's get to work. I've mentioned finding buddies, and I've mentioned *Priceline.com* so far, so let's put that stuff together and find some cheap places to stay for the next couple of days. Now, before hitting the road, it should be said that it is very important to look ahead when touring. Alliances are key here. Swallow your pride, and before you leave on your trip, start emailing friends who you haven't seen in years, folks who you went to high school with who, it is rumoured, moved out this way after school. Or think a bit as far as relatives go: is there an aunt or a cousin who has a place somewhere up in the B.C. mountains? As well, perhaps at home you have put up travelling bands whose towns you might be passing through. Do a trade. Getting a good hook-up with a three-day stay almost anywhere, especially if it has its own kitchen, is what you are looking for.

Having explored all of these ideas and having come up short, it is time to hit the hotel sites. Now, it could be said that cities like Montreal, Calgary, or Kingston, Ontario, are a real ball-ache when it comes to cheap accoms. It is almost impossible to find cheap places to stay in these towns, and as you have already found out, a lot of the time smaller towns can be almost as bad. Remember Brandon? But it will probably surprise you that upon giving the bidding sites like, say, *Priceline.com* a go on some afternoon when you have Internet and know generally which direction you are going in, you can get some remarkable deals. Bid low, say, $45, maybe up to $60 for major centres. You might get lucky. Now you have a couple of days to kill, so in this case, try some low bids in Vancouver, and if that doesn't work, just start bidding on rooms in towns that you could make east of Vancouver. If it is still early spring, it is not tourist season yet, so maybe you will find some deals up in the hills, where the tourist hotels are begging for deals. Keep an eye on the map so as to make sure you are going to be able to make it there. I know we have found some pretty great deals in towns like Toronto, Winnipeg, and, yes, even Vancouver. Once we also lucked out in Jasper and got a condo that slept seven people and it cost less than a $100 and we had a fireplace. Wow! That was a nice night off.

As I have weaved you across Canada, I did try to land you in towns where it is possible to kill your days off. I must admit that I did leave you in Montreal for a couple of days, and so I must point out that Montreal is a bad town for the hotels. That is a town that you are going to have to find someone to put you up, but fortunately Montreal has a very healthy population of musicians who have arrived from elsewhere in Canada, so if you are not from there, there is a good chance you know someone who lives there. Make sure you research that out before you leave.

Back to the mountains

Weaving back out of Vancouver on Highway 1, you bid *adieu* to the flat land. Your vocalists should mostly have their voices back, and the rest of the band has truly been enjoying feeling like superheroes for the last week or so. The farmland rolling by between Chilliwack and Hope behind you, you once again start your climb back up into the mountains on Highway 3, the Crowsnest Pass. You watch the altimeter climb as you take in some stunning mountains and pass the day happy as you push from mountains to high plateau country, wilderness giving way to farmlands, vineyards, and then ranch country. I found this transition to be surprising and a good reason for taking this route, rather than the Trans-Canada with its mountainous up and downs, traffic, and severe accidents. The 3 does unfold as you reach the top of each hill to have a particular, diverse beauty that I was not aware was contained in Canada.

The trip from Vancouver to Coleman, Alberta, checks in at a thirteen-and-a-half hour drive, so I would say unless you had some cushy accoms back in Van, I would cut the trip in half and find some cheap accoms around Osoyoos. In the off-season, this tourist town is mostly empty and has a slew of motels. It will take about a half hour to figure out which one has the cheapest rooms. Don't go by the posted signs. Bands with more than three people may find that these motels might have different-sized rooms that may accommodate larger numbers. It must also be said that the mom and pop places, as family owned, are not going to sell out that night, so some dickering may be possible.

This brings on today's travel tip: dickering. Dickering, or

haggling, over prices is very difficult for most people, but there is that segment of the population that is good at it. Those are the folks who don't mind looking you in the eye and saying, "No, come on, how much do you really want for that room?" The person who can be convincing that they are going to leave and try it somewhere else unless their price is met. Now most of these cost-conscious people are nice folks to the general public, but if you are in the service industry, you will know them as *The Dick*. That is why they call it *dick*-ering. So, today's tip is: if you have what a bartender would refer to as a *dick* in your band, that is the guy who should now be promoted to "Accommodation Captain." He is most likely going to save you a ton of money on accoms. Here is the second part of that tip, though, the cautionary tip….

If you have identified the dick in the band, that person willing to go the extra mile to save some dough, well, that doesn't necessarily mean he should be in charge of all the band's business. He should not be in charge of getting paid by venues. That job should go to the more politically minded in the band, *The Mom*, the one who stops fights and smoothes things out. Getting paid is a political matter; getting paid and leaving a venue with a good relationship is paramount to continuing your career. So, when getting paid. it is good to be firm with bar owners, and don't get walked on or ripped off by any means. But I always found that diplomacy works when someone in the music industry does not meet their financial obligations. For example, you have an email that says they are going to pay you $500 for two sets of music, and that night the bar only wants to pay $250 'cause the night went bad. It's worth having that talk, but in reality, I have found taking the

$250, not having a big fight, and not burning that bridge, usually works out in the long run. Burned twice is another story, but at this point, the right idea would be to say, "Thank you. We had a great time," and then never deal with that venue or that band again. Don't talk bad about them outside of the band, and don't send nasty emails. Just write them off, don't book with them again, and don't send other people to them. Just go on your way. It is two strikes and a quiet, "You're out."

So back to Osoyoos, the "*dick*ering" having scored you guys a reasonably priced room, you bed down early and get some sleep, the clean, thin mountain air lulling you to bed.

Up reasonably early and back on the road passing Castlegar, you are now in virgin territory. Laying out this route, I have tried to minimize the backtracking, but in reality, Canada is a big old rectangle, a long thin strip of population located close to the American border. You will do some backtracking, but I have tried, for the sake of morale, to keep covering the same highways to a minimum. Virgin country will get folks in the van to be more alert, talkative, even excited. Covering the same ground that you have already covered will in fact breed heavy drinking on tour.

For instance, when sitting in a motel in Portage la Prairie, Manitoba, one night after a long day's deadhead drive east, one could easily decide that getting blotto tonight is a good idea. I will have fun and then be zonked out for the entire ride to Thunder Bay tomorrow. On a personal level, this can be a good decision to make because, man, that drive sucks, and I'm going to sleep through it. From a band morale point of view, it can be said that too many of these days of everybody in the van silently nursing hangovers can be brutal on the longevity of the band. Try whenever possible in the planning stage to avoid a large amount of backtracking, and life in the long run will go better.

Back to the road at hand. Having passed Castlegar, you are looking at a couple of days of stuff you haven't seen before. After passing through some memorably idyllic beauty, and the rough-around-the-edges towns of Creston, Cranbrook, and Fernie, you will pass over into Alberta again. Don't forget to honk and adjust your clock. Oops, it just dawned on you that you just lost an hour, and it is now an hour later in the day. I mentioned this earlier in the book; touring east is a bitch. For the most part, I have designed this tour to minimize this problem of the always-advancing clock by giving you fewer shows to play on the way east than you did on the way west, while covering time zones as well as utilizing the dead days of Sunday, Monday, and Tuesday to cover vast distances as you drive against the clock. This will mean a few long dead-head travel days but less stress about making it to shows.

For the bands who live in the west, it must be pointed out that playing the slew of shows should be done on the way home. Simply reversing the bookings while heading east is not a good idea. Most of the gigs I plotted on the way out are tight travel distances on the way out and losing hours instead of gaining them could quite often mean getting even less sleep and maybe even missing gigs altogether, especially if travelling in winter. I have heard western bands complain about how tough it is to make the Calgary-to-Saskatoon drive during a snowstorm. It's a real roll of the dice in a snowstorm, and even if you make it, you are worn out and will probably play badly.

Keep a real eye on the backward clock while booking from west to east.

Plunging headlong back into Alberta, the first thing of note is the Crowsnest Pass. You have been on the highway for two days now, and finally you make it to the pass. The pass refers to its being a low spot in elevation, which is a small break for the original engineers to save some time and money while building railways, pipelines, and, eventually roadways. Not just a break, but actually making them possible. You will remember the Kicking Horse Pass? I guess *pass* referring to this is the only place in hell you are going to be able to build something. This pass uses the Crowsnest Valley to make its way across the Continental Divide.

Here you are back up in high country again, but this time things will be easier. You should not have acclimatized completely having been back down at sea level for the last two weeks, and the repair time your body enjoyed will go a long way towards making this part of the trip more than bearable. As well, you will be playing tonight in high altitude, but it is only one show, and then, after that, pretty much every show after this will be at lower altitudes on a decreasing basis for the rest of your trip. After tonight, you are home free and rolling downhill.

Rounding a corner on Highway 3, you arrive at Frank Slide, previously know as the town of Frank. Previously, because back in April of 1903, Turtle Mountain fell over on the town of Frank and crushed about a third of it, killing close to 100 people. If you react fast after seeing the sign, you will be able to make the turn that takes you to the interpretive centre. If you have time, do it, the view is wild. Winding up the hill to the interpretive centre, you park and have a pretty good view of the century-old scene of carnage. It looks like a big old field with a whole lot of rocks scattered all over it, but after a little while, it sinks in that about half of Turtle Mountain just sheared off and fell right where you see it now. The remains of the town and the people who perished remain buried underneath the boulders. Fearing a repeat of the incident, they moved the whole town down the road a little, and all has been fine since. The only part of the area that was cleaned up was, of course, the right of way for the railway, which took them three weeks to reopen and cuts a strangely unnatural path through the scene. This place is a must-stop. It's kind of gruesome but a natural marvel just the same.

Coleman, Alberta

Coleman is an ex-coal-mining town of just over 1,000 people. There is about a block of town that will give you the idea that this is the Old West, but for the most part, this village tucked into the bottom corner of Alberta looks like a suburban town sitting on the upper part of a mountain valley. Lacking in tree-lined streets or stately homes, the core of the town sprawls out with some strip mall development here and there. The outer edges of the town sport ruins of a bygone era, and the downtown is unimpressive and dusty. The vistas are nice, taking in the mountains that surround it, and the high altitude will give you a bit of a sluggish feel as you climb out of the van and plod your way through load in to the Blackbird Coffee House.

The Blackbird is an oasis built from an old church. Man, I love churches. Well, I love churches once folks have found an appropriate use for them, and in this case, the folks who run the Blackbird have. Open only on weekends and when they have a good reason, this homey bistro/café does a pretty good job of bringing music to this region. It is a fair-sized space that could hold 150 folks if it had too. The night we played there, I think we pulled in around fifty, and the place looked full with its hodgepodge of mismatched furniture including a lovely wood-burning stove. The Blackbird fits that middle-of-nowhere venue ideal. The town of Coleman is small, probably not big enough to support a venue, but fortunately Coleman is quite a way from anywhere else, so they pull folks in from as far away as 100 kilometres. There isn't a lot of competition for things to do out this way. Add to it that the venue is cozy and intimate, so the folks who show up don't mind paying a little more at the door 'cause they are going to get to see you in a real nice place and share smokes with you on the front porch post-show. For the band, it's a great place to play. This room is a great version of good room/bad PA. The room sounds great, but their tiny four-channel Peavey PA really is a piece of junk. Fortunately, the room more than compensates for the lesser quality equipment. Once you manage to get the vocals bussed into the board, and get the squeaks and squawks worked out, you will find that the room sucks up a lot of the bad sound coming out of the speakers and a warmth takes over. Good-sounding rooms can make bad PAs work fine, and this is the case here. Sound check limped through on sore fingers. Having taken a few days off, there are more than a few cobwebs that have crept over the joints, fingertips, and vocal cords, but the fireplace is nice, and I believe there was some decent food involved in the deal, so the aches and pains of the road were left to be worked out in the first set.

I remember the most notable part of the evening was the fact that the show was all-ages. It didn't really sink in at first, and it wasn't until we got a few songs into the set that it was pointed out to me that there were ten or so kids ringing the choir loft that was behind and above the stage. It was just at the point in a regular song set-up that I would start saying things about death and sex, and Filly, knowing what was about to come out of my mouth, pointed to the angelic group that was wide-eyed and wide-eared, waiting for me to complete my thought. Being the professional that I am, I think I completed the now-irrelevant song set-up by mentioning that puppies were, ah…good. This sent the show into an impromptu child-friendly vein. After several rough and bawdy West Coast performances, with each show getting a little more coarse and slightly more filthy-mouthed, the return to family friendly was difficult, but once the gears were switched, it all went fine.

The other great thing about playing the hottest gig for miles around is merch sales. Yep, these small, not-much-going-on venues are always great for merch. The folks, not having a lot of other places to acquire music, dug deep that night, and we made almost as much money selling CDs as we did on door.

We spent the time post-show drinking beer by the fireside and talking with the locals and some German tourists. I remember thinking that if I could possibly change myself into the kind of person who could live outside the confines of a big city, that I would very much want to own a place like the Blackbird. There are a heck of a lot of defunct churches out there across our fair land. Here is the tip: before putting $38,000 down on some broken-down church in the middle of nowhere and opening a café/indie venue, please take a look at the map. These places are what the Canadian music scene is going to be made of in the years to come. But before buying one, make sure you are on the way from someplace to some other place. Coleman works because it is on a fairly direct route from Vancouver to Calgary. The big downside to this venue is that they have not quite committed to doing week-night shows. If you put work into getting your patrons to come out on a Wednesday night, they are going to get a bigger show for their money. Big-money bands make their big money on the weekends just like everyone else. They do okay on the Sunday through Wednesday but are definitely willing to deal on a lesser night, and if you add this to the fact that you are on the way to their next well-paying gig, and your club is cool, you can actually attract bands that you may have thought out of your reach. There are a few clubs around that play this strategy, notably the Neat Coffee House, the Black Sheep Inn, or say the Boathouse: they book the harder-to-get shows earlier in the week and in some cases the more local shows toward the weekend. It's a good mix that gets the local listening public a far greater bang for their buck and a lot more access to big name talent.

Head-Smashed-In Buffalo Jump, Alberta

This part of the world is the lower corner of Alberta. It's high and flat country. There are windmills; there are straight roads and the occasional beef jerky shop; and there is Head-Smashed-In Buffalo Jump, a mountaintop cliff known for running animals to their death. It's a weird part of the world but not altogether unenjoyable. Jerky hanging from your mouth, the salty goodness spreading through your taste buds, on a sunny, cold day, you can really cover some miles as you speed towards Calgary.

Calgary, Alberta

Entering Calgary, there are two things that strike you: one is that those hills that ring the town are in fact suburbs and not second-growth tree plantations. I'm not kidding! My first time through town, it was a couple of days into it before I really noticed that the neatly plotted patterns up on the hills with the backdrop of mountains were, in fact, very neatly laid, out housing. After realizing that, I started to feel hemmed in by this city. Perhaps it's the way the terrain unfolds to the north, east, and south surrounding Calgary, or the way it splays out with the Rockies off in the distance to the west, but it can give you a claustrophobic feel, sort of a back-up-against-a-wall or box-canyon sensation.

The other difficulty with Calgary for the outsider is its street address system. This probably came up while you where booking the tour, but after sweating through entering the club's address into your itinerary, you then forgot about it. Now, driving along in your van trying to successfully enter said address into your GPS device, you are completely lost as to what that address means.

Here is an example: 1410 4 St SW. Yes, to the outsider, the address system of Calgary can seem like binary code. I'll break it down for you: 1410 is the street number, 4 St means it's 4th Street (not to be confused with the Avenues, which run perpendicular to the Streets), and then there is SW, which means you are in the southwest section of Calgary.

If in fact you are in your van and did correctly enter 1410 4 St SW, you will end up in front of what used to be A Bar Named Sue. That bar, sadly now defunct, handed us to Calgary one fine night in February. It started months before, when Filly was calling around to bars in Western Canada trying to fill holes in our upcoming tour. Some folks online had suggested, Bar Named Sue. It was a small place, and most folks agreed that it would be a good fit for us on our first time through town. So Filly called up and asked to speak to the manager. Now, keep in mind this was before most of the bars started booking almost completely by way of email, the two-thousands being that grueling transition time between pre-modern and modern indie tour booking. It was that changeover time when not everybody was online and you still had to call places and try and talk to the manager, who got a lot of these calls, so he really didn't want to talk to you. I don't miss those times at all. So here is Filly trying to put the sale on this bar manager who was mostly just kind of humouring her at this point when Filly notices that in the background she can hear our band's first CD playing on the bar's PA system. Being a quick and resourceful girl, she realizes that so far the conversation has not allowed her to mention what band she is trying to book. She then quickly throws in that she is with the United Steel Workers of Montreal. Don't get me wrong—even at the high point of our career, throwing our name around didn't usually mean that anybody would actually know who we were, but she was pretty sure that was our music playing in the background. This probably marked the first time dropping our name actually worked. The manager sort of jaw, drops and mentions that he and the assistant manager were just at that moment drawing straws to see who had to work while the other drove up to Edmonton to see the United Steel Workers play next month at the Black Dog. Within a minute, Felicity worked out the details with the club, and we had a Monday night filled for Calgary. Nice.

A couple months later, with this story in our heads, we entered A Bar Named Sue. It was a small place with barnboard paneled walls, a stand up bar, some thrown-together furniture, and a working model train that wound its way around the bar on a track suspended ten feet above the floor. The first thing that hit me was the food menu. Stapled to the wall under a sign that said *FOOD* was the front cover of a Swanson's Hungry-Man dinner. $6.95. Yep, just behind the bar was a fridge, and on top of the fridge was a microwave, and for $6.95, they would toss a frozen dinner in the microwave and you had a piping-hot Hungry-Man chicken dinner at low, low bar costs. I asked if they sold many of those, and the bartender replied, "You'd be surprised." The way he said it led me to believe that, in fact, yes, they did sell quite a few. Wow, what a great way to offer food at very little inconvenience to the bar. A quick peruse of the menu led me to find that they also sold pot pies. This being late in the day, and me being in my very first throes of altitude sickness, I unfortunately had neither, but I look forward to the day when all bars serve such delights.

The band installed on stage and sound check finished, we played that night to a pretty damn fine crowd. Keep in mind this was our first trip out this way, and the small bar was packed out, maybe sixty-five folks. Not bad for a Monday night. The bar had given us a small guarantee, like, say, $200. We figured, it was a Monday, so what the hell? The shock was when we finished our first set and ten people came right up to the stage and said, "What do you have for merch?" We said, "These two CDs, these two stickers, and T-shirts." I think all ten of those first people, and then the majority of the folks for the rest of the night all said, "Yep, we'll take it." We said, "Take which one?" They repeated, "We'll take it….all." A few of the songs in the raucous second set were videoed and hosted on YouTube, and to this day, they are still some of our most-viewed videos. By the end of the night, we had sold $800 in merch. This, at a financial low point of the trip really got us over the hump. It also instilled in us a problem that plagued us throughout the rest of our touring career: our biggest and best-paid shows in Canada were 3,500 kilometres west of our home base in Montreal.

Calgary, from the first show to the last, was always out front for us. We had some good shows there, with great crowds and some great times. This is Calgary: it's big, cold, and a long way from home. It also holds the record for the town I've almost got my ass kicked in, something like eight times. It always seems that, winter or summer, semi-famous, or unknown, every time I stepped out for a smoke after nine p.m., I had some dude in a dress shirt, white cowboy hat, and black boots get all up in my face just because I was standing there on a sidewalk. People in my face is tough for me 'cause I have a big mouth, and even though I have never been one to actually ever punch anyone, ever, I will tell you to f. off at the drop of a hat. Bad strategy in this town. Fortunately, every single time, the dude had a buddy who pulled him away before he had the chance to actually dismember me like so much Wing Night BBQ. Today's travel tip: always watch out for the dudes.

As for the town itself, Calgary has a slew of venues, festivals, and occasions to perform at. Clubs like the Palomino Smokehouse, Broken City, and more recently the Ironwood Stage & Grill make this town a backbone for your Western Canada tour. The folks here come out to shows, and while there, they buy merch, so bring merch, lots of merch.

On the food horizon there is a must-mention here in town, a not-to-be-missed Calgary exclusive known as the Tubby Dog. Located at 1022 17 Ave SW, this hot dog stand and cultural legend is the place to fulfill your hot dog dreams. I always found their fries to be burned, but this was easily overlooked due to their big old dogs with crazy toppings ranging from your standards like bacon and cheese to out there with things like Cap'n Crunch and fried eggs. You have to eat there. The memory of the event will haunt your travels as you try to figure out why every town in Canada doesn't have a Tubby Dog. It's full-on junk food done right, so give it a go.

Fort Macleod, Alberta

Located near the confluence of Highways 2 and 3 is the town of Fort Macleod, named after the actual fort. The fort, built in 1874, was named after Northwest Mounted Police Colonel James Macleod. This rough-around-the-edges western town with its wide, windblown streets will definitely evoke the Wild West. Driving down the main drag, which takes about a minute and a half to tour, you will feel as though you have been transported back in time. It would not seem the least bit out of place to see a gun fight or a cattle drive taking place. In reality, the Fort Macleod of today has an abundance of pickup trucks. This rundown town has not really seen a heyday since the CPR pulled out and moved to Lethbridge 100 years ago. The only reason this town has survived is because the Alberta Culture Committee thought it had some nice architecture, which it does due to the fact that the town burned down in 1906 and they rebuilt it with sandstone. Unfortunately, the buildings outlasted any boom and they still sit quietly awaiting something businesslike to happen in Old Fort Macleod.

The stately Queen's Hotel stands watch on the corner of 24th and Haultain Ave, the nightlife capital of this small town. From the back door of the Queen's, an establishment that doubles as a liquor store, I believe on an average Wednesday night you can see the whole world go by. From young kids huffing and trying to buy beer, to drug deals, to local drunks getting kicked out and arguing whether they have been barred from both hotel and liquor store or just the bar. In the background are cars spinning tires and near drag-race police chases and fisticuffs a-brewing. It's the closest to the Wild West you are likely to witness north of Montana. The highway runs you through most of the town, but please, while passing through, jump off the highway and take a quick tour of Fort Macleod. It's a neat place.

As a band, we got real lucky and had the chance to stay there for a couple of days. A while back, we were booked into the South Country Fair, which was one of our first western festivals. It's a great festival, which got us three nights of accoms at one of the town's finest local motels, the Heritage. Yes, it's rundown and old but a comfortable and a friendly stay to be sure. The added bonus for us was rooming beside a local man—I don't remember his name, so we will call him Willy. Now, Willy's story was that he had driven in there a year back in his early-seventies Cadillac. The Cadillac, I believe, is still there according to Google Street View. The cream, coloured beauty with the over-burdened rear suspension up and died on Willy in the parking lot, and the owners of the Heritage Inn took pity on him, and he had been living there for several months when we met him. Willy was a storyteller, and perhaps the de facto mayor of Fort Macleod. Wanted or unwanted, Willy's stories filled the air, and he would even follow you into your motel room and continue his dissertation on the history of the town and his family's place in the surrounding folklore. As mentioned, I don't think he ever got the old Caddy running again, and judging from the Google map, he may still be there. Who knows? He was a pretty old dude then, so maybe the Caddy is now some sort of shrine to an old man that just ended up there.

Having spent three or four days in town, I got a chance to take a walk around a few times and found one of the most surprising food places of all time. Johnny's Restaurant is located at 225 24th Street, just down from the Queen's Hotel and beside Tru Hardware. The sign in the window says *Johnny's Restaurant Certified Chef Western and Chinese Cuisine.* Well, ding ding ding, and I'm there. Entering into the sunny little diner and sitting at a table, I peruse the menu. Lo and behold, although it is Chicken Ball fever that brought me here, my eyes catch sight of the Reuben Special. It being late morning, and I was kind of looking for something in a breakfast mode. Yes, Reubens are breakfast food in my book. Any-

thing that can be eaten between three a.m. and noon is breakfast to me.

So there I am, wondering if a Reuben sandwich could be
any good way out here, seemingly light years away from any
Jews, and then my knowledge of the symbiotic relationship
between Chinese people and Jewish culture fills my head, and
there is the waitress asking me what I want. I stammer....
"Ah...give me the Reuben." I swill a decent cup of coffee as I
await my sandwich. The entire time, I see Chinese food coming out the kitchen door and going to the other patrons. It
looks good. Have I made a mistake? And then it arrives. It's
small, not the Broadway Deli half-a-cow on a cracker sort of
affair New York's Upper West Side has to offer, but a good
looking sandwich nonetheless. I chow down, and bam! Man,
that was the second-best Reuben sandwich I ever had. Who
knew? The brisket, if not actually pastrami, was great; the
kraut, the rye bread, and, yes, the dressing. Man, that was
good. If you stay another day or two, give the noodles a go
and let me know if the Chinese menu holds up.

Lethbridge, Alberta

The drive between Fort Macleod and Lethbridge takes
about a half hour, and the scenery is comprised of rolling hills,
desolate ranches, and big skies. It's cow country, and the road
is mostly straight and uneventful. Short drives on the cross-
Canada tour don't come that often, so savour this one, and
maybe even set the cruise to five kilometres below the speed
limit, just for fun.

Rolling into Lethbridge from the west, you will at first be
wowed by the Lethbridge Viaduct, a 894m train trestle. The

trestle spans the valley, which was cut through this part of the terrain by the Old Man River. The unique valleys out here are called *coulees*. The land is mostly flat—even the rolling hills are kind of flattish—and then you come to a coulee, and the earth just sort of drops off. A river or spillway or drainage ditch just sort of cuts right through this otherwise uninterrupted land without warning. They are dramatic.

Now the Lethbridge Viaduct cuts way across one of these, and if you get the chance to pull off the highway and make your way over to the foot of the bridge, then do so. In the Prairie country, you never really have to wait long for a train, and anyone who is into trains is going to want to see a train go over this baby. I know you're thinking, ya, sure, watch a train go over a bridge, but, yes, even if you are not a man (being a man really does predispose you to being enamoured with trains), you will see this bridge, and you will want to see a train go over it. It's the longest train bridge in North America. Seeing something that long and that heavy come barreling across the open land blowing its horn and then just sail right across a valley completely uninterrupted. The big old train looks as though it is running a tightrope. The feeling that immediately hits you is the thought of the engineer being on the front end of all that as it sails off the cliff, with only a thin and seemingly insignificant strand of steel playing out to the other side. It will give you the goosebumps.

Having now witnessed the engineering feat of the day and the second-coolest train encounter of your life, you turn your attention to the fact that you are now in Lethbridge, Alberta. This less-than-bustling town, originally called Fort Whoop-Up, will shock you because night or day, winter or summer, it will seem to be almost desolate and empty. Maybe it's the western feel, with wide streets and low buildings or its far-flung suburbs, but to me, this town always seemed spookily empty.

Putting that on the back burner, your second stop upon entering town is the Mr. Lube on 3rd Ave. It is now time to come to terms with the fact that you have put about 11,000 kilometres on your van over the last two months, leaving you 6,000 kilometres overdue for an oil change. What do they say? Pay now or pay later? Well, Lethbridge is as good as any place to pay now. With the help of our GPS, we located a Mr. Lube on 3rd Ave and found the family-owned and-run establishment to be super nice, efficient, and thorough. They did the oil, our rear end, cleaned the windows, and lubed our door locks, as well as serving the driver a cup of coffee. Door locks are going to be a problem if you are touring heavy because all that winter salt and summer dust knocks the shit out of your keyholes. It is a real good idea to get yourself some lube and routinely use it every week that you are on the road to prevent getting locked out of your van just before load in, which has happened to us.

We found WD-40 really let us down, and on Flipper's advice, we went with Jiggy Lube. That shit rocks. The price of our Lethbridge oil change was completely reasonable, coming in under a hundred bucks, and keep in mind that that included changing our differential oil too. That actually was a must because we had dried out our rear end a ways back on a summer tour when we hadn't noticed a very small rear-end seal leak. It fried the "dif," burning across the hot Prairies, but to the credit of Ford Motor Company, we put another 40,000 kilometres on that E350's rear end before having it replaced.

It got loud, but we made it through and just kept changing the diff oil. I think without the rear-end trouble, the bill would have been $50 or so: a good investment.

Oiled up, we wound our way into the downtown core in search of the Slice. We have played a few other places here, but it really wasn't until we found the Slice that we started to have good shows in Lethbridge. The Slice is a funky pizza restaurant that doubles as a venue. The cool part about playing a pizza bar is that when it comes to dinnertime, you get to eat pizza, and this place has great pizza. Whether you are getting free pizza, or a deal on pizza or having to pay full price, not having to run around after sound check to find a slice of pizza is going to make your life better. Besides, if you play your food card right, and you are not a big pre-show eater (I never was), have a couple of slices and stow the rest backstage for after the show.

Loading in, we set up for sound check. Jesse, the owner, is a little curt...one of those guys that you will meet at four in the afternoon and get a tiny feeling he isn't real into you, but by closing time, you will be thinking of putting him on your Christmas card list. He is a good example of Lethbridge itself. Upon entering, you will be certain that no way this dead-ass town is going to lead you to having a good show, but then the folks arrive and mill about, there are sort of fleeting moments of enthusiasm mixed with reluctance, and by halfway through your set, they are awesome. By closing time, you are very drunk from all the free shots and have a handful of email addresses for your now new-found friends. But for now, there is sound check.

Sound check this far into the tour can be a ball-ache, as

well as a complete necessity. By now, everybody in the band thinks they are a soundman, they think they know more than the guy running the board in his own room, and they are just not going to take suggestions from another soundman on this trip. With good reason, mind you, because by now you've probably had a lot of bad sound. Clubs in general are a real hodgepodge of sound, and you have now witnessed it all. That said, please try and keep your shit together through the back half of the tour, because getting pissy isn't going to help. The Slice has a pretty good system if you manage to ignore a weird roll-back that comes back at you from a beam in the middle of the room. It's there, it is probably going to stay there, so don't go beating up the soundman about it and looking like an ass. Just ignore it and all will go fine.

We tear off after sound check and head for the motel at the other end of town and check in, have showers, and then make our way back for pizza. The show goes as expected: there is the wringing of the hands as to whether folks are going to show, but they do, and generally in greater numbers the more you play here. By second set, the room is full, and folks are dancing and carrying on and having a great old time. You finish up to a resounding encore, and with the exception of the designated driver, you all get drunk. There are lots of locals clapping you on the back, there are a lot of CDs purchased, and shots of whiskey. Returning back to the slightly smelly and stained-furniture non-chain motel you are staying in, you bunk out for the night in preparation for the long journey home.

The Long Drive

Back in the van come morning, you have packed up your gear for the ride home. The ride home can be done one of two ways: you could ignore the entirety of Northern Ontario, The Sault, and Sudbury, and just head for Southern Ontario, which means you could do the run home stateside. Keep in mind that everybody in the van would have to have a valid passport, and the van would also be held up for a search at the border, so all illicit materials would have to be cleaned out. Don't forget that any band hangers-on may have rolled a joint in your back seat and left a baggy stuck down behind a seat cushion, or somebody might actually be carrying their Communist Party of Canada ID card in their wallet. These are things to consider before committing to the long U.S. road.

The long U.S. road does offer some upsides, though, once the border is crossed. Gas will be 35 percent cheaper, hotels are easily 60 percent cheaper, the scenery of the northern states is definitely worth a look, and then there is the fine American cuisine offered by the U.S. truck stops. With all that in mind, jumping into Montana with its 75 mph speed limits awaits you just a half-hour south of Lethbridge. We have taken that trip, and although we didn't in fact save any time driving across the U.S., it was worth the effort. This all leads to the tip of the day.

When deciding to run home by way of the U.S., don't play shows. This might seem enticing because finally getting some access to the U.S. markets can seem worth going for. Well, it might be, but doing it illegally really doesn't seem to be the way to go. Gone are the years when you could sneak across the border and get a couple of gigs in. It was a couple of years ago that the U.S. border guards figured out Facebook and the like. If you play on the U.S. side and anybody talks about it, there is a better-than-average chance that the U.S. customs service will be able to find out about it. My take was always: never play a show unless folks know you are doing it, and so playing a stateside show and not telling anybody about it would be without purpose. There have been some pretty high-profile examples of bands that found this out the hard way, which basically ended their push for the brass ring in the U.S. by being barred entry for a minimum of five years. My advice for U.S. shows is: do them legal or don't do them. You have to consider the costs of visas and legal expenses, and any band members' personal brushes with law enforcement over the previous years.

All that said, let's get back to the Canadian experience. As I said earlier, your run east will be against the clock with the time zones working unfavourably to your sched. That is why you should finish up your Lethbridge show on a Saturday night, get a good night's sleep, and head full-tilt for Sault Ste. Marie on Sunday morning. You should be able to make it to the Sault by Wednesday night and kick off your last three weeks of the tour through Ontario.

Rouleau, Saskatchewan

For your first day of the long drive, you are going to want to put in about twelve or so hours, which would put you in Portage la Prairie at the end of your day. That said, detouring an hour out of your way and taking in Rouleau, Saskatchewan, may or may not fit with your plan. If this does fit, due to everybody's getting up early and in the van with their gear when it can still be safely called "morning," you could swing by this must-see tourist stop on the way home.

This quest came to us on a whole other leg of our touring. While we were in Europe, it so happened that I had five seasons' worth of the TV show *Corner Gas* loaded on my laptop. This was a show we mostly had made fun of, the way Canadian folks will sort of poo-poo our own Canadian culture. Admittedly, I really didn't get into the show until it was mostly over. Well, the band's disdain was overcome on one leg of our Europe trip when we were held up in a guesthouse in Vorselaar, Belgium, with way too much time on our hands and only non-translated Belgium TV to occupy our time. The band as a unit got into *Corner Gas,* and we watched most of the five seasons. It was travelling across Canada later on that we found out that the town where it was filmed was located just a half-hour south of Regina. We arrived to find that, yes, the set, which consisted of the gas station and diner, is still there sitting right across the road from a grain elevator that sports the name *Dog River*. Like good tourists, we all got out and took pictures of our band van parked at the pumps and had a good look around the property before hopping back in the van and taking one cruise up the main drag of Rouleau to see the Dog River Hotel. Then we were back on our way. We didn't take a lot of these sojourns while touring, but this one did line up for us one trip, and we had a lot of fun.

110 kph east

Getting your ass out on the big road and setting the cruise on 110 kph, which is the posted speed limit, you have a long way to travel and a short time to get there. You have three advantages working for you: one being you have no shows, so your time is just about getting down the road. The second is that the highway is smooth and mostly straight and flat, and the third is the tailwind. One would think tailwinds are the sort of thing that only affect sailboats and maybe airplanes, but it really is going to help you too. When tearing across the flat land in an easterly direction, you will notice that the prevailing winds are generally coming out of the north and west, which means for the next two days at least they are going to push you across the Prairies at a rate far quicker than you were able to maintain heading west. This will increase your fuel economy a lot and help spread the distances covered between fuel stops. Fewer fuel stops means fewer chances for the band to purchase beverages, which will mean fewer piss breaks. You will cover vast distances as you deprive your band members of precious fluids. The van will be quieter because everybody is kind of worn out from the trip thus far and thinking about home.

This is downtime, time for you to start thinking and retracing the tour in your head, figuring out the mistakes, and the successes. You plan and you work things out, you take stock and have some time for debate. You also now know your realities, money and otherwise. Chances are there is at least one member of your band who has put in his notice, stating that when he gets home, he is staying there and not continuing on this strategy of being a professional musician. Don't get down, folks leave. At this point in the tour, expect folks to realize that in order to make it in the Canadian music industry, this tour you have just done means that you will have to do it again, and again. This might just be a little too overwhelming for every member of your band right now. At this point of being overwhelmed, they might in fact be leaving, or they might not. That is to be worried about when you get home.

In the meantime, take stock. The first thing that you probably should have noticed during this trip is that merch was a really important part of the money-making experience. Merch is very key. There is just no reason at all to leave your hometown without it. Playing road shows is fun, but without a CD to sell and thus leave in that town, there isn't really a lot of point to touring at all. Touring is a reason to sell CDs, and leaving CDs in the hands of someone who just enjoyed your show means that he or she will play that CD for their friends, and then you come back six months later and there are more people at your show. Shows that you sold merch at can predictably expect to be bigger on the next swing, and shows that you sold no merch at you can expect to have almost the exact same turnout for next swing through town.

As well, keep in mind that promo-ing your CD is good, so leave a copy or two at the bar in hopes of its making their playlist, but for everybody else, sell, or at least trade for, your merch. Free CDs generally never get listened to. It's weird but true. If people hand you a CD, the chance that you will ever listen to it goes to roughly 12 percent. CDs that you pay for get listened to upwards to 98 percent, so sell, don't give. Also feel free to trade discs with the other bands you play with. Most of my collection of music has come to me this way.

On the merch end of things, I have also found that having more merch on the table means you will sell more merch as well. Two or more CDs, T-shirts, stickers, buttons, and anything else you can think of goes a long way to keeping people at the table longer. The longer they stand at the table, the greater chance they will buy something. As well, every show has at least one whale. Whales are those guys who saw your show and really connected with your band. They are very excited about your band and want everything you have. They want to help you out and put as much money in your pocket as they can, so they take it all, and the more you have, the more they will buy.

Merch is also the reckoning for the indie band. Here in this era of digital downloading, online music purchases, and pirating, this is where the music fan comes to relieve their guilt about having stolen your music. Keep in mind that the only reason these folks have any idea who you are and came to your show is because they were able to listen to your music for free. It's kind of the way radio used to work, sort of. Well, now they are at the show, and they have seen that, yes, you guys do a show worth paying cover charge to see, they want to pay you back for all those tunes they have been listening to over the previous six months before your arrival. I have had the comment so many times—I would say maybe even at every show—"I got your album from a buddy of mine. I love it, and I came to your show so I could buy the actual CD and give you money."

This is the new era of the music business, an era that the major, and for the most part minor, labels have yet to figure out. People are more than willing to pay for music: they just want to put it in the hands of the actual people who make it and see the artist touch the money and hang onto it at least for a short period of time before the industry gets their hands on it or it ends up in the gas tank of their tour van. If you are just starting out, you might have this feeling that this all sounds way too business industry for you. "Selling my music, and making sure I get paid! That is selling out!" If that is, in fact, your issue at this point in your career, then just wait till you get home and find out just how much money you made. Two and a half months on the road, if everything was done right and went very well, will net your band far less than if you had stayed home and just worked at Starbucks over that same period of time. Selling isn't selling out; it's survival, and it goes against what you are collecting as an hourly wage being a musician. In the beginning, you will be making twenty cents an hour. At this point of touring, maybe you will get it up to a buck. Someday you will be paid the exorbitant amount that Starbucks pays people to schlep coffee, and you will be playing music instead of schlepping coffee, slinging beer, call centres, lawn maintenance, teaching high school, or the other million ways musicians get through between tours. Just remember you are selling something you made with your own hands; that's better than schlepping for some big-ass company any day.

Now I've got you worried, so, the other way to increase sales is to always have your merch out, every show. It sounds funny, but this will go by the wayside as you tour and the show and time take a huge toll on your day. But it is the most important part of the tour. Now that you are three-quarters of the way through your tour, it is time to take into consideration whether you have figured out a way of ensuring you are selling your merch consistently. Is the merch table getting set up before every show, and is it being manned every show, and is it open for business for the whole night? Now is the time to consider having a road manager, or maybe even a "Merch Girl." Certainly, the first time you go out on the road it would be difficult to believe that paying someone to sell your merch would be worth it, but in reality, having someone whose job it is to sell the most merch possible can be very worthwhile. Also, if you did in fact buy the idea that selling merch is the most important part of the tour, then paying someone to move that shit would become very important.

Give it a thought: having a road manager who has a driver's license and can pull some or all of the designated driving detail, do the running around for the band, booking hotels, running errands, and being in charge of selling merch, can really take a load off the band members who are doing this stuff every day. This rigmarole does take a lot of energy while on the road and can go a long way to burning out the Mom person in the band. The funding for such a person could be seen as coming directly out of the merch budget. Thinking about the possibility that the merch will get set up every show and manned for the whole night, if you sold five extra CDs every night, then that is probably what you are going to pay the tour manager, maybe the band kicking in, say, $25 out of the door to make sure the manager does all the things that make being on the road easier.

If that is too far out of the dreamscape for the first tour or two, maybe grabbing some traveller, or friend who isn't doing anything, and taking them on the road for, say, a percentage of their sales might fit. I know punk bands have always done this. Grab some guy who would be couch-surfing anyways, and say, "Hey, want to come see all of Canada for free?" They generally would make enough money to pay their food, and you can put them up wherever the band stays. Once again, here it is about moving merch, and the more you sell, the more people are listening to your CD after you leave town. The more they are being played, copied, and introduced to people, the more people who will be at your shows next time you come back, meaning larger door take and more feasible touring, maybe even the band making a living. But that, of course, is a ways down the road.

This is the Canadian music industry in a nutshell: Record a CD, get in the van, and either turn right (east) or turn left (west), repeat, each trip completed getting you maybe 5 percent more successful. Repeat these steps until famous or the band breaks up.

Two trips across Canada, and you will become aware that you are not going to be discovered. The record labels and agents and radio play, if they ever come, will only come after you have no need for them. They will all get on board once you have proved that you have no need for them, once you are moving a lot of CDs, filling rooms, and getting good press, and making money, money they can now tap into. Labels aren't inherently bad. Labels and agents can be a game changer to your career, but they will be nowhere to be found until you have made sense of your band, monetarily and spiritually. Your band must make sense before professionals get involved with you, because professionals only want to work with professionals, and until you are one, you are locked out. These things are now swimming in your head while you are doing the seemingly endless drive across the Prairies. It's dawning on you: it's a long road metaphorically as well as realistically, made only slight easier by the fact that at least it is straightforward.

By Medicine Hat, you have already figured out where you lost money on merch, and which buddy of yours you are going to talk into coming out on tour with you next time, and how you will make him do all the hard driving and hulking.

Swift Current has you dreaming of a bigger van, maybe one with bunks in it. Touring always starts out with you driving whatever you can find for a vehicle, anything that you and your gear fit into. After one tour, you start refining your needs. The size of the vehicle depends on the size of your band. We were six and had a stand-up bass, so right off the bat, we were renting full-size vans. We quickly traded up, well down actually, to a $400 Chevy of our own. Four hundred dollars was a great price, and then it took us $4,500 to get it roadworthy, and then about $1,000 a month for the next year and a half to keep it on the road. In the end, we bought a three-year-old Ford E350 fifteen-passenger van. We removed two rows of seats and added a deck to stow our gear under. We bought the van from a rental company with no money down and paid $350 a month on a five-year loan. We fixed everything as it broke and did a lot of maintenance to keep it in shape. Whenever the band had extra money, which wasn't often, we paid chunks of the $19,000 off, and four years later, after the band split up, we owed $2,500 on it and sold it for $6,500. This all sounds expensive, but this is what it actually cost to drive a band up and down the road. You can buy new, or old, make payments or spend money fixing an old van, but this is what it costs. The upside for us was we got pretty good fuel economy and had a warm and dry ride with comfortable seats. All bands dream of the tour bus some day, but that is a different biz altogether. Tour buses are expensive, and although we look at them as affluence, the truth is the bus is used to get everybody up and down the road. Successful bands use tour buses because they are playing seven nights a week for weeks on end and must get from place to place quickly and have everybody rested when they get to the other end. They are also havens that give the band somewhere to hang out away from the fans. Big-name folks can't chill out at the coffee shop across from the club 'cause folks will bother them, and that is work.

The Grass Mountain Hobos covered the middle ground very well. They found a twenty-person half-bus for sale. It was a diesel and had overdrive, an extra gear that can lower the RPMs at highway speed and save fuel. They found it was a good-sized vehicle for a six-person band, with room to move, and had a bunk built in the back over their gear. Due to its being a diesel and having overdrive, they found if they drove reasonably slow, they actually got better gas mileage than any minivan they had ever used. Minivans are generally underpowered pigs. They got very lucky with their van: they paid very little for it and, other than replacing the transmission at one point, had very few problems with it. If I had to do it again, I'd probably go that route.

Moose Jaw finds you auditioning replacements for your

drummer who has put in his notice, due at the end of tour. In your head, you have narrowed the list down to five possibilities, and weeding them out now is based on who smells the least, and which one of them has a job that they can and will quit at a moment's notice and come out on the road. From one tour, you have heard your entire band get 100 percent better as players, just from doing all these shows. So when replacing members you now know that being a shit-hot drummer is not the issue because everybody gets good on the road. Talent is not the issue; being able to tour is paramount—getting along with everyone else, and then can they hold a beat? Excellence is for the weekend-warrior band: they don't play six nights a week, so they have to *be* good. Road bands *get* good, and get good quick.

In Brandon, you stop at one of the crappy truck stops you have already eaten in, and guess what? It still sucks. It didn't get better in the last month, still serving canned vegetables, rubbery meat, and canned gravy. Once again, you eat where you know, and you now know Brandon. You might even know the waitress's name by this point. You pass pleasantries with her, and she remembers you from your trip west but as of yet hasn't had the chance look up your band, but she will. Already you realize you are getting acquainted with the road, and this thought gets you through your day.

Back in the van, you run through the mileage on the GPS, and you are pretty sure you can make Portage la Prairie by 11 p.m., time enough to get checked into a motel and put the feet up. Yes, you have bitten off a pretty huge chunk of the Prairies today, and Portage will probably do you for the day.

Portage la Prairie, Manitoba

Rolling into PLP late at night, you check into the Econo Lodge and go in search of some food. It's early in the week, and this Prairie town, made up mostly of farm equipment dealerships, closes early. If you are lucky, the liquor store and the Boston Pizza is still open. Once again, eating what you know kicks in, and you go to the BP, that middle-of-the-road, every-town-Canada establishment that has taken over the strip mall district in every town over 10,000 people. Boston Pizza on a Sunday night is the cultural high-water mark of most towns it invades because everything else is closed, and this town is no different. The BP in PLP is bumping, maybe with fifteen dudes eating chicken wings and downing pitchers of Coors Light. The music is fair to loud, and the myriad of big-screen TVs clouds your brain as you search the menu for something edible. The pizza is terrible, which is not surprising since this place accurately takes its name from a town synonymous with bad pizza. Boston is number two in North America for bad pizza, the top honour going to Montreal. The pasta is small and watery, and so even though the chicken wings at the next table are tiny but alluring, you settle on the very over-priced Caesar salad, vowing to eat a vegetable today albeit a vegetable slimed in fatty garlicky dressing. The Caesar will let you down. Today's tip: don't spend the extra $3 on the spicy chicken topping because it will let you down more, and that $3 could take you halfway to your second Coors Light.

The band is worn out from the day's travel, and the conversation is a dog's breakfast of concerns stemming from everybody remaining in their own heads all day, being quiet and thinking about all the things I have mentioned, and of home. There is no getting around this. You are in the home stretch, and everybody is itching for home. By next week, these feelings will have been put off or morphed into something different with the rigours of the final weeks of your tour, but for now, everybody is sitting between tired and excited. Tired and missing home and wanting to get away from each other and the road. Excited about getting home and having this accomplishment to brag about. The thought of getting back to their local and telling everybody about the tour is very hot in everybody's minds.

The food arrives and lets everybody down. More beer is ordered in hopes of alleviating the letdown, and then the bill comes and everybody is pissed off. Writing off the bad experience of Boston Pizza as the only place in this town to eat at eleven p.m. on a Sunday, you trudge off into the cold, dark Prairie night and head for the Econo Lodge for a night's sleep.

Up early and gone

Having gotten to bed reasonably early the night before, say, two a.m., it is just not unconceivable that those who eat breakfast have been up early enough to catch the meagre continental breakfast and had a muffin, coffee, and maybe some dry cereal. Man, Canadian continental breakfast really does pale in comparison to those in the U.S. The U.S. chains rarely offer them, but when they do, there is always a waffle maker and some form of breakfast meat. Here in small-town Canada, we make do with maybe granola and some fruit. Not bad things to eat while on the road, really.

Today's travel tip: maybe stash a Thermos in with your gear. I have never been the one to carry a lot of infrastructure on the road with me, choosing to travel with the bare necessities only and wear my dirty jeans for weeks on end rather than lug around extra clothes. It can be useful, though, secretly spiriting a Thermos of coffee out the door of the hotel along with a big ziplock of granola and as many bananas as one can carry. It really will take some weight off your per diem and make you feel as though you didn't over pay for the night's stay. Getting to know the different hotel chains across Canada and their level of breakfast offerings really will play into your band budget. One hundred and twenty dollars a night per room can be offset by six people not spending $12 each and an hour out of your day finding a truck stop. It is a ways into your travels that you realize that it costs a lot of money and effort to get a band up and down the road. Smaller and younger bands may have what it takes to sleep in the van and drive all night and play endless shows, but it is my experience that staying in safe places and getting a night's sleep when one can goes to longevity of the band as a whole. It is usually the younger bands, and younger musicians with the balls-out mentality, who risk premature burnout in the world of professional music. Get some sleep and pay for it. Save where you can, and pay the rest of the time.

Busting back out of town and down the Trans-Canada Highway, the wind at your back, you have the early morning Monday road to yourself. You are cruising just slightly over the 110 kph posted speed limit, and it is less than an hour to the city bypass of Winnipeg.

Coming into the Peg from the west, it is easy to glance at Winnipeg and see it as the sprawling hulk of city it really is. Entering from the east is far more romantic. Today had nothing to do with romance, and you catch Highway 100 to the south for the trip around the city. It is at this point that you see its burbs, and if this majestic city in your memory had ever begged of you "Why don't I live here?" then the suburbs will now have you shaking your head and wondering why people live here on the outskirts of Winnipeg.

Skipping around the Peg, the bypass dumps you back on the main highway east, and it's a straight shot to the provincial border. The reverse to your entry is noticed as you pass the Welcome to Ontario tourist office, which has reasonably clean washrooms and a whole lot of tourist pamphlets for touristy things that won't be open for a couple more weeks, it being off-season. Never mind the cruise control for the next couple of days. You will not need it as you are plunged back into Northern Ontario. Turn the radio off too, 'cause you are back into the two-lane experience you already know too well. If you're driving, ration your coffee. If you are riding, read a book or catch up on email.

This leads to today's tip: if you are managing a band, then use an email management program. It was a ways into the laptop generation that my bandmates noticed that I was always answering emails while we where on the road. They said, "Hey, how are you answering email in the van?" I responded that I used Entourage on my computer and thus downloaded my email in the morning before we left the safety of our hotel. Then I had two hours of work to keep me busy for the long trip. In reality, I was only composing emails. As of yet, I don't have a cellular uplink while on the road, so I compose and answer my downloads while in the van, and then later that night when wireless service is found, I upload. Then I get to spend all my limited Internet time surfing or using Skype instead of desperately trying to manage some Hotmail account. The system works well with the hours spent in the van methodically answering emails instead of rushing sporadic responses. This approach to communication kept me mostly up to date as the tour continued. It also relieved a lot of the boredom found on drives like these.

Up one hill and down the other, make it past one logging truck and find another, get past five of them, and then someone has to pee, and you watch all five trucks pass you while you are relieving yourself. Get back in the van and start over. It's posted as a nine-hour drive on Google Maps, but after getting stopped in Kenora for your second contribution to the OPP's traffic fund, and stopping in Ignace for the pot pie, your trip is going to be more like ten or eleven hours. Without the race to make a sound check, you will find it even harder to get folks back in the van. You have all day, and you will be stopping in Thunder Bay tonight, so you have time if the band finds something to stop for, maybe birdwatching or to pose in front of a statue of a very large mosquito. By all means, take the time. Don't rush, speed kills on this road, so take your time. You still have three weeks of road agenda in which to risk your life and limb. Today, there is no hurry, so don't.

Thunder Bay, Ontario

Rolling back into Thunder Bay after dark, you are back in the womb of the Apollo. If you showed yourself to be of good mettle on your trip west, then you and your band have been offered another night in the T-Bay. We always aimed to arrive Monday night, and if the sched was possible, we would take that night off and play the Tuesday night. You could play either night, really, but playing Tuesday meant not having to rush on Monday, and having Tuesday to sleep in. This Tuesday night show, though, will have to be toned down on the post-show revelry due to having to be up early for the long drive to the Sault. The drive across the top of Lake Superior is long and always strewn with a minimum of ten-plus hours of inclement weather. Obviously, winter is worst, but in summer as well, it always seemed to be raining at least. The summer also brings the RV traffic, which slows things down considerably. So play the show, have a nightcap, and go to bed, sweet prince.

The second consideration for a Tuesday night show would also be this: if given the Tuesday off, the band will do one of two things. Either someone will be itchy to get on the road and will talk everybody into leaving Tuesday for a Wednesday night show in the Sault. (This will mean paying for accoms, which might be worth it: more on Wawa later). Or, the band could decide en masse to spend the entire day drinking, which will lead to the band inevitably drinking into the wee hours of Wednesday and causing all kinds of other problems on your long rip across the lake. All of this taken into consideration, the safe bet is to arrive Monday and play Tuesday.

Marathon, Ontario

If at all possible, give Restaurant Thunder Bay a miss this morning of your trip and hit the Timmy's on your way out. Roughly four hours up the road, and two hours after hitting virgin territory on the low road across the top, you will see the sign for Marathon. You have to pull off the highway altogether and traverse the two-kilometre distance to the bustling downtown of Marathon. This former pulp and gold-mining town, boasting a population of less than 3,500 people, offers the exact type of restaurants you would expect up here. It has an A&W, a Pizza Hut, and a couple of mom and pop places, typical fare for the locals and travelers alike. It was quite surprising that on one trip west I was able to talk the band into trying the Chinese restaurant, and I, at least, was suitably impressed. Wok with Chow, located at 83 Evergreen Drive, did fit my bill as the lone Chinese restaurant, and, as of today, Subway has not unseated it from the locals' hearts.

We were happy to find the darkly lit restaurant to be quite cozy. The wait staff were actually Caucasian, usually not a good sign in a Chinese restaurant, but they were nice, and the food was better than you might expect.

The low road

Highway 17, the low road, is prettier than the high road you took on the way out. If the weather is uncharacteristically nice and it is daylight, this can be quite a beautiful drive. There are near mountains to traverse and some fantastic vistas to take in. The entire road is two lanes, and you will pass through many small roadside villages, without stopping. I say without stopping because you should not need gas for this trip. If you are smart, you filled up in Thunder Bay, or Nipigon, or Marathon. As previously mentioned, gas stops are sporadic across here, so be safe not sorry. Even gas stops that you used last year may have gone out of business, or be closed due to holidays or the off-season. If there is any chance you will need gas sometime over the next 250 kilometres and you see a gas station open, take the time and fill up.

Wawa, Ontario

To the folklore of fuel stops in Northern Ontario I will add an encyclopedia of things-gone-wrong stories. Previously mentioned was the 79.4 litres of fuel in an eighty-litre tank story, but there are many folk tales about fueling in Wawa. Wawa is a couple hours north and west of Sault Ste. Marie and generally a gas stop for most cars heading west, and probably most cars heading east. Over the years, I've encountered at least three people who have said they had to spend days in Wawa due to car trouble following stopping for gas there. The assertion was that the guy pumping gas did something to their cars while fueling. The most exaggerated story involved a guy who swears he had to stay in Wawa for six months, working as a waiter, because his transmission fried ten miles out of town. After a tow into town, repairs were assessed and work begun. He suspected all manner of tampering when the very polite gas bar attendant not only fueled his car but also checked his oil. Maybe, while under the hood, the attendant took the opportunity to put some sugar down the dipstick, or maybe sand. The long and the short of his story was that it took him six months of working in a local diner to make enough money to pay for the repairs so he could continue his trip west. Now I do not know the truth of this story, and do not mean to soil the good name of the local gas station attendant or its owners, and this story could be an urban myth, but I know when filling up in Wawa, I pump my own gas and check my own oil.

The other unmissable stop in Wawa is the Wawa Goose. Don't worry: you will not miss it. It's a huge statue that dwarfs the highway, and, like all good roadside attractions, there will be plenty of time to pull off the main road and visit the info centre. A note to the wise: the info office also has a second-hand book rack, located near the bathrooms. The books are cheap, maybe a couple of bucks each, and Matt sifted through the plethora of romance novels and found a copy of a great Walter Mosley book for just $5. Matt was real cool and actually let me read it, which took up a lot of the trip across one Canadian tour.

Books are good to take with you. When your laptop, or iPad or iPhone, is down and there is a lineup for the one cigarette lighter the standard van is equipped with, you will always have a book. If you are fussy about your books—if you are the type who hates spine-crackers or dog-earers—then leave those books at home and bring trash or books that are already semi-destroyed. On the road, they will get passed around when the lighter is occupied and you are out of battery life.

Today's tip: install at least one other twelve-volt outlet in your tour van. One will not be enough. After-market twelve-volt outlets will work fine, and with the band using the main outlet for the GPS, you will need one to run the power inverter to recharge all the cellphones and laptops that you will find you have once you are on the road. Maybe it's even a good idea to figure out how to install one in the back of the van, and then the folks in the back of the van are not bothering the driver. Not bothering the driver is good, and is safe. The more things you have in the back of the van to keep the kids happy, the longer you will go without stopping, thus the happier you will be.

Driving just south of Wawa, you will see a sign for the High Falls Motel and Cabins. If you have booked the Monday night at the Apollo, and you are nine hours into your drive, feel free to overnight here at the High Falls. It's a great little place, and at least during low season we found their cabins to be affordable and nice. The true experience was when we found out that they have a gazebo sort of building in the middle of the front yard where they have a nightly bonfire. The place is hexagonal, and the tin roof cones upwards to become a chimney. It's a great please to have a fire even when it is raining. You sit on built-in benches, and under the benches is neatly stacked firewood. Sitting around the glowing fire, it was an awesome night, until the unlimited firewood was too tantalizing for us semi-intoxicated city dwellers and we built a fire so large that the owner of the motel had to come out and ask us to avoid burning down his gazebo. He was nice about it, but he did give us the idea that any and all damage to this property would be put on our Visa card.

Morning comes, and the wise ones amongst you bought breakfasty stuff the night before and the morning meal was cooked in the cabin's kitchenette, thus saving money and a lot of time running back into town for food. Although it must be said that eating at the diner in Wawa may help out some poor sod who is trying to make money to pay off his new tranny, but getting down the road yourself might be a larger priority. All that said, I don't think there are a lot of dining options on the road south to Sault Ste. Marie, so eat before you head out.

Sault Ste. Marie, Ontario

Ah, the Soo. *Sault* means rapids in French and is pronounced "soo." This sprawling northern town of, say, 70,000 folks actually dwarfs its American sister directly across the St. Marys River. Sault Ste. Marie, Michigan, is a dinky little affair of, say, 12,000 folks, and looking at it on the map, you have to realize that it is a small town stuck way up in the dead-end, northern part of the Michigan peninsula. There really isn't much happening in the southern part of Michigan, so it would follow that the northern part of the state would be exponentially desolate, and to my knowledge it is. The only thing that the U.S. town has going for it are locks. The Sault Locks are the lynchpin to all the Great Lakes shipping, and the Americans have the run of the commercial locks there, the big and important locks. They handle the freighters that run on Erie, Michigan, Huron, and Superior. These ships are way too big to fit into the Welland Canal locks down near Niagara Falls, so they spend all their days in these four lakes. Excluding the three months of the year when the lakes are frozen over, these waters and the Soo Locks are busy with mammoth ships traipsing to and fro, laden with bulk cargo.

Sault Ste. Marie, Ontario, not having the commercial locks to keep itself busy, has been the mainstay of the steel industry over the last sixty or seventy years. This rapidly dying industry still manages to employ most of the town, with other residents working for the Ontario Lottery Commission, three very large call centres, and the usual big-box stores on the outskirts of town.

The latter will explain a lot about the Sault. Just like every other town in Canada when the eighties rolled around, there was a big recession. The town's "powers that be" decided that what they were going to do to kickstart their economy was to start building malls and strip malls. The town sprawled out in all directions, and a deafening sound could be heard from the downtown core. That sound was a whoosh of air as the downtown emptied creating a vacuum. The main drag just up and emptied out. This is a pretty fair-sized town, and unemployment doesn't seem to be rampant, yet the main drag has yet to rebound twenty-five years later, with the exception of a few restaurants, maybe a shop or two, and the shinning light called Loplop Lounge.

In a back parking lot, a lot that stretches the length of downtown, stands Stephen, a married guy in his late thirties with a lot of energy. Stephen was, and is, the smart kid in the room. Stephen bears an uncanny resemblance to Andy Richter from the Conan O'Brien show. Although thinner, he has a similar laid-back energy. Stephen is a hard worker, he's not a martyr, and he is smart and successful. I have no idea why he called his club Loplop, but he runs the f. out of it. This town can be a lesson for all those interested in running a successful establishment.

The Sault, by all accounts, should have no nightlife. It has suffered the same as every other small town in Canada, it's in the middle of nowhere, and all of its inhabitants gave up on live music years and years ago. Then came Stephen. He noted that the downtown was dead, which means that it was cheap, and that you could do what you wanted and nobody would complain. He also recognized that Sault Ste. Marie was on the main road across Canada, a stop on the Trans-Canada Band Tour, and a ten-and-a-half-hour drive from Thunder Bay. This is the next logical stop for any travelling band. So, he has a cheap place, and bands, and all he needs is a crowd. So he starts doing an entertainment-esque mag. It's not really a magazine, it really is just a calendar for his bar, but it's slick and has interviews and bios of the bands that are coming through town. The mag is supported by a pretty decent website too. The vacuum created by nothing else going on in town and this mag gets the folks interested, and after a couple of years of booking all the great bands that travel back and forth, the folks around town start to expect to see live music in their town, and bam, you have a music scene again.

Loplop may have a bit too much of a bistro feel, or maybe a martini-lounge feel, but it is comfortable, and the layout does offer a genuinely intimate feel when only twenty people come. There is a big couch area up by the stage and tables up on a riser farther back. It can hold 150 on the occasions the crowds show up en masse, so in general, whatever night you show up, whether the crowd is there in good numbers or not, you have a good show, and you slowly build your audience, and Stephen builds his clientele. It's win, win, and, of course, win. The band has a chance to build this into an actual paying gig, Stephen keeps his bar afloat, and the good folks of Sault Ste. Marie have a music scene. Voila!

Loplop is a believer club. It's not come to full fruition as of yet, the slow build is still underway, but it is getting there. Stephen goes that extra mile and has worked out a deal with a local hotel to offer a decent reduction on hotel prices, and he has in the past even gotten us this deal on cheaper accoms on nights when we weren't even playing his bar. This solidified our relationship with him, and I look forward to playing his venue every time I head west. The whole idea is to build. You are starting with nothing and going from there one relationship at a time.

Going against him and the rebound of the town's core would be the "magic bus." It is just real dirty pool here, but it is rumoured that on weekends, the bar owners of the Sault, Michigan, actually send a bus over to the Canadian side to pick up customers and drive them over the bridge, for free! Once across the bridge, they will find $1 shots of Jack and $1.50 Budweiser. Man, this is what Stephen is up against.

Sudbury, Ontario

On the drive over to Sudbury, I am thrown back to my early truck-driving days. This part of the country is scrub Canadian Shield, slightly post-apocalyptic the closer you get towards Sudbury, although I have seen it transform over the last twenty-five years.

Sudbury was one of the first long-distance runs I ever did. I was working for a pop company out of Toronto, an outfit called Brio Chinotto. With them I was routinely sent north to service North Bay's, Sault Ste. Marie's, and Sudbury's Miracle Food Marts. It was my job to take the long drive north to deliver a trailer's worth of pop and bring back the empty bottles. The drive was a meandering piece of winding, hilly two-lane. It was the typical cottage-country scenery: trees, rocks, and roadkill for hour after hour once the 400 highway has played out just north of Barrie, Ontario. The tree cover and hills lulled along until you got to the top of Highway 69, just thirty minutes south of Sudbury. The trees just stopped, the scrub brush stopped, and the land took on a lunar surface motif for the rest of the drive into Sudbury.

Here's why. Sudbury over the years has done a lot of mining and smelting of nickel…a lot. Proof is that Big Nickel you are going to drive past on your way into town. The fact that the town is known as the "Big Nickel" should be a tipoff too. Back before they built the really big smokestack, I mean the really, really, really big stack, the super stack, all those chemicals coming out of the then-smaller stacks, all those acids and that eye-burning stuff just came out the top and sort of hung around the area. This seems to have burned off all the surrounding vegetation for about a 100-kilometre radius around town. It really did look like the Moon. Fortunately, all those nasty chemicals were dealt with when they built the super stack. It got all the chemicals way up into the atmosphere where they could do no harm at all…well, to the people of Sudbury anyway. About thirty years ago, the scrub started growing back, and then later, a few trees actually struggled their way towards the sky. It is by no means attractive, but it is a remarkable transformation. Seeing it for the first time now, I'm sure you will just think, "Wow, kind of ugly scenery really," but now you are in the know. When driving into Sudbury, just imagine no vegetation at all and just see what nature can do when it has thirty years to bounce back. Still ugly, but getting there.

Rolling to a stop in front of the Towne House Tavern, you are immediately assaulted by two things: prostitutes and cold northern air. There always seems to be a storm in progress or, at minimum, a-brewing on the horizon every time I've been to Sudbury. The other omnipresent thing would be the super aggressive hookers that frequent the immediate area. Both situations can be managed with a little perseverance, an umbrella, and an unflappable spotter to watch your gear while loading in. You enter the hallowed halls, under the roof that

Tom built. Stompin' Tom, that is. Yes, Stompin' Tom spent the seventies wandering around this part of the world picking up gigs. I'm sure there are gin mills in Northern Ontario that were more important to his career than the Towne House, but they are all closed since the eighties. The Towne House is close to the last man standing representing the Ontario hotel bar. There really are few left. This place is a bastion, if not a memorial to the once-great Ontario music scene. As mentioned before, all these hotel bars closed in the eighties and were bought up by the banks in the nineties, except for the ones in towns that had universities, like Guelph, which has the Albion, and Sudbury, with the Towne House. I guess the student population has made it just feasible for these old taverns to stay open. College students love to slum in old man bars. The Towne House is historic but still fighting for survival and relevance in this changing music scene.

Taking advantage of being on Canada's main drag, the Towne House still even offers a guarantee, which is great, but over the years, economic realities have lowered it to something like $300. It's still a guarantee, nonetheless. Unfortunately, the place has stagnated a bit. A typical show will see a $5 cover charge with 100 folks coming through the door. They will walk past the stage, which is sort of sequestered off to the front of the bar, and just stream right past to the back of the bar where the pool tables are. The place has just sort of mucked through for a couple of decades, without really giving much thought to the way bars or music venues and their patrons have changed. Perhaps this handy little nook of a stage served the purpose back in the seventies, and though it really is cool standing on a stage that Stompin' Tom stood on, in the very spot he stood, with today's shag carpet suspended over the very hole that Tom wore through years ago with a boot heel, this set-up just doesn't work for today's crowds.

The typical show at the Towne House has you playing to the seating area and dance floor immediately in front of the stage. Maybe twenty seats, and you could fit fifty people up there if things really got going. Usually, the case is there are 100 townies back at the bar and hanging around the pool tables, and you are actually playing a show for ten people, usually folks from out-of-town. This on its own is weird, but pretty much every time we've played there, there were folks who had driven down from Abitibi, or folks who drove up from Guelph, to see us at the Historic Towne House. The layout of this place really has to be changed, though. Over the years, we started dreading the Sudbury show and being about 100 feet from our audience. That said, return we did, many times. The other oddities which probably kept us going back to the Towne House, were the PA and the accoms. The PA is awesome, sort of. Well, it's super loud. I wouldn't say it sounded good, but loud, yes. The even more awesome part is that they have two PA systems. The first is the one that points at the audience and is loud, and the second PA system is the 4,000-watt behemoth that is aimed at the band.

The biggest problem for any band, night after night, is the monitors, those small wedges propped up in front of the singers. These are speakers the band uses to hear themselves, well, mostly to distract themselves from what they would be hearing from the mains, which is usually not the sound they want to hear. It has a completely different mix and in a lot of cases has a bunch of reverb or, say, echo on it, which can make it sound out of step with what you are playing. The music that is coming out of the PA system, or, as they are called, the mains, is actually coming out slightly delayed from what you are actually playing on your instruments. This depends on the room size and just how reverb-fixated the soundman is. To battle this, and yes this is a battle, the band usually wants to hear themselves in the monitors so they can tell were they are, and then the mains for the band just sort of adds power to the show.

At the Towne House, they have gone to the other end of the universe on this battle and set up a massive and loud PA system, just like the mains, but it is onstage and facing the band. If you want a loud stage sound, then this is the place for you. It can work well. We usually have played Sudbury on the back end of our tours, so by then you are pretty worn out and limping. Having this massive PA at your service can be fun: just whisper into the mic and it sounds as though you are screaming bloody murder. Simply form a chord on your guitar, and even think about hitting a string with your pick, and you are booming like you are playing a 50,000-person stage show. Yes, it can be welcoming, even easy, but generally when you are playing with that much power things get out of hand, and by halfway through the set, things are all out of whack and the overall show ends up being a raucous bunch of noise. It's worth experiencing, but even upon your second visit, it starts getting old. In all cases, good sound would in fact be better than loud sound.

The second oddity about the Towne House is its ghosts, which are located in the basement. The place is known for the accoms. And I'm pretty sure I am safe when I say the Towne

House Tavern's band accommodations are easily the worst accoms on the planet! This alone is a reason to play   the Towne House. Built some time over the last forty years, the basement of the bar was once some kind of flashy hip lounge, a Las Vegas-esque private clubroom located below the main stage floor. The gaudy decor includes, I think, a fountain and ornate fake-wood paneling, and probably even a marble statue of a boy pissing into said fountain. That said, I'm pretty sure the room was used during the seventies as a den for the bar manager to snort coke off of a waitress's ass, but the seventies having passed a while ago, and the rooms were given up to the bands years ago. Today, it is a windowless basement with a hodgepodge of decor and junk. The bathrooms are destroyed with the exception of one working toilet—one out of four, and three urinals. There are holes punched in the panelling, a bunch of broken-down three-legged couches, an assortment of broken exercise equipment, dangling electrical wires and burned out light fixtures, and a stairway that dead-ends into the ceiling. There are two bedrooms, one small room with an itchy bed, matted carpet, and a view of the next room courtesy of a hole punched in the wall, and a larger L-shaped one with four beds and a viscous poo, maybe even viscous bloody poo, mixture of something oozing down the wall. I'm not even kidding here. The carpets are matted, the lights sporadic, and the beds always itchy. Back in the main room, you bear witness to the devastation that thousands of bands can wreak on a room that the management gave up on years ago. Most of the flat surfaces in the room have band stickers on them. Yep, from one end of the room to the other, the walls are covered with band stickers.

Today's tip: do not leave your hometown without band stickers. You will be able to get the band to fork out the money to produce a sticker by mentioning that you will be able to sell these small self-adhesive beauties at a 800 percent mark up, which will probably only net you a dollar anyway. They are in fact good advertising, as they get stuck on people's cars and other bands' guitar cases. But once out on the road, you will see why bands really have band stickers. They are for leaving your mark. All the good venues in Canada have somewhere, either in the green room, or backstage in the bathroom, or in the accoms, a place that it is okay to affix your stickers. Here is where your band gets to leave its mark. Please don't be a douche: don't go putting your stickers just anywhere. Don't f. up a well-kept dressing room by actually graffiti-ing the space, but when you see the stickers you will know, oh, here on this wall it's okay, and there you will leave your mark. As you travel Canada from one end to the other, here and there on stages and bathroom mirrors, you will see names of bands you know, and bands you won't, and amongst them at least for the next couple of years, you will see our band's white-on-black USWM.CA sticker gleaming out at you. In the basement of the Towne House Tavern, the room I lovingly refer to as the "Shania Twain Memorial Hymen Suite," you too will be able to post your band's logo for all history.

Your sleep at the Towne House will be rough, with the itch of the mattress, the only semi-muffled sounds of the last remnants of your band partying until nine a.m., because there are no windows to point out to them that it is the next morning, and finally, after they calm down, the ghosts will start moving around the outer reaches of the room. The slight thunks and moans will be present in your dreams as you drift off to sleep, while trying to make sure that in your sleep you don't move around too much to prevent your foot touching the gross stuff coming out the wall beside your bed.

You awake the next afternoon, late, very late, 'cause there are no windows to let you know the next day has started. You are groggy but exulted by the feeling that you have slept in the Towne House, in the room where Stompin' Tom wrote "Sudbury Saturday Night," right below the room that inspired it, right below the stage where it debuted. You have slept in the room rumoured to be where Shania Twain lost her virginity. You are now part of the Great Canadian Experience. On this cold, dreary morning, it's official that you are a road dog, and nobody can take that away from you, ever. Shake out your sleeping bag and carefully check all the seams for bedbugs, roll it up, tie the strings, and put it back in the van with your gear. Get going—you are hours late, if, in fact, you have not missed your next show altogether.

The land of classic rock

Booking your way down Highway 69, you are in a hurry, a big hurry. You are heading straight for Windsor, and it's Friday night. You've already decided you are going to be pulling in late, so you really have to make time. You've made the decision to avoid Toronto and its weekend traffic, so you are going to do a cross-country maneuver to avoid the big city. Google Maps will have this adding an hour to your trip, but trust me, the Toronto traffic will cost you more than that. Also, it must be said that there will be very little reason in the future to see this part of the world, so now is a great excuse to see the rolling farmland that is Southwestern Ontario. This can be done, but it will take getting out the Rand McNally because your GPS will continually be sending you back to Highway 400 and thus back to Toronto. It's analogue for the afternoon, and you will have to plot a jagged course across the top of Western Ontario. All the roads sort of drift north and west, and there is no best way to do it. Avoid all of the large towns and stay on the B roads, but first you must make it down the 69.

Getting down closer to Barrie, Ontario, you start picking up radio stations, and having exhausted all the playlists on your trip across the mostly radioless north country, it is at this point that you find yourself worn down by arguments against classic rock. You just can't hold your own against the arguments from your bandmates wanting to here some classic rock, and you are now in the land of classic rock. Yeah! Hurray! With the possible exception of the Maritime provinces, you will find no better place in Canada to spin the dial and land on a radio station that for the last thirty years has not changed its playlist. These stations have been pumping out that same old pap year after year. You are bombarded with the Rolling Stones, Led Zeppelin, the Doobie Brothers, ZZ Top, and, because you are in Ontario, it took only two channel changes to land on Kim Mitchell. Yes, this is the backdrop of Canadian music.

I've had this argument dozens of times in the last twenty-five years when talking to either someone who is still reliving his high school days or, even worse, a twenty-year-old kid who is trying to turn me on to Led Zeppelin or the f. Beatles. Man, I have lived through four complete revivals of the Beatles catalogue. I am so tired of them I wish my ears could puke. I also reject the idea that they are the best songwriters ever! My reaction would be, how would we know? Their music has been so omnipresent for so long, taking up so much of the mass media, that who knows what happened out there over the last forty years? In this Beatles-rich atmosphere, we had little to no access to the millions of bands that have come along since them, bands that were not heard because the f. Beatles, the Stones, AC/DC, ZZ Top, Led Zeppelin, and all that other tired crap was taking up the entire dial.

My argument is not with Paul McCartney: Hey, buddy, give'er, take that career to the end. Keith Richards: Keep going, dude, while you still have quasi-blood partially running through your hardened veins....

No, my problem isn't with the bands, it's with the purveyors and our lack of understanding of the forces that are behind it. Radio works like this: you play the music and sell advertisements. Now, advertising generally tries to target the largest group that it can, so.... Who is the largest target audience ever? Yes, the baby boomers, meaning there have been more of them than any other group of people for the last thirty years. So what did we do? Well, we just kept playing, and playing, and playing the music that they wanted to hear, over and over and over again. What music did they want to hear? That's easy: the music they got laid to for the first time, or the music they listened to on the way home from the big game where they caught the game-winning ahh...goal, the music that they listened to when they were thin and beautiful. So we just kept playing the music, and the folks who advertised on those stations got to have access to all those aging boomers, and the rest of us just had to keep listening.

Plus, a lot of exposure to any song generally means that that song will find more people to like it. That song will get under more skins and, thus, eventually become what is known as a successful song. Come on, "MacArthur Park" was not a good song, yet, played constantly for many, many years, it has become a very successful song. That is what classic rock is all about—it's not good or bad, it just sells acne cream, hamburgers, cars, Pierre Trudeau, more expensive cars, hemorrhoid cream, old-folks homes, and then yes…funeral plots.

The overwhelming presence of classic rock has led Canadians to ignore the music that surrounded us, that was played by people we knew, people we could go see, maybe even have a talk with post-show. Music should not only be a magic thing, played by people you will never meet. It should be all around, inspiring kids to learn to play music and to see it as something relevant to their lives. The monolithic domination of a particular kind of rock hurt us all and helped collapse many of our music scenes and helped isolate the artists it inspired and made them all move to Toronto. With less and less competition, classic rock just kept getting bigger.

But *classic rock is coming to an end!* Take a hike, Burton Cummings! Soon we will not have "These Eyes" and "No Sugar Tonight" rammed down our throats! The baby boomers and the generation just after them are dying. Sorry for not feeling bad about that, but I have had to listen to your demographic f. up our culture for too long. I will not mourn you, but will mourn the loss of potential that died on the vine while your crap filled the airwaves. You are soon to be done, please turn off your amp and go quietly.

The new era will belong to the Canadian indie musician, so run quick and join a band. Get your ass on the road 'cause here it comes. As Keith and Mick die, finally folks will not have to save their entertainment budget for $500 a pop Stones tickets. Having just downloaded a bootleg copy of their legacy album, folks will now have that $500 to spend on music that has something to do with their lives today. The folks who sing about the roads they live and drive on, their politics of this day and not that, the colours that our lives have become. Not a thirty-year-old, disjointed take on the sixties, but current music about things that are happening today. Not just politics but love that is happening today, frustrations we are all having today. I do realize that the music I've spent the last twenty years creating will in fact be forgotten in the mad rush to be immersed in our now non-sentimental current culture, but I'm okay with that if it means not having to relive my awkward childhood through the songs that were the backdrop to all my embarrassments and misgivings. If I do want my voice heard, I suppose I will have to go out and come up with new music to force into the machine. So be it.

Having decided for myself that this is the way things will go, I actually enjoy hearing "Riverboat Fantasy" as I drift from Highway 69 and onto the 400 and then cross-country, all this argument blaring in my head, blaring like so much Fleetwood Mac. Yes, I said it. Fleetwood Mac can blow me. I hate them, but they are going away.

Windsor, Ontario

Arriving late in the Whiskey City, a town built on booze and bootlegging, originally named Walkerville, after the booze conglomerate, you pull up in front of the Phog Lounge. It's a small but hearty club, and they seem to have the inside on Windsor here. This surprisingly music-centric town boasts a large and eclectic scene. I've wondered over the years how it is that this town has a scene and its neighbours in Southwestern Ontario don't seem to. Perhaps it is the demise of London, Ontario's music scene that has very much boosted and insulated Windsor's. People kind of have to stay in Windsor unless they want to move to Toronto, and it's nice and surprising when you find folks that didn't want to move to Toronto. And U.S. immigration being what it is, aspiring musicians can't head out for Detroit, either. Thus the magic of being right next to the big city, in this case Motown, but without that city's ability to draw off the cream of your crop. It is a unique place to be.

That said, I was pleasantly surprised to find Windsor has its big-boy pants on when it comes to music. There are an outstanding number of bands here, and Windsor seems to even have a bit of what one might call its own sound: sort of alternative, but acoustic, punkish and thoughtful, worldly. The town's music seems to have grown up out of the last decade, which has found them on their own because fewer and fewer road bands have been able to make the trip out to the far west end of Southern Ontario. Years ago, more bands could eat the long drive and the low pay, 'cause they could pick up a decent gig in London, thus cutting the costs. For the most part, those London gigs are gone and so Windsor has been left to its own devices for a while. This separation from Canada has served Windsor well.

The Phog Lounge with its glowing painted TV signage is

small and slightly rough around the edges but welcoming. The stage is low but adequate, offering a rough-and-tumble, let's say intimate, show. It's "self-sound," so the band plug themselves in. No soundman to get in your way, so tonight you get to fuck up your own sound, and you do.

Post-sound check, you run out to find food, and on the main drag you find fish and chips. You are in the promised land. The fish has that central-Ontario-Protestant flavour of lard, flour, and understated self-repression. The crunchy batter from Sir Cedric's Fish and Chips does in fact transport "you" back to "my" youth. This is not the "be-all and end-all" fish and chip experience, but it is close, and you now feel appropriately sluggish as you head back to the club.

Back at the club, the show is underway, there is a line up, and the opening band, the Locusts Have No King, is warming up the friendly-as-f. crowd, and you drink beer while trying to shake off the lard that was dinner. The heat of the room, winter or summer, is what gets the fat moving through your veins thus avoiding a heart attack. By the third song of your set, you are on the ball again. A big dinner, a long drive on little sleep, and the folks of Windsor get you going. The folks here expect a show, and with their enthusiasm, you give it, and you are duly tired at the end. Pouring into the van post-show, you then pour into a motel room and spend every cent you made tonight on accoms. But it is Friday night, and Windsor has surprised you; you will return some day, as soon as you figure out how to cover the losses you incurred driving all the way down to this end of the province.

London, Ontario

I knew some guys from London, years and years ago when I lived in Toronto. Dan Kershaw and Dave Pedliham of the Brothers Cosmoline fame, had moved up to the Big City of Toronto back at the end of the eighties. We lived together for a couple of years, and they filled me with stories of their youth: the bands, the scene, the bars, clubs, and the garage shows, indie zines, and girls with long black hair and safety-pin piercings. Arriving in London years later, on our first tour early two-thousands, we played a show at the Wick, a rough-around-the- edges Ontario hotel bar. We were playing an off night, early or mid-week, and it was a summer tour. Summer is a stupid time to play clubs, shows, or bars. Nobody is there because they are on vacation or they are saving their money for the music festivals. That said, the bar wasn't packed, but I remember there being an enthusiasm for our music. We were even able to compete with the terrace that, at that point, was the new style of smoking lounge, Ontario's indoor smoking ban having only recently come into effect. Yet, we were still able to hold their attention. There were musicians in the crowd, and cool kids: not a big crowd by any means, but a great demographic, a group of folks to build on.

It was not that long after that show that I found out that the Wick had burned down. Our next show in London was harder, and the show was a little less fun. The cool kids were still hanging on, but the musicians were not there, having either moved to Toronto, Montreal, or, say, Windsor by this point. The next run through town found no cool kids and no musicians, and that is when we started rethinking our playing in London. By the end of our tenure, we were actually turning down offers from the club Call the Office, a club we had been trying to get into for years, because we just didn't really feel the town anymore. We knew nobody would come, and we would play in front of maybe a couple of folks, and there would probably be a fight, maybe even a knife fight. This is what the town had become: a big, IV-drug-addicted knife fight, and the kids, the bands, and the normals just either left or started staying home. We played our final show at the highly sought-after London Music Club, a venue that was somewhat impenetrable until we got an agent in our final years, but by then, we were just kind of done with the town musically.

Now, that said, all is not done in London. We did travel all the way down from Montreal a couple of years ago to record at the famed House of Miracles, an undercover little place hidden away near the downtown, a place without a sign, and a place that probably few of the locals even know is there. In fact, it's not there anymore, having relocated to Cambridge, Ontario. Our host, and the owner of the place, Andy Magoffin worked, yes, miracles on us as we spent a long weekend in London recording our third and final album. Andy, of the long-running band the Two-Minute Miracles, in the final stages of our playing in London, gave us a window into what it was that we missed. Yes, this had been a great music town, and then it went away, and the drugs took over, and the local university just kind of divorced itself and started staying on campus and never ventured out to the downtown core. Sad: gone are the days.

Other than a heroin problem that dwarfed Toronto's intravenous drug statistics, and maybe some bad times on the recession front, nobody has sufficiently answered my question as to what happened to London. Where did that town of my friends' youth go? Was it drugs? Was it recession? Probably not, because they did seem to have more work out that way than most. Did the middle class just squash it with malls? Did the university just roofy and date rape the scene out of existence? Nobody has said. But the one thing London does have is Walker's Fish & Chips. You've been waiting, and you thought I had forgot, but here it is: Walker's Fish & Chips, the best, or at least tied for the best, fish and chips in Canada. This completely landlocked chippie is the quintessential fry shop. They have done a pretty damn good job at staving off the flash-frying, burned-on-the-outside-raw-in-the middle hollow of flavour that has become chipping over the last twenty-five years. They have damn good fish and chips. If you score a show in London at the Music Club, then leave yourself room to hit Walker's. Walker's, you are the one.

Trevor of safety

Waking safe and sound, the bed is soft, and there is sun streaming in the window. The window looks out over rolling farmland, it's noon, and nobody has bothered you at all with the exception of the sound of frying potatoes and the smell of freshly brewed coffee willing its way into your dreamscape. All is peaceful as you descend the stairs and bid a good morning to Trevor. Trevor is a mid-thirties indie photographer. He is mild mannered, he is soft spoken, he eats no meat, and he is more connected to the Canadian music scene than any other person, living or dead.

Trevor's family owns a lovely B&B located about a twenty-five-minute drive north of Hamilton, Ontario. I will give you no more information on the location than that, so you will have to find your own way into Trevor's house and his good graces.

As stated, Trevor's folks run a B&B, and they are also sailing enthusiasts, which means that come fall and winter, which is when bands tour, they close the B&B and head south to the Caribbean. There they spend the entire winter sailing and not being twenty-five minutes north of Hamilton.

This allows Trevor to take over the place for the slow season. Come the winter months, Trevor makes the place available to touring bands as a safe house from which to conduct their Southern Ontario tours. Get out a map and drop a pin just north of Hamilton and see what shows are available within a 100-kilometre drive. This radius around Trevor's place takes in London, Kitchener, Guelph, Brantford, St. Catharines, Hamilton, Toronto, and, stretching some, Peterborough, Oshawa, and Cobourg. Trevor's rate is a floating scale, a pay what you can. For the signed bands, the bands with an accoms budget, funded bands, he charges more. Down the scale to the second-time-out-and-still-scrimping-by bands, if he likes you, he can get down to very cheap, and certainly well below hotel accoms. In this case, the money goes to cover his costs of eggs, bread, and potatoes.

He does what he can to cover costs, but his objective is to help out. He is not the only one out there—there are rumours of others—but he is the guy who found us, and that is generally how it works. Trevor takes pictures for a living, and great picture, at that. He does a lot of band shots, and is available to go out and do tours if, of course, the budget is there to pay him. His rates are reasonable, and if he likes your music, there is a good chance that Trevor has already reached out to you. Due to his situation, he has his finger on the pulse of the touring scene and routinely contacts bands that are touring and offers his services. I don't believe he accepts bands that call him. He takes referrals and does his research to decide who he is going to help out.

We have done a few Southern Ontario tours based out of Trevor's house. Rip thirty minutes up the road and play Kitchener, then return to Trevor's, sleep in, wake up, have some locally sourced breakfast of eggs and potatoes, hang out, download your email, chill, take a walk on the farm. Come evening, you jump back in the van rested and go do your next gig.

The real cool part about all of this is that Trevor has done this with dozens of bands over the years. He knows everybody, and that makes him a true window into the music scene here in Canada. He is friends with everybody and has spent time with everyone doing the long, hard road in Canada. I believe the idea for Trevor is that he will do this for the next fifteen years and then publish a book of his photography, which will eventually be considered the complete visual bible of the Canadian music scene with staged and candid shots showing everyone who was involved in music from the two-thousands on.

Trevor makes you feel at home and safe…safe except for his love of bonfires. I'm not sure if it was just us, but, man, every time we showed up, he had set up a fire for us. Winter or summer, there was a pile of brush or wood just waiting to be soaked in diesel and set ablaze. This alone, the chance to spend a couple of hours gazing into the fire post-show, or on a night off, restores your soul.

Trevor's music library is extensive, and you can add to it by leaving your music with him in the knowledge that other bands will hear it and maybe copy it.

You don't have to be an indie photographer to do what Trevor is doing. If you are conveniently located near a music venue or main road, or even better, many music venues, and have room for a band, safe storage for their gear, parking, and the will to meet everybody who is important in music, you too can be Trevor. Simply contact bands that are coming through your town and offer up your services as a place to stay. The first couple of attempts will probably go unanswered until you have got a few bands to stay with you and they find out that you were cool and didn't get all creepy with them. You can do it, and you can even charge. Bands pay at least $150 a night to stay in a shitty motel, so if you can do it for half that, if you are willing to help and to meet people, and try to make ends meet, you will start making friends quick. People with quiet farms near large cities will find bands looking for places to kill their downtime. If you're handy, you can have a front-row seat. Keep in mind you will have to figure out a filter system so you don't get a bunch of jerks trashing your house. You will have to set a vibe for the place. In Trevor's case, it is chill, and safe, and homey, and welcoming. We love Trevor. Everyone loves Trevor. Go be Trevor! Go!

Kitchener, Ontario

If you are a go-getting band, you got up early today being Sunday, and you managed to talk Kevin at the Boathouse into giving you a Sunday afternoon spot. If you are a normal band, you have the day off and plan on playing Kitchener on Tuesday night and blowing off Brantford.

Always to be encouraging, let's go with go-getter here. It's tough finding the Boathouse because the address just doesn't seem to show up on your GPS. Try putting Victoria Park into the machine, and it will get you there.

Pulling up in front of the public bathrooms in the middle of Victoria Park, you see your standard Ontario small-town park: maybe ten acres in size, and located in a stately part of town. The old trees and semi-sculpted landscape show off the water feature, which is an old, dirty, manmade lake. The bathrooms are located dead centre to all this, so you stop to take a piss, and at the back of the bathroom you notice a door. You walk through that door, and you are surprised to find you are in one of the best music venues Canada has to offer. Yep, it's weird. Here in the middle of this stolid, although slightly down-at-the-heel, park, in the old residential part of town, located in the back part of the public bathroom, is this great little rough-around-the-edges, almost quasi-punk, bar.

The Boathouse is about 1,000 square feet in a near perfect rectangle. It has a beaten-to-death six-channel PA, either Behringer or Peavey, I can't remember. The mic stands are bent and broken, there is one 58 and a couple of Behringer mics and some tangled XLRs, but you will find that this room sounds great. Now, having spent some time in the recording industry and having produced a few albums and engineered a few more, I am acquainted with the golden ratio of room size. You don't want equal dimensions with this rule, you want longer than wide, and ceiling height coming in at somewhere between the width and length but not equaling either. That's all technical, but I think this room has accidentally hit it. The

PA sucks, the stage is kind of beat-up, but once you get the squawks and feedback out of the PA, this room sounds nice, real nice, surprisingly nice. The room is softly lit and inviting.

Added to the sound, there is the staff. They are rootsie, tattooed, and just damn nice to you. This bar has that family feel that all bars go for and almost never achieve. They know their regulars and they know the regular bands. It's homespun, and naturally comfortable, and welcoming to bands and clientele alike.

The bar itself screams *unfeasible*. How could this great little down-to-earth place exist here, renting space from the town of Kitchener, in the middle of a public park, blasting all manner of loud music, underground, mainstream, folk, rock, what have you? I'm not sure how they pulled it off, but my guess is years ago there was this space, and Kitchener, like most places in Ontario, was in a downward spiral, and nobody else really wanted the place, as the park filled with drugged-out kids and the ills of society. My guess at the time is the park was awash in crackheads, and the town's folks really didn't spend much time there, so the Boathouse folks picked up the lease. I'm not saying it has all been easy for the bar, because as of late, the club had to go to the mat with the town council, but they won.

Recently, the town of Kitchener has rebounded from the ills of the eighties and nineties, and for the most part has gotten comfortable being a bedroom community for Toronto. This means the middle class has started to infringe on this place's ability to be the best damn club in Canada. Yep, the high-end folks who live on the edge of the park, having renovated the old, beleaguered houses in this once depressed town, and now sitting out in their newly refurbished back-yards, could, if they listened real closely, detect music wafting across the park. So, they decided that the music was too loud and the place itself and the folks it attracted had become too unsavoury for their safe little rebuilt lives in this gentrified part of Kitchener. The reality is that having a club in the middle of the park actually made the park less attractive to the glue-sniffing masses and is probably what made this open area habitable after years of neglect. But the re-energized park and the renewed state of the area kicked off a battle at the town council that lasted the better part of a year. This one event should actually be formally documented and become the bible for all cultural spaces that are threatened by annihilation by the stupid shortsighted powers that be.

The long and the short of it was that the bar itself had done such a great job of endearing itself to the community that the townsfolk came out en masse many times and filled town hall meetings and argued until they were given their re-prieve. Nice to see. I really don't remember the last time the good guy won. Good on you, Boathouse and your staff, and the folks of Kitchener.

The reality was that this was an all-or-nothing fight. I've played other rooms in Kitchener, and if this place went by the wayside, then that would be it for music in this town. Kitchener very well might suffer the same obliteration of their culture that London endured.

I think the success of the place has been a simple combination, and could also be a blueprint for music venues all across this land. These guys have a lot of music, six nights a week, and the most important part is that they do a great job of booking a perfect mix of local and touring bands. As well as the dimensions of the room, they have hit the golden ratio of supporting local talent and allowing it to grow, and giving the locals the expectation that if a band in Canada is touring, they will pass through Kitchener and play this club. This all became very important to the people, and they were organized by the bar to fight the all-too-prevalent tide.

I have booked this show on a Tuesday, but it must be said that on your first couple of times through, maybe a weekend would fit better. The beauty of this place is the fact it took us very few Thursday or Friday shows to build enough of a crowd to get to the point we could play here on a Tuesday night and fill the room.

Once again, here comes the dimensions. The room is small, and I think eighty folks is the top end here. This works well 'cause the place generally looks pretty busy even if there are only twenty-five people in the room. This makes for a good show even on a slow night, and as discussed earlier, good shows are a big part of building your audience. Within four plays in this place, we were pulling decent money to play there on an off night, leaving the weekend to play towns like Hamilton or Peterborough, towns that are ill advised to play mid-week.

This is the magic of this club. It works, they have a following, and folks are used to coming out on whichever night of the week someone they want to see is playing. The out-of-towners are booked well in advance, and local bands, of which there are many, fill in the empty spots as the dates get closer. It's a great system that bolsters the music scene, and generally goes toward making the place successful. If you are opening a bar/venue, maybe drop Kevin a line and see if he will let you intern for free at his bar for a month to see what it takes to make this all happen. No, actually, leave Kevin alone because he has enough on his plate running a great bar.

We eat dinner supplied by the Boathouse kitchen staff. The food is a nice mix of salads and nachos with some fries and adventurous specials. They are not shy on the portions, and one must moderate oneself in order to leave room to play later. In good weather, you eat sitting on the patio, which is beside the lake. It is rumoured that the patio and the lake have been refurbished lately, but as of yet, I've not witnessed it with my own eyes. I have heard bits and pieces online that allude to the fact that the lake doesn't stink as much as it used to, and the terrace is even more pleasant. If it's towards the weekend, there will be a band on stage playing a very loud afternoon set, and you will have a couple of beers whiling away the time until your show.

We take the stage to a packed house. The crowd is easy to split into two: get the folks from Kitchener to good-naturedly rib the good folks of Waterloo, and your night will go off without a hitch. It's a small room, and the stage, which is more than adequate, is still fairly low to the floor. Take advantage of this intimate space and maybe make your way into the crowd. The folks are warm and a real mix of demographics. Young, old, and in the middle, they all play well together.

This goes to my ultimate conclusion on local music scenes in Canada: it only takes one dude, in this case, Kevin Doyle, the owner and shepherd of this little but very important venue. He is the dude that made a scene here, and he keeps the scene going. Larger places can have more than one of these people, but it takes that one person to create a focal point, a rallying place. It is this place that makes it possible for our cultural spaces to exist and to defend their existence in the face of folks buying condos and not liking the noise, in the face of the local governments that don't understand that the ills of our societies come from a lack of these spaces and not from too many of them. Towns that have no music scenes are quieter, but are also generally given up to rough bars, strip clubs, and gambling and drug culture. Towns that have no place to play have a bunch of folks walking around high, angry, and/or drunk with nothing to do. Thank you to the Boathouse for, yes, saving lives and giving music a place to displace the ills of the world, or at least Kitchener's ills, and this town has many.

On that note, try to avoid getting pizza in Kitchener's downtown area post-show. I have almost been knifed waiting for a slice on the main drag. Leave late-night treats to a grab and go at the gas bar and eat in the van on the way back to Trevor's.

A tragic footnote: After many years of shows and battles with the local government, the Boathouse finally closed its doors in September 2013, the city citing non-payment of back rent. I leave this chapter unedited in hopes of truly showing what it is we have lost, and just what our music scene and culture is up against. Here's hoping a new club rises in its place and continues the outright battle to keep live music in small-town Canada.

Monday morning sleep in

The day arrives back in the safety of your accoms, and the sun streams in through the window. Today is sleep, relax, and catch up on email. Have a coffee, go for a walk, and maybe make your way into the nearest town and get groceries for tonight's meal. Home-cooked food is a godsend on the road, especially if you get to cook your own. Not having a place to make food for yourself on the road will be a surprising ordeal. Realizing how easy it is to make and eat food at home is a real shock once you hit the road, and there is nothing like a kitchen to cook your own food to help mend your psyche and prepare for the final push of your long tour. The band is feeling the end coming near, and after the long trip back from the west, you are on familiar ground: only a six-hour drive from home. A drive that is going to take you another week to complete, but you are running downhill and the band is tight and the shows are good.

Brantford, Ontario

All anyone ever knows about Brantford is that Alexander Graham Bell invented the telephone here, and that Wayne Gretzky was born here. This town is pretty forgettable. Standing alone in central Southwest Ontario, about fifty kilometres north of Lake Erie, this part of the world is seemingly unexplored by development. The uneventful small towns of Port Colborne, Port Dover, and Port Stanley are gateways to Brantford, their larger but unremarkable brother. Having grown up in Southern Ontario, I am quite surprised to realize I know little about this part of the world.

I am drawn to Brantford's semi-empty downtown. The sprawl of the suburbs has created a void, and the almost complete lack of traffic in the centre of the city leaves you worried about tonight's show as you pull up in front of Two Doors Down.

It must be said that our band only ever played one Tuesday night gig here in Brantford. It was a great night, and we had a local opener, but unfortunately I can't remember their name. The room was full, and the folks danced, jumped, and sang along. There was beer, and tons of folks buying merch, and we were a fifteen-minute drive from where we were staying for the night at Trevor's. For the life of me, I have no idea why we never played Brantford again.

The patchiness of my memory is due mostly to the fact that I am pretty sure I was hammered that night. The good folks of Brantford got to see a rare show played by me when drunk. Now, I'm not saying I was dropping my pants or anything, but I do believe there was some imbibing going on, on that leg of that trip.

Toronto, Ontario: the good?

Many folks in Canada have maligned the centre of the universe. Hell, I have, many times. Toronto has taken a shellacking over the years. I lived there for quite a while in the eighties before Montreal easily enticed me away. I remember being a kid and coming into the Big Smoke with the "Old Man" back in 1979. The population sign located at the Rouge River read 1,400,000. This, to a kid, was as big as the mind could conceive, and I remember bragging to my school chums that I had been to the city. Today, they have moved that sign back about seventy kilometres, and with amalgamation the Greater Toronto Area stands at a population of 5,583,064. This low-density city has become a Los Angeles-style blanket of civilization that sprawls from Kingston to Niagara Falls. It's the black hole, yet it's the black hole that has somehow come into its own in the last couple of years.

I have no use for the burbs, and I wouldn't give you a nickel to live in Mississauga, Brampton, Scarborough, or the like. Sorry, Brampton dudes. That said, having lived in Montreal for twenty years now, the arch nemesis to Toronto, I am going to go out on a limb. Here comes the hate mail! It looks like Toronto is actually getting around to being a cool place to be.

Toronto is cool if you are below Eglinton, okay, below Bloor Street, west of the Don River, north of Front, and east of Roncesvalles. This town's traffic sucks, and it will always suck, at least til they plow under the Don Valley Parkway, and the Gardiner Expressway and build an actual city bypass. But, til then, if you live within walking distance of stuff, and don't own a car, Toronto has become cool.

In the last couple of decades, with a revival of music, food, bicycles, bars, and art mags, this city has bounced back. The music scene kept going throughout the eighties coke party, even though coming into the nineties every band sounded exactly like Blue Rodeo. It's still expensive to live in, but the constant flow of new folks into Toronto has kept it alive and even rejuvenated it. It is easy to say that most of the music business in Canada has centralized itself here, the last straw being when everybody in Vancouver finally said f. it and packed up their indie labels and moved east. Not speaking French, the music industry types stopped when they got here, and avoided Montreal. If you are a musician and you live in Canada, you will at some point have to decide if you are moving to Toronto and then deal with the results of that decision.

It's Wednesday night, and we pull up in front of the

Dakota Tavern. It must be said that there are a ton of venues in town: the Horseshoe, the Silver Dollar, Bovine Sex Club, Rivoli, the Drake, and Rancho Relaxo to name just a few. It must also be said that all of them are staffed by folks who would rather stick burning nails into their ears than hear one more band play one more show, all with the exception of the Dakota and Rancho Relaxo. Rancho Relaxo is probably the hardest-working music bar in the scene: fun, cool, and stuccoed. Yes, the walls look sort of like old cottage cheese. I like Rancho. Toronto is a big town, but I'll mention two bars here. Rancho is the dirty little brother hanging around above a Mexican restaurant. The staff are good to their regulars, the regulars are good to the bands, and all works out, even with a bad PA, and a dangerous staircase for load in. I would play any day at Rancho, any day except for today, when I have managed to get my ass into the Dakota.

I mention both bars here because they are excluded from the reality that every other venue in Toronto will give you: the feeling that they don't want you there. The weirdism of this town is they seem to respect seniority when it comes to their staff. Most folks working behind the bar at these clubs have worked there since the eighties. As a forty-seven-year-old bartender, I get that it must be nice for a person with years of experience not to have to fight their way through their career against nineteen-year-olds. However, the staff at these place have seen it all. That is the downside. Man, the folks who serve in TO are really tired of serving people, and even more tired of serving bands. We have been treated badly by venues, and not just a couple of them but by all of them. I mean things like being screamed at when asking for a glass of water after playing a one-and-a-half-hour set to a packed house. Even with a toonie displayed in my right hand when ordering…yep, screamed at. Eddy Blake was almost thrown down the stairs, although that was a case of mistaken identity. Felicity almost came to blows over a tab twice. Doormen threaten to have you towed while loading in, gear stolen from the stage when staff decided to move it to unprotected areas on a whim, disputes over cover charge, bad sound checks — yep, we have seen, heard, and felt it all. And I believe we have gotten off easy since we generally get along pretty well with folks. I know other bands that have horror stories worse than us. Add to that terrible load ins, impossible parking, thievery, and low pay, and you have the Toronto live scene down. The upside is that there is a big old music scene here, and it ain't going anywhere. It is installed in granite that not even bad government and condos can shake.

Talking about the Dakota, I'm not saying they have solved all of these problems, but they have created something that stands outside the normal Toronto show. The Dakota has bad parking and bad load in because it's a basement one flight down and parking is insane, but once that is conquered, all gets better.

The Dakota is a new place, and the good folks who run this saloon bar have taken up the task of running a country bar in downtown Toronto and making it hip. One reason is that the Blue Rodeo Problem is pretty much in the past.

Let's go back to the eighties when Toronto was becoming less of a backwater, having stolen a vast chunk of Montreal's population in the seventies and eighties. The city was really becoming the centre of Canada and the centre of the music industry. They had every genre of music here including rock, rap, funk, jazz, pop, and, yes, a big old country scene. Then came Blue Rodeo. Those guys played the Can-Con rules right and started knocking out countryish pop tunes that obliterated most of the charts. I'll be the first to say those guys could write a song, but, man, they were wall to wall on the radio: commercial, college, I couldn't even avoid them listening to Radio One. They even spilled into the U.S. market, and their success was felt by all.

By the end of the eighties, everybody in Canadian music wanted Blue Rodeo's success, and so, soon, every band in Toronto started to sound like them. It was impossible not to. They were everywhere, and their music was like acquiring an accent after living in Scotland for a few years. Before you knew it, country—well, let's be serious; this wasn't country, but a happy pop, alt-Canadian country—and it sucked in the pop, rock, folk, and singer-songwriter folks. Nowhere on earth did that become more concentrated than Toronto, and on its, till then, vibrant country scene. Well, into the nineties, there was no country scene in the city at all, as the folks in the know spent a decade arguing about what country music was. By the end of the nineties, all had decided that even though everybody liked Blue Rodeo, it was not, in fact, country music. Once they figured that out, all the hip and fast kids set about rebuilding the country music scene, and jams sprung up all over the place. Bam! Five years later, Toronto has become the Nashville of the North, big enough in fact to support an actual hip, urban bar that professes to caters to country music alone. Really, the bar embraces the spectrum of country and music somewhat influenced by country, yet still Toronto has a unironic (and that is the important part, unironic) country bar and it is the Dakota.

The Dakota's other wily as f. maneuver is making this place hip and somehow keeping it hip. This is difficult in a city where being successful usually means you are past your prime thirty seconds after reaching it. The young hipsters in this city take great pleasure in discovering new, hot places and getting all their friends to frequent them instead of hanging around the place they decided was cool last week. But the Dakota seems to be holding its own and continues to attract the intelligentsia of the country, alt-country, singer-songwriter, folk, folk rock, and roots rock hipsters. They manage this and still seem to be down to earth. The Dakota has never been a hangout for me when in Toronto, so I really don't know the ins and outs of their scene, but I do know they have always treated me right as a musician. Word to the wise: one can keep the hipsters' fickle attention if they are continually drawn back to your club because folks they want to see are playing there, and nothing breeds loyalty from bands like being treated like a person. No, not a rock star but a person.

The Dakota is bigger than it looks. It has a great small-bar feel, with the bar running down one side and the stage running down the opposite wall, leaving a big area in which to crowd and see the show without getting in the way of the business of selling drinks. The stage is lit from lights located at the front of the stage floor and gives the bands playing a creepy feel, but at least the lighting can be said to be purpose-ful and unique in that it does look as though someone has put thought into your show. The PA isn't too bad, although I be-lieve the board is digital. I've always had a problem with the way digital boards compress acoustic guitars, making them muddy and, in the absence of drums, causing a fair amount of confusion as to where one might be located in the 1-2-3-4 of playing music. That said, though, generally the sound is better than the usual bar experience. The club seems to take its fire code capacity very seriously, and you will find it not very crowded for your show even when there is a lineup down the block. The staff is nice, and the crowds are cool, hip, and surprisingly less pretentious than you might expect. Possibly, these very same people act like asses in other bars, but this well-orchestrated room seems to bring them down to earth, and the night goes well.

At the end of the night, you will find out if you fit this place or not. You might have had folks liking your stuff, maybe even dancing, but come the end of your set, if the staff liked you, they will want to have a drink with you, and you will probably be asked back. If that doesn't happen, well, they will pay you and say nice things, and you can go about your business knowing you had a good show.

I like the Dakota 'cause it runs and works differently than the other clubs in TO. They book bands based on their liking the music and not so much on whether your band draws or not. They do not pander to masses or what's seen as hip, although some of their bands are quite hip for sure. The Dakota folks just run the place well, which attracts their friends and their friends' bands, and the rest of the folks come because the place is busy. The public are treated professionally, and that fills the bar. It's a nice mix of regulars and the public at large. A lot more clubs could run like the Dakota, and we would be okay.

Filing out of the club after a blockbuster show, your shoulders still ache from all the folks clapping you on the back. Toronto folks are not timid and really do a nice job of putting themselves in front of you and letting you know how happy they are that you played. It is a misconception that Toronto folks are rude. They are not. It's quite the opposite really: in fact, they are so polite that in the absence of alcohol it is considered rude to even make eye contact with their fellow citizens. One must not strike up a conversation with a Torontonian on the street because it would be seen as an invasion of their personal space. Now, alcohol generally takes those walls down fairly quick, and you can expect to hear from your fans in Toronto, and they will be exuberant.

Fleeing the club in search of food, you run into the be-all and end-all of late-night food, street meat! Located on at least every other corner of Toronto's streets is a hot dog stand. Well, not a hot dog stand, exactly, because they don't always have hot dogs. They serve sausages: the Italian, the spicy, the mild, the chunky Charlie, the veggie, and they are all grilled on a gas grill and served with a variety of condiments. There are probably 12,000 of these hot dog stands in Toronto, and they are all pretty similar. Busy corners may sometime have two or three carts all crowded within twenty feet of each other, and the prices are about the same, so the real rewards go to the cart that has the best fixin's. Ketchup, mustard, brown mustard, pickles, onions, black olives, green olives, slaw, mayonnaise, bacon bits, grated cheese, Cheez Whiz, and hot peppers would be a cart I would stand in line for. Loaded up with a Chunky Charlie, I kick some yellow mustard, a little mayonnaise, pickles, Cheez Whiz, and some bacon bits on there, and if I'm drunk, probably green olives, and once again I am in heaven. With the tough but juicy sausage with grease projecting everywhere with each bite, a Coke stuck in your pocket, extra napkins wrapped around your dog, this is the only meal I concede to eating while standing up. Someday, due to health reasons, I will have to quit smoking, drinking, and eating fried foods. Actually, that "someday" is pretty much now, but when in Toronto, I will always have a street meat.

Here and there across Canada, you will find hot dog stands, including the illustrious Tubby Dog of Calgary, but Toronto alone is the Canadian pinnacle of dogs. I must agree that when it comes to clean, these ragged little kitchens can be a little daunting, but I've eaten hundreds of Toronto street dogs with absolutely no dire consequences. This food is good. Get one in ya, and then get out of town.

Up the next morning, having stayed on someone's floor in the downtown area, you grab breakfast at one of TO's many fine breakfast joints. Yes, Toronto is all about breakfast. I think breakfast eaten at a restaurant fits Toronto perfectly: the demographic for a healthy breakfast community seems to fit towns that are expensive to live in, and Toronto is that. Folks who live in expensive places have absolutely no chance of ever buying their own homes, so they seem to spend their meagre disposable incomes eating breakfast. We are never going to save enough for a down payment on a home, so let's eat like grown ups and go out for brunch.....

Today's tip: food eaten and everybody happy, the wise folks will make their way up Bathurst. Avoid the Don Valley Parking Lot and go straight up Bathurst to Highway 401. There is a gas station just before you hit the eastbound ramp, so glance at your gas gauge and, if needed, grab some gas 'cause it's going to be a while before you see an easily accessible gas station. Filled up and onto the 401, you will probably immediately run into traffic. The 401 is always stop and go, twenty-four hours a day, 365 days a year. Every year, they add another lane to it, making it wider, and every year, the car companies build the appropriate amount of cars to fill it. This is a never-ending cycle as Toronto sprawls out farther and farther with this low-density wasteland splaying out in all directions, including a healthy amount of filling in Lake Ontario to make even more room for condos.

It must be mentioned that those condos do not seem to be threatening Toronto's nightlife in the same way that they killed Vancouver's scene and Halifax's bars, and are threatening to kill Montreal's culture. Nope, Toronto is actually poised to be the only city in Canada to continue to have a music scene in the years to come. This is probably due to the fact that most of its overdevelopment is expanding outward instead of trying to take over the cool parts of the city that have been there for years.

The Shwa: Oshawa, Ontario

Pulling up in front of the Atria in Oshawa, a frayed at the edges community known to the inhabitants as the Shwa, you step out on King Street. It's bleary, windy, and probably raining. The Atria is not attractive. Its redone façade of new brick and sheet metal, although cleanish and newish, screams absentee landlord. The street is not particularly bustling, and you leave one of your crew on the sidewalk to watch the gear while someone goes in to see if it is the appropriate time to load in. Street types start circling your van almost immediately, bumming cigarettes and casually checking out your ride.

Oshawa is a hell hole. An auto town, known only for its auto plant, its workers known grudgingly to the rest of the people of Southern Ontario as the folks who got the good jobs. I'm sure the town is probably not such a bad place, but living thirty miles away and on pogey for most of my young adult life, like most of Southeastern Ontario I was led to believe that these high-and-mighty, well-paid auto workers were a bunch of sucks, making the big money as we scrabbled around to find a way of getting by.

The truth was that those union guys organized, and cut their deals, and made what people should make for the basically shit job of spending ten hours a day putting one f.n part on one car at a time, day in and day out. The envy, the claim that they were whiners, was misinformation designed to help GM crush the strikes that would come up every so often. Regardless of spending the last twenty-five years giving a shit about my fellow man, organized and otherwise, has left me realizing that Oshawa was probably not all that we had been led to believe her to be. Oshawa is rough around the edges, sure, down at the heel, yeah, filled with bike clubs, strip joints, and the like, but not devoid of culture.

In the wake of the eighties downsizing of small-town Canada, the removal of music from local towns by way of the dance club/mall consortiums, towns across Canada were obliterated and changed overnight, weaned on to classic rock and fed chicken wings, a product not heard of in Canada until 1983. Not sure what we did with all those wings before that. Oh yeah, we ate them along with the rest of the chicken. I wonder where they now get all those chicken wings from?

Sorry, yes, this all happened, and Oshawa was in no better shape than the rest of us. They had jobs, but their shit closed up on the main drag as every one moved out to the OC, or Oshawa Centre, the largest mall in Ontario east of Toronto.

One thing I do know of the Shwa is that having lived in Montreal for twenty years, all these really great musicians keep showing up on the doorstep of the bar I work at claiming to be from the Shwa. Like a few other towns across Canada, including Saskatoon, Nelson, Dawson, Charlottetown, and St. John's, Oshawa is not only breeding musicians but giving them at least some will to work and travel. How did the Shwa produce so many awesome musicians, all whom seem to have evolved with very little influence from their big brother to the west, Toronto? Bands like Lee Mellor and the Mudhounds , Trish Robb, the Stables, Poor Pelly, Bradleyboy Mac Arthur, Wayne Petti of Cuff the Duke, and don't forget the enigmatic Doug Hell. Was there something in the water that spurred a scene here, or was it as simple as there was just a place to play that didn't close?

You load in to the Atria, thus getting the gear out of your van, stow your bags in the van out of sight, and order a few beers and wait for the night to take off.

Sound check goes well. The local band arrives, and handshakes and welcomes from road friends take place. The Stables, the local band, load up on stage and start sound check. They have played this place before, and so getting their washtub bass with a hockey stick for a neck to sound good takes very little time. They finish sound check, and more beer is consumed as we talk shit about other bands we have crisscrossed with over the last year. The Stables did the tour several times, and it was our pleasure to follow them a few times cross-country. There is pleasure showing up at a club and seeing the posters of the other bands that are on the same tour, on a day-to-day basis checking their progress, their tour weaving slightly different than your own, their band having found slightly different places to play in certain areas than you. Of course, we would have only played with the Stables in Montreal or Oshawa. In Montreal, we could locally support them, and in the Shwa they could support us. The bull session continues till show time as strategies and lies about the two bands' travels volleys back and forth. This exchange is what I always lived for, two road bands talking shop.

The night gets out of hand early as the Stables take the stage. The small Thursday crowd, drunk even at ten-thirty, start, bopping about and slamming to the punk folk styling of our opener. A brief respite taken to smoke, and we hit the stage to a small but ardent crowd. This is a newbie show for us, probably the first time we have played for them, although not the first time they have heard of us. As we play for the first time in this roughed-out club, the folks are singing along, a sign that folks in Oshawa have searched us out. This is a town that has a scene, a scene that has folks looking around for other stuff that isn't on the radio. They sing along, they dance, pogo, and drunkenly lightly slam their way through our set. At the end of the night, there is back-clapping, handshakes, and a bunch of people buying our CDs and saying they are here to buy 'cause they had downloaded it two years ago, but now want the money to go to us. Keep coming back.

We didn't. The Shwa, I feel as though I failed you. You did bring it out, although a small crowd. It took me years to get around to booking you, and then we never got the chance to return. I'm sorry for that, but just after being through your town, we got signed by a big-time booking agent, and Oshawa fell off their map. When I have to do it again, I will. Given a chance, I think this town could very well build to a decent-paying night. The folks who came out were the cool kids, the intelligentsia of the scene. It's a city beyond most, so play the Shwa.

Central location

It's 2:15 a.m., and we make our way back out to the 401 for the trip back to Trevor's. The traffic is light for the most part, and the time between two and four a.m. is the only time you will see this stretch of highway sparsely occupied. Even the stretch across the top of Toronto, excluding the summer months when they do all the construction, zips along with few holdups. This two-hour window, just after the evening traffic dies down—yeah, no shit, the evening rush lasts till two a.m.—and the four a.m. truck traffic starts, allows you to jump back over to your safe haven relatively quickly.

If you don't have a safe haven, finding a cheap mom and pop motel to give you a weekly rate and basing your operations out of this area might actually work. Choose a ground, level affair, someplace in which to park safe or at least someplace to back the van up against to avoid unloading every night, or, that aside, an easy load in to accoms. It sounds crazy doing the drive every night back to the same place, but finding new digs every night, dealing with security of gear, loading your bags every day, all adds hours to your day. Central location really works if all the needs are met. And centrally locating yourselves does give you a little better leeway when booking to make sure you are playing the right towns on the right night.

For instance, all clubs are going to want you on Friday or Saturday. You really can't hang around Southern Ontario for three weeks trying to get all the shows in, so here is my thought. Hamilton must be played on Friday or Saturday because those folks really do work at five a.m., so they aren't coming out to see you on a Wednesday night. Peterborough needs a Friday generally, and Oshawa no earlier than Thursday. Toronto can get done any night, really, although Sunday and Monday are going to hurt some. Kitchener and Brantford, as already stated, could be pulled off mid-week, although Kitchener only after you've made yourself known there, and Brantford with a local opener.

Once again, finding a place to stay that is easy to get in and out of will give you the chance to book these places in an orderly fashion, spreading out like a rose to hit all the clubs easily and not worrying so much to do them all in a linear order like the rest of your tour. Certainly, after hauling ass all the way across the country, the thought of having to haul from Oshawa to just outside of Hamilton, taking forty-five minutes at two a.m., even if it takes more than twice that during the day, will seem pretty luxurious.

Back at Trevor's, we break into our squirreled-away beer stash, the stuff that got hidden away till today's big official box was gone, and maybe a mickey or a hip flask comes out to put that last bit of booze in you to take the buzz from the road and your show off your brain. This is late in the tour, so the big parties are behind you. Winding down, at this point you are merely maintenance drinking. If this was your first trip or you are in your early twenties, you might actually be worried about your drinking at this point, but several tours later, you realize this is your life and brush it off. A couple of beers in you, maybe a board game, and you are off to bed and don't need to be back in the van til, say, five p.m. tomorrow.

The Hammer: Hamilton, Ontario

Ah, the Hammer, the beleaguered, the looked-down-upon, the gritty, the seat of all things organized crime. Once upon a time, this industrial hub was the biggest Canadian industrial mob west of Montreal. But it has seen its share of downturn, with the successive governments of the last thirty years doing everything they could to put the kibosh on its life. From the anti-labour governments at the end of the 1880s to the current pro-American Tory agenda, this town has taken on all comers, and now seems poised to be the next big cultural mecca. As the alternative city to the vastness of Toronto, old Hamilton, in its recent post-industrial phase, is attracting all the smart kids. Sitting here at home in Montreal, I have been wondering where the next big scene is going to spring up, and the smart money is on the Hammer. It's forty-five minutes out of Toronto, the rent is half, and there are six towns within an hour's drive to play. Add to that a couple of decent venues in town and an art scene that is really coming into its own.

For our band, Hamilton was always a tough slog except for the last two years when This Ain't Hollywood opened. Before that, we had been playing in a place downtown, a restaurant, and it seemed like every time we went there twenty-odd folks would come out to see us, and then four months later, a different twenty-odd folks would show up, and then later on, more of the same. It just seemed that we couldn't manage to get all the folks who liked us, which seemed to be a substantial number, into the room all on the same night. Then Hollywood opened and they all seemed to come out en masse.

It must be said that we have always had a great amount of support from the steelworkers union there. The boys at Local 1005 actually bought two boxes of our first CD and even booked us to play at Copps Coliseum for a steelworkers rally. This when we were only three years into our career. Yes, the union folks did us fine, but never so fine as our last trip to Hamilton.

It was stuck on to the end of our last western tour, in early spring a couple of years ago. The Local 1005 was on a lockout from Stelco, or what Stelco had become, U.S. Steel Canada. U.S. Steel had locked them out after a long, protracted court battle dealing with the "buy American" policies of the American legislature of the day, as well as a long battle over the company's trying to steal the union's pension, which the union won. So, here are all these guys locked out, they have the tents, and pickets all set up at the closed-down foundry, and they want us to come down and give a concert for them. I must admit, we were daunted by the idea, but we knew that they were giving us the chance to do what Pete and Woody had done fifty years ago when they played the gates of Stelco, so we stuck our chins out and played a show for them.

This was not a massive rally. There were maybe fifty or sixty people there, there was no PA system, and we stood on some plywood underneath the overpass across the street from the gates. It was cold and our fingers hurt on the strings as we acoustically belted out our most worker-friendly material.

Post-show, the folks all came over and shook our hands and thanked us for coming down. The day was sombre but heartfelt. The fact that we did this on one of our last cross-Canada tours seemed very fortuitous, near the end of this long road we had inadvertently started ten years before, after that fateful day when Sean B'y Moore offered up the name the United Steel Workers of Montreal. I told the guys that were in the band at the time, "Hey, I hope you know that if we name ourselves after a union, I think we can probably expect to end up having to play shows for unions and left-wing causes and such." They all said, very off-hand, "Yeah, sure, whatever. I like the name." I liked the name too, and that fateful day was the start of the road that led us to Hamilton on a cold and rainy day to play for some workers while standing under an overpass, a place that it is rumoured that Pete and Woody played.

Over the years, the members of our band had many fights over politics with some pretty heated discussions, but in the end, there on that day, I looked around and for the most part almost the entire band was proud to be there. I was very proud to be there. To most in attendance, it was probably a reasonably forgettable show, but for me it was a high point in my career. A lot of people who have picked up an acoustic guitar have been drawn to music by folks like Woody Guthrie and Pete Seeger. Some may have had an easier time, a more comfortable time, with the music, looking past the inherent message of going down the road feeling bad, just thinking of it as, say, a blues tune, but I always saw it as a work tune, and a workers' tune. To the folks who bristled at singing the song "Union Maid," I say I gladly sing the song for its content as well as its handy tune and fun lyrics. I believe in this stuff, and I got to add my two cents to the debate with my own work tunes, in a place rumoured to be where Pete and Woody played theirs.

This land is your land, this land is my land, and I didn't know it was a pinko commie tune until much later in my life, but now I know, this land is your land, this land is my land. The day was definitely a high point on my road.

Back in the van, we ran the maze of Hamilton's difficult topography and found ourselves back at the front doors of This Ain't Hollywood. This is a place that was definitely an old-man bar back in the day, a gin mill, a place that probably didn't allow women into it until at least the mid-seventies. These old places haunt the cityscapes of most Canadian cities, their owners for whatever reason never updating them, possibly using them as a shelter for tax reasons, or some other den of vice that is less than savoury. These heavily romantic places nestle on the rim of working-class neighbourhoods, most of which have gone away. I have my eye on a couple of them in Montreal that I am waiting to come up for rent. The boys down here in Hamilton managed to get their hooks in one, and away they have run. They are not the only place to play in town, but they have managed to garner if not solidify a lot of support from the burgeoning music and arts scene. They do the tried and true mix of local bands and road shows that find their way through town, and although it can be said the place is best played on weekends, they are slowly but surely changing that and raising a crowd of fans that can be expected to support any night of the week soon.

Doug Smith greets us at the door. Doug is *the* soundman

and rivals Ian Dearborn of Saskatoon as being the most likely to have become the seventh Steel Worker. We know Doug from the days when we played Pepper Jack Cafe. We grew to respect Doug because Pepper Jack was a tough room. Behind the stage was a two-storey glass wall, and the room it projected into was a low-ceilinged, tile-floor affair, with a big old structural column, about eight feet in diameter right in the middle of the dance floor. You couldn't have found a worse room to do sound in, and Doug made us sound great there. I don't honestly know how. When Peppers folded up and all the kids streamed over to This Ain't Hollywood, we were very glad to see Doug land there too. From right then and there, our shows in the Hammer started going real well.

Doug plugs us in, and sound check is short and sweet, even with a bad amp. Gus's beleaguered Ibanez 30-watt, an amp we got on a deal from Ibanez for being low-end famous, picked this sound check to check out. I had its twin, and we had been running them on thirteen for a couple of years. Post-show, upon inspection, we found that the speaker cone just finally completely detached itself from the magnet. "Upon further examination" meaning we flung the old girl across the green room, where she ended her tour of duty. I think we paid something like $50 a piece for those amps, and they were great little amps, albeit very much smaller than we should have been using. They really took the rock and roll beating as we shoved a ton of acoustic thudding through them. Rest in pieces.

Springing into action, Doug reroutes Gus into a DI, and we go with monitors for him. It must be said that Gus had been having a lot of equipment issues on that tour, and by the end of the night, his Taylor guitar had to be replaced by my mini Martin. I finished the set on the bar guitar, a baby-blue Strat that was probably the heaviest guitar I have ever wielded, and the first electric guitar I ever played onstage in front of people. I've since opened my career up to electric, but it must be noted that it was not that night or that baby-blue Strat that did it for me.

Post-show, hanging around on the patio with a slew of locals, a varied collection of musicians, artists, unionized factory guys, non-union guys, and a couple of hipsters thrown in, folks we had been collecting for years here in the Hammer and its environs, smoking and drinking and sitting around on a nice night. Man, it's good to have found a home in a town that I have wanted to have a home in for years. Sit back and watch it grow, folks.

Petertown: Peterborough, Ontario

Bidding goodbye to our saviour, Trevor, we head out once again across the top of Toronto. The traffic is predictably bad, and the brake-light festival continues all the way across the top, through the Rouge Valley and past Pickering, the town that glows with radiation, sulphur lights, and the ghost of the man I refer to as "the old man." Eddy Blake shouts "nuke," getting one more point on his collection belt, and we wing our way through Ajax, and then the Shwa once more. Its dirty brown outskirts morph almost unnoticeably into Bowmanville, and then we get to Clarington, where we exit onto the 115, the highway to the Kawarthas. A quick rip up this affair finds you running through scruffy farmland, forests, and a non-stop dotting of single-storey homes tucked back off the service road to the highway. These are the bedrooms of

Toronto, and this region is rife with the folks who believe that spending fifteen to twenty hours a week sitting in your car listening to classic rock is a just add-on to earning a living. These folks have managed to make themselves believe that it is worth it to do all that driving rather than just try and make a go of it in the country. The whole region is rife with the stress created by half of the towns' residents living in their cars, probably spending more time there than they do in the town they call home.

The highway ends in Peterborough, the outer limits of the distance folks will travel in which to gain employment in the city of smoke. Unfortunately, this town marks the gateway to the Kawartha Lakes, a massive band of cottage country that extends 250 kilometres to the north, west, and east of this mid-sized community. That fact creates even a larger influx of traffic come the weekend, and even more so come summer's long weekends.

That apart, Peterborough manages to have stayed a pretty good place all these years, being only a stone's throw and a bad commute to the T.dot. "Petertown," coined by Roger Dawson (second bass) oh so many years ago, is also known as the Patch or P-town. It's a university town, home to Trent University, and the downtown boast, five or six music venues, a slew of restaurants, cafés, and a couple of thousand musicians. No shit, this town is filthy with music. Like Hamilton, it's within a quick jump to play a Friday night show in the city, but its property values and rents are far below that of Toronto. As well, the university seems to give it lifeblood culturally.

Having said that, I will take this time to mention for the first time in this entire book that I'm not sure why universities manage to help the scenes across Canada, since in all our travels, we have seen precious few students at any of our gigs. Maybe it's that the school keeps the locals from leaving en masse come high school graduation. Most places breed the kids in such a way that once grade 12 is attained, you are either staying or going. In university towns, I guess that just is not so cut and dried, and some of the university's graduates will hang around too and start actually adding to the culture of these towns…I think.

Peterborough is the town that we have played more than any other town in Canada, besides Montreal. Our first tour, way back in the day, found us doing a non-stop fourteen shows in fourteen days rip from one end of Ontario to the other. On that tour, we did two shows with a bunch of kids. Well, they were kids at the time, and I'm pretty sure about half the band weren't even of drinking age.

Filly found them as she randomly searched the Web for local bands, and when we called them, the United Steel Workers of Montreal calling the Unionist Ministers, it all just seemed to fit. Those guys actually booked us two shows with them, one at the Sunrise Café and one at the Spill. Wow, our first two-nighter.

We showed up at the café, which turned out to be a renovated Harvey's restaurant, early evening and loaded in. We started plugging into a very rudimentary PA only to be stopped mid-plug and told that we should wait for the Ministers, 'cause they would be opening for us. We dutifully set our gear aside and waited. Not that much longer after that, they started arriving, and arriving. We really didn't know that much about these guys. We knew they were young and knew they had a slew of instruments, but that was about it. Well, they started plugging in, obviously all of their instrument requirements were not met by the PA, so some of them were just playing acoustically and some through the board. It was pure chaos, wires strung everywhere, mics screeching, instruments tuning, arguments, brown bagging, and test, test, check, check over a cacophony that continued for thirty minutes. At some point, we realized that they were actually on their third song. It worked as a stage show, or it just kind of culminated into a show after a fairly drawn-out plug and play, never really announcing that they were starting. This would later become known to us as the way the Ministers worked. Most of the band didn't want it to work that way, but nevertheless it did.

We finished off the two shows with these guys, our hosts to the Peterborough scene, and that started off a relationship with these young miscreants that lasts to this date. Now the band consisting of Mike Duguay, Bryar Gray, Cory Mumford, James Plouffe, Max Power, Ben Rough, and others grew from these beginnings, later known as the post — Silver Hearts era of Peterborough. These kids became all that Peterborough became, spinning band after band. The Patch being a small town, most of these dudes did time in any number of bands, and it is these kids that I remember from our first show in town. I have subsequently seen, and toured with, them all over the world. Having played many shows with Peterborough's own the Burning Hell, it is easy to forget that I first met Mike Duguay at that Sunrise gig eight years ago, or running into Ben Rough in Montreal at the bar I work in, or seeing Bryar Gray backstage at a festival side-manning it for some loudmouth from TO. Plouffe makes it through town with his

Shotgun Wedding Band a couple times a year, and it is always nice. Man, those kids, now approaching age thirty, are everything Peterborough ended up meaning to us.

As I've said, I grew up in Cobourg, Ontario, many years ago, a town that kind of forced me out. I wanted to stay there. I tried hard, returning back from Toronto every couple of years and really giving it a good go. I was a Cobourg boy and always saw myself settling in with a good job, a wife, raise some kids, pay off the car, and kick back. Cobourg and its surrounding area leaves no reason to own a cottage, or commute. The treed wilderness abounds, and the topography is idyllic. Yet, even in my early twenties, the town just kept offering me none of those pesky things one needs, like a job, companionship, or stability. My family was "come from away" sorts: my mom and dad brought us up from Ohio in the early seventies, and even after my father died at the age of thirty-seven, and my mother remarried "the old man," even he was from Toronto, so we had no nepotistic hold on the area. Folks who were from there got the jobs 'cause their father got them their jobs. "The old man" wasn't from there, so the opportunities did not abound. The opportunities that went along with the job—a car, a house, and actually a wife—were also pretty scarce too. It was a hard old life for the "from away" kid, and I found myself breaking the cycle of Toronto dependency by moving in one fell swoop to Montreal. The pull of the area is still great for me, though, and it is my memories of Saturday nights spent in Peterborough at a roller rink that have me drawn to her loins.

The town dates back for me that far. When you are sixteen and just got your license, Toronto is way out of your grasp. But Peterborough, well, that is a town, and we flocked there, as did many kids from the far-flung small towns surrounding it. Peterborough is a second city to be sure.

When I was nineteen or twenty, I was a roadie for some friends of mine in a band called China N Guns. They were the typical university types, broke and carless, so I was brought on to help haul their rhythm section up from Toronto to play their show at the Underdog. The drums and bass cab easily squeezed into my 1977 Caprice Classic. Once there, I had never been witness to things so cool in my life. I knew these guys 'cause they were friends of my brother, and they had a band in high school, but their university days saw them taking their band seriously, and I really liked their stuff. I saw a lot of their shows in and around Toronto, but I remember hauling their gear to the club in Peterborough and helping them set up in the basement of the Red Dog, a space called the Underdog. The club wasn't packed, but they did get a pretty good crowd, and they knocked it home that night to a late-eighties bunch of college-type hipsters. I was duly impressed and later started my second band, the Po-Folks, with China N Guns', bass player, Dayle Stolicker. It was a duo, actually, and we had a cassette tape that eventually became part of my first CD, entitled *Gern f.: Why I don't write*. I have realized only now that what has become the whole of my life was just trying to get me back to the Underdog.

The twelve, or fifteen-year absence between then and that first show we had at that café saw the town bump along, me oblivious of it and it of me. They had some grand times surviving the cultural wars of the eighties and nineties, once again spared by the fact that Peterborough is a university town. If not for bands like the Silver Hearts, however, the town might have blown away in spite of its affiliations. When glancing at the town, mid-two-thousands say, from the rickety hay wagon that served as a stage for the Backmeadows Music Festival, a two-day event that took place at James Plouffe's parents' farm, of fifteen bands on the bill, ten of them local, one could easily see that the Silver Hearts were big, unwieldy, and completely out of place for their time. The late nineties really wasn't ready for a band with an accordion, a tuba, and two theremins. But this band touched off what I refer to as the Peterborough Sound. The Silver Hearts, which still exists on a part-time basis, only ever did one real tour, and generally, by all accounts, the first and most influential version of the band died just as soon as it was getting known, but they influenced everyone they touched. They not only made every band in Peterborough sound like a crazy bunch of acoustic insanity, but those bands, having made it past the beginning stages and touring, set off what I would say became a lot of the Canadian indie scene we have today. I am willing to go out on a limb and say that if they don't sound like Blue Rodeo, then you will find their roots in the Hearts. Yep, few people have even heard of these guys, but their unique power infested everyone it touched, even our own band, who actually started two years before any of us had ever seen them. One trip across Canada and some well-placed shows here and there over a couple of years, and gone in Canada were the three-piece rock bands. Everybody now needed an accordion, a fiddle, and something else weird to stick in their band. Suddenly, it was all different, and all bands had to be big, at least a six-piece, and that became the new way things went.

That all came out of Peterborough, and keep in mind that Blue Rodeo has their studio up near town too, so that is like saying Peterborough changed it all, and for the most part without anybody even knowing it.

We load into the Red Dog, which is upstairs from where the Underdog used to be. It's close enough for me. Sound check goes bad on some seriously bad Peavey mics. We get ours done, and the local opener comes in. It's the Burning Hell, and Mathias pulls me aside and says, "Hey, this is gonna be great tonight, but, man, this should have been booked at the Montreal House. That's where everybody is going these days." It's the two-venue-town paradox again, and the show goes off great. I'm sure it would have been better at the Montreal House. Back in the day, the Burning Hell gave a twelve-piece rock show featuring two bass players and a full horn section. More on how bands stay together later. The Hells, back then and now, are a force to be reckoned with. We have toured with them a fair amount, with road shows here in Canada and in Europe, and in many of the band's incarnations, it is best suggested to not have to follow them. Their live show is that good. They will wear you out as they are slaughtering the audience with killer alternative pop tunes, amazing stage banter, and every trick in the book including, I think, fire from time to time. While they play, you should be backstage, okay, back alley, stretching, warming up, and throwing in a couple of Hail Marys just to be sure. You take the stage, and the audience is that worst-case scenario. They are hyped up and ready to go but now not the least bit easy to please. You really want to bring your best guns out for this show. Having done maybe twenty shows with these guys over the years, and maybe having to follow them, say, half the time, I'd say we managed to not embarrass ourselves at least eight of those times. Keep in mind, we had a lot of fun on the other ten shows where we opened for them, making sure they had a hill to run up. I loved playing with these guys. If you follow them and don't get booed, then you are a good band. They are a good band, and I love every one of them…all thirty-five different members I've seen over the years.

This night in Peterborough was one of the nights we followed them, and thanks to their energy, we blasted right through our set, and the night was memorable to all. And this just one flight up from where it all started for me, years before. It was the place that gave me the bug, the place I saw how it worked, the place where I figured out, hey, anybody can do this. I think I might try.

Lying low

You wake up on a floor in Peterborough. It's Sunday, so splash some water on your face and get down to the Only before they stop serving breakfast. Over eggs you, decide where to kill the next couple of days. Your next gig is in Cobourg on Tuesday night, so there is here, on some more dirty floor, having promised someone in a band from town that you would put them up in Montreal, or say in your home town next time through. Go find some relative in the area—come on, this is the centre of the universe! You have relatives in Ontario, everyone does. The other option is that it is still off-season, so maybe surf around online and find a cottage rental place that is open and cheap because it's still early and folks don't want cottages on Sunday and Monday night. We pretty much had most of the above covered over the years, so I don't have greater insight than that on hiding out. Like I said, there are a lot of bands in Peterborough, and most of those bands tour, so alliances made in advance could really help. With all this in mind pre-tour, maybe when you see bands coming through your town, be proactive and introduce yourself to them and offer them a place to stay. Peterborough is a place you will pass through, and folks from there will pass through your town.

Cobourg, Ontario (hometown)

Well, I certainly have been scornful of this old town throughout this book. Sorry, Cobourg: you have been my whipping boy here, and you probably don't deserve it. I've discovered that most small towns in Canada suffer the same ills and do the same damage to their young. But what small-town boy who goes to the big city has anything nice to say about home? If we spoke highly of our past, then we would come dangerously close to acknowledging that moving away could have been a mistake. Maybe I should have stayed in Cobourg and made it better. Maybe I should have put all my energy into developing a venue, promoting shows, putting up bands as they travelled across Canada, and using my skills to build rather than tear down. Yeah, I should have. I should have stood against your ills, looked your demons in the eye, wrestled the town council, and fought the good fight. I did not. I am sorry. I apologize to those who stayed, tried, and failed. Mind you, then you would have had to hear me ranting for the last twenty years, and now I would probably be apologizing for that in these pages. So, well, there is that.

Pulling up in front of J&J Steak and Burger on Elgin

Street, my mind is in disarray; I know this place to be on the other side of town, but that location on William is now a fish and chip joint. To be honest, I am doing all this online as I sit in a café in Montreal. I haven't been to J&J's since it moved, but that said, I pull up out front and we enter. The floors are tiled, the decor sparse and prematurely aged. Once again, I'm guessing here. I walk up to the counter, and a young Greek teenager takes my order. Cheeseburger and onion rings, with a can of root beer. I feel comforted in the fact that even though this place has moved, it is exactly as it always was.

This is mid-Ontario, and every town has one or even a couple of them. It's the non-franchise fast food restaurant run by a Greek guy, and in this town, it's JJ, or J and his other brother J. I've never met the man, but I think I have seen him. Late-forties, looking dude, muscular physique, good hair, tanned even in January. There are gold chains, rolled-up short sleeves showing off muscular arms, and a friendly but businesslike manner. He is the ringleader here—not usually on cash, sometimes on the grill, a lot of the time working the phone. He leads his troops, two young men, maybe eighteen or nineteen. Kids you never knew in school, kids that have migrated here from, probably, Oshawa and doing time in their uncle's restaurant. Also there is a dyed-blonde woman in her late fifties working the cash, and some old guy mopping up. They are a team as they sling out a non-stop cornucopia of simple fast food. Harvey's has stolen its menu from these places. J and J, or JJ, have those unmistakable frozen hamburgers grilled on the gas flame. Yep, Harvey's stole this from mid-Ontario, and then dumbed it down and made all the portions smaller and thus less satisfying. I'm not kidding; folks from Ontario are all with me here. I'm not sure where these great guys, with their burger joints, get their food, but it all tastes like Harvey's except better. It's weird, like a secret franchise, a subtle franchise, but it is all the same. Their fries are hand cut, their frozen onion rings are the large, skinny kind, and their pickles garlic dill, always cut lengthwise, the way God intended.

I get the cheeseburger with ketchup and mayo, and my pickles on the side. The cardboard box is overflowing with the onion rings, and I stop beside the garbage container to fill the side of the box with ketchup. Sitting by the steamed-up front window watching the traffic go by, a background of bad radio and food orders. Having talked about fish and chips all through this book, going on and on about breakfasts, but, yes, it is the Greek burger joint that I go right to whenever I'm in town. It doesn't even have to be JJ's because there are four places in Cobourg that are identical to this place. In our small-town big-otry we all believed they were owned by the same guy, but who knows? Maybe they are. We don't know 'cause we just eat at these places and rarely get to know the owners, or the employ-ees. These places are staffed by family, I think, so no one you went to school with worked there. It's all just speculation.

Lunch done, you head for the gig. Although I have ac-cused Cobourg of being devoid of music, there are some gigs to be had, sort of, under certain conditions. The first is Kelly's Bar, my local, my old-man bar, and the bar I aspired to drink at when I was eighteen and still illegal. It's a bar I long to drink at to this day. This old-man bar with its separate male and fe-male entrances, a tradition that died out only in the late eight-ies when the second generation of Kellys started taking over.

The pickled-egg bar, the bar with one draft tap, although I'm sure that has changed too. But still, Kelly's is still Kelly's. The original owner's son, Pete (I think), having seamlessly taken over years ago. In the last while, Pete has started booking shows. I have not been able to play there, although I really wanted to, but, alas, reality says that those shows are only on Friday or Saturday night, and this show is really not going to be successful enough to warrant a Friday night on your tour. But if you do have a dangling weekend, give them a go.

There are a couple of venues in Cobourg. The Oasis Bar and Grill is a small, very small, restaurant that will occasionally do a dinner show thing. We had a lot of fun there with me finally getting to play in front of my high school chums, and random locals, my first hometown show.

The Oasis is the place where I got my all-time favourite show thrill. Here we are, playing in front of friendlies, and I'm going on and on between songs, really painting a picture of the folks that I have written about in my songs, Cobourg having played a huge part of my songwriting. Specifically, I am setting up a song called "Small Town Banks," which is about three guys I knew from grade school who, in their late teen years, decided to rob banks as a summer job. They didn't do too well since the banks they robbed were pretty small-time. It is rumoured that they netted very little money and eventually got caught.

I took this story and made it a little bigger, mentioning that the spree lasted for two day, because the three small-town banks were only open on odd days. On the days they were closed, the staff were sent to the next town up the road to work at the other bank. This was, in fact, how it worked back in the day. So I spun it into "Imagine the surprise Mary Ferguson went through when she got robbed on Tuesday in Grafton, a traumatic experience I'm sure, only to be robbed by the same guys on Wednesday in Colborne." I closed the story by saying that the boys were eventually picked up at the Grafton Softball Tournament Dance, which takes place at the end of the summer. This dance is definitely the social high-water mark of the year, a not-to-be-missed event. It's so unmissable that even these three lads showed up, and were arrested by off-duty O.P.P. officers who where being employed to work security.

I had told this story many times, and I am not even sure how much of it is based in reality. However, it's one thing to tell this story all over the country and get laughs and what not, but here I am going on like I normally would, and here tonight there are actually folks in the room who were there back then. Folks who were well acquainted with the folks in the story. So, yup, pretty much one beat after concluding the story, a comment arose from the bar, a semi-muffled reply.

"Hey, maybe it's not good to go talking about folks that are still doing time, folks that are getting out soon." That said, two, maybe three, beats of uncomfortable silence and an instant bead of sweat running down my brow as we plunged into the song. That comment was rolling through my head as I ran through a song I had sung hundreds of times, giving it new meaning.

It was later, after the show, that I ran into the man who had made that comment. He meekly approached me with the "you probably won't remember me" opening line. This was a guy who wasn't one of my friends in school, but I did know him, and he was actually a friend of the guys I had just gone on about. I've always had a goldfish memory, but, surprisingly was able to blurt out, "Hogger!" He blushed a little, having eluded that nickname years ago, and I was actually expecting him to kind of start giving me shit about bad-mouthing folks he grew up with, but he didn't. He just told me the story of how he had arrived at the show that night. "I was just walking down the street and saw the sign The United Steel Workers of Montreal Tonight," he said. "You see, I'm a tin-knocker, unionized, with a local out of Oshawa, so the name just struck me, and I came in to see who was playing. It wasn't until halfway through that I figured out we had gone to school together. Good show, man."

I've had similar confrontations with folks from my past life over the years, but it is this one that takes the top prize of pride for me. The distance in time, the fact that nobody from my hometown even knew I played an instrument since I really didn't when I left, the fact I changed my name, gained 100 lbs, and aged twenty years. Most folks from Cobourg do not have a lot of access to indie music, so it has always been the greatest pleasure to be recognized by someone at a show who showed up 'cause they liked the music, only to later realize that they actually had long ago known me as another person. That is the fun stuff.

That night at the Oasis was my hometown play. The old friends who had never seen me play live got to. It's self-indulgent, I know, but it is the thing that drives music on a very sub-basement level. It's the feeling that, hey, yeah, I know you wouldn't sleep with me when I was seventeen and gross, and I don't blame you, really, because I was a mess, but, well, look at me now!

The Cat 'N' Fiddle doesn't do live music often, and even less so early to mid-week, but they did in fact host us once or twice. It's an English pub affair and the very first place I ever drank Guinness, underage I must now admit. A live show is kind of weird 'cause the place isn't really set up for it, but we did do a nice job of filling it up one Tuesday night.

Accommodation in Cobourg can be expensive, so it's a good idea to ask the place that booked you about a room deal. That aside, my favourite place to stay in town is the Breakers Motel on the Lake. This renovated motel, located on the beautiful Victoria Park Beach, can be the cheapest accoms in town but in the off-season only. Come spring, the rates climb, but off-season, these folks are very accommodating, and the rooms are nice. If you end up staying in the rooms on the east side of the parking lot, peer out the windows and into the backyard of my independence. The house located right behind the motel is one of the only good apartments I ever had in Cobourg. I spent two years in that ground-floor granny flat, the only apartment I ever had that had a pool. We drank a lot of beer in that backyard, located just steps from the beach, and that beach was where I learned to play guitar and sing. The usual Saturday night was to return home post-bar at two a.m., drunk and dejected from striking out with the local girls, and grab my guitar and head alone for the beach. I would stand on the deserted beach and belt Pogues tunes into the surf for an hour or so before the local security staff would eventually roll by and tell me to go home. That is the backdrop of my young adult life: rejection, repression, and drunkenness, and then I became a road musician.

Colborne, Ontario: who wants pie?

Making your way out of town, take Highway 2. You are
not in a hurry, and Kingston is only 250 kilometres up the
road. Take this chance to find out what Ontario looks like
when you're not ramming yourself down the 401 at 112 kph,
sticking close to the guy in front of you, eyes peeled for stray
O.P.P. who are looking to give you a speeding ticket. Nah,
you have time, so take the two-lane. On Highway 2, you will
pass out of Cobourg heading east and roll through the small
town of Grafton, where I went to school as a young, awkward
boy. Moving along, you will pass through Wicklow, and just
after passing the Wicklow General Store, on your left, or the
concrete pad that used to be the general store, a little farther
up, look right and you will see Knight's Appleden, a long tin-
covered building, an apple warehouse. Round the back, you
will probably see a bunch of big, shiny, red tractor-trailers. I
drove unit number six for a few good years of my life. That
was a long time ago, but my guess is that truck is still kicking
around. Old man Knight never got rid of anything, and generally kept his trucks in top nick too. Don't scratch that
bumper or you're fired!

Bombing along Highway 2, you will eventually run into
Colborne, where you'll have to slow down. Bank on into town
and get down past the LCBO, then hang a left around the
park, and there on the corner of Percy Street will be the
Queens Hotel. They haven't had shows in there since I can
remember, but it is a good example of the small-town hotel
bar I've been going on about. Hang a left on Percy and exit
town north back towards the 401. A mile or so up the road,

just before you get to the 401, you will see an Ultramar gas station on your left. Just after that is Orchard Road, so hang a left on it, and the first driveway maybe take a right and into the parking lot of the Big Apple.

Every trip you take between Toronto and Montreal, you will pass it. The Big Apple. You will see it, that big fifty-foot tall fiberglass offering to a forty-storey-tall Adam, a present from a forty-storey-tall Eve. It's the forbidden fruit, a land-mark the locals refer to as "that big cock-suckin' apple up there by the highway." Let's stop here and get some pie.

Here's the story as I know it. I once knew a guy named Groovy…yep, Groovy. He owned a trucking company just up the road there. You passed it on the way in. The building says Durham Transport, and I believe that business was actu-ally owned by one of Groovy's brothers or a father or uncle or someone. I didn't know Groovy that well. I did a couple of runs for his company, National Freightways, back in the day. He had a bunch of trucks, the old-fashioned kind, the shiny ones. Groovy liked shiny trucks, but most people did, I guess, shinier the better. So here is Groovy, and, no, I don't know why they called him Groovy, but they did call him that to his face, so there's that. So he's running this big shiny trucking company, and as I heard it, his wife was all getting tired about never seeing him, him always down at the yard polishing his big trucks. Well, Groovy got tired of the nagging, so he set his wife up in this business so as to keep her busy. He threw some money at it, and her idea was to make pies. Well, she did, and good pies at that, and a lot of them. Before you know it, she is selling more pies and making more money than Groovy ever did running shiny trucks up and down the road.

We are talking millions of pies, and the sign outside says so.

It took a couple of years, but, man, she really got that pie business going. It was no surprise a few years after that when I was driving by and noticed that all of Groovy's trucks were gone. I guess in the end she found a way to keep old Groovy home: make more money than him, a lot more.

I don't know if any of that story is true, but National Freightways is gone, and there is that "big cock-suckin' apple," so it's a good story that has a guy named Groovy in it, so... there's that.

Go on in, it's a big old place with a huge gift shop and a big cafeteria. The cool part is that the pie factory is behind glass just as you walk in, so you can watch the assembly line. It's kind of cool. Oh, and get some pie, it's great, and the apple cake is even better. Before you leave, make sure you run around to the other side of the building and see the Big Apple in all its glory. There is a museum inside, something to do with growing apples, or the neighbourhood history, or something.

After the pie, as you exit the restaurant and turn onto Orchard again, keep in mind that if you have a steel guitar player in the band, then you are going to be turning right on Orchard and run, that way for about a mile or two. On your right-hand side, somewhere around number 566 Dudley Road, which Orchard turns into after a while, you will see the Steel Guitars of Canada workshop. This is one of only a few steel guitar shops in all of Canada, but I probably don't have to tell this to anyone who has ever owned one of those finicky, impossible-to-understand instruments. If they own one and need a part, which they often do, it probably came from this guy. And yet it is here in Colborne, Ontario, just up past the pie shop.

Back on the road, you head east. Now you are running a little late 'cause you did all that f.'n around at the pie shop, the guitar shop, and back-roading, but everybody is filled up on sugar and they are happy as clams. The road rolls out in front of you as Kingston is getting closer.

Kingston, Ontario

Kingston has one and only one positive attribute: the Arby's. It is a sad attribute, due to the fact that most bands having tried Arby's once have had to make a rule about not going there again. It's sad. I love Arby's, with that fine, thinly sliced bit of roast beast magic, on that onion bun, the Arby's sauce so tangy and delicious. Trouble is, there is not a human alive who can pack down two of those sandwiches and not spend the rest of the day pungently farting their brains out. Well, it's the truth, and rules are rules. Arby's has unfortunately been relegated to the very few times I have passed through Kingston on my way to elsewhere and I am by myself, and of course it is warm enough out to have the windows down. That kind of works because usually the gas has passed sufficiently in the two and a half hours it takes you to get from here to either Toronto or Montreal. Just be kind and do not take in Arby's while travelling with another person. Or maybe, if you have managed to pick up a hitchhiker and you want to have some fun 'cause he got annoying somewhere around Brockville, but good manners has stopped you from saying so. Pull in, load up, and just blast his racist ass right out of the passenger seat. Hmmm... cool. I'm going to do that someday.

Now that's the upside of Kingston. Honest, that is the upside. The downside of Kingston is its many industries. Let's see: Queen's University, a military base, a military college, and five prisons. This pretty United Empire Loyalist town is a great place to come to on a class trip. Take the tour; it's pretty and whatnot. But come nightfall—you know, that time of the day when you play shows, when musicians live—and man, this town gets a wee bit scary. I was going to be nice here and just not mention Kingston at all, but the truth is you will end up playing here at some point, so I'd better give you the heads-up.

So it's night, and all the reasonable locals, of which I'm sure the town has many, all go home just before dark. Now it's the zombie apocalypse. With all the reasonable folks at home, locked in until morning, there is almost no one on the streets. Almost no one except the hordes of drunk university students, drunk military students, drunk military dudes, or the drunk prison guards, or the drunk parolees, or the drunk escapees. Wow, what a combination of revelry, each and every one of them just out boozing and ready for a fight. This is just not a comfortable town.

Fortunately for you, once you have gotten your gear into the club, you will not see these folks at your show, mostly 'cause nobody is going to be at your show. Doesn't matter how often you come through town, no matter how many local bands you play with, no matter who is now running the bar, no matter who is postering this show, or what radio station is talking about it, outside of the four relatives that it turns out your band has in town, and that one guy who buys vinyl on line and wears the black trench coat, nobody is going to come to your show.

Why are you here? Well, I'm not sure. The first trip

through town was bad, and every show after that was bad. Every time, the bar owner says, "Well, next time it will get better," or the soundman give an excuse, or says maybe your $5 cover was too high. It's terrible, but for some reason, even after my telling you this, you will be somehow tricked into playing here. Your agent will lie, saying the gig is in Paris, and at some point, you will plug it into your GPS and it will turn out it is not in Paris but in Kingston. In the end, this makes sense because who would book Cobourg, Paris, and then Ottawa? Man, I should have looked at that fine print. It will happen to you. At the end of the night, you will be handed $12, which is fair 'cause no one showed up. You will go check into the $120 a room chain motel with the mouldy walls and drink yourself into the unfounded belief that your band sucks and the even more unfounded belief that you will never play this town again, cause you will.

Up early from the possible bite of bedbugs, you get back in the van and get the f.' out of town. This is two slow nights in a row moneywise, and you need a gig to come through. You need folks to show up and want to see you play. You need a believer club, and fortunately you are heading for one.

Back-roading

Winding your way out of Kingston, it would be easy to just hop back on the 401 and head over to the recently built Highway 416. That is the way the GPS is probably going to take you. The 416 was a great idea, a highway that actually runs into the capital, but it's far more boring than driving cross-country.

The winding road unfolds, and you follow the GPS as the

road turns this way and that. It's beautiful farm country, and getting up this way can be quite idyllic. Hey, look, a hay barn. Bet you thought those were all torn down and sold to China. Well, not all of them, and thanks for noticing. Lots of cows up here. It is now in your trip that you realize that you are in cheese country. It's going to take some research to find them all, but there are a lot of cheese factories up this way, and if you did choose to take the cross-country method and you are heading up through Perth, plug Balderson, Ontario, into your GPS. At 1410 Lanark, or Highway 511, you will find Balderson Village Cheese & Country Store. Load up, baby. If you know this is going to be your stop, maybe go light on breakfast, grab some crackers and some juice, and spend the afternoon running up to Burnstown munching cheese and crackers. At some point, I will assemble a map of cheese factories, which should be superimposed across the touring map of Canada. Cheese factories are a great band stop. With the exception of the lactose impaired, everybody loves cheese, and most cheese shops have enough of a selection to intrigue everyone in the band as well as provide a lunch that is at least different from your usual burger stop.

Travel tip of the day: all cheese stops need rules. The first rule is everybody buys cheese and shares. The second rule is nobody is allowed to buy cheese that is older than three years. You are in a closed van, and cheese really starts smelling like baby shit once it passes the three-year mark. Now, a taste for poopy or foot cheese can be developed, of course. I myself can find it enjoyable in certain settings, with the right side dishes, maybe a nice full-bodied wine, and some coarse bread. The wrong place to open up a big pile of smelly-poop dairy product is in a van with five other people.

Please be kind and stick with the two-year-old. It's plenty strong, and don't even try smuggling the real old stuff in 'cause someone will find it and think it's a good idea to open it. There are rules, so stick to them.

Burnstown, Ontario

Rolling into Burnstown, a town of fourteen residents, two cafés, a couple of art galleries, and a church, you pull into the Neat Coffee Shop. The Neat is a dream. It's a dream for the owners, it's a dream for an indie band, and it's a dream for the townsfolk.

For its owners, it has also been a whole lot of work. They moved up here from Ottawa, I think, and looking for that dream in the country, they put that boring old big city that is our nation's capital in their rear-view mirror. Move out to the country, start a business, put ourselves on the map, have folks come to us instead of hiking it in to the big city, ending the commute to work to entertainment to culture. If you build it, they will come, and they did.

Although I don't know all the realities of opening a chi-chi little café out in the wilds of Central Ontario, I'm sure it starts with cashing in one's retirement fund, and in this case, buying an old schoolhouse and then putting every ounce of energy you have into the place. The Neat was one of those nineteenth-century one-room jobbies that used to dot the countryside. This one has been captured and reused and turned into a cultural centre for the town once again.

Located across from the church, the coffee shop is at the crossroads called Burnstown. It's not quite a village, maybe a hamlet. The Neat is open as a place to get coffee and baked goods during the day, grabbing the commuting crowd on their way into Pembroke, or even Ottawa. In the evening, they do dinner. They sell beer and wine, and the café, which operates out of the back of the schoolroom, provides an on-going business that keeps the place connected to the surrounding community. Once a month, the doors to the hall open wide, and the folks come in to see the bands.

It's a great arrangement. The bands who swing by have a great room to play in the hall with its high ceiling and antique surroundings. There's a homey, almost house concert feel, but grand enough to feel professional. The folks who may not have heard of your band trust the owners Kim and Adam to book acts that they will like, so night of show the folks from the surrounding area come into town. In a lot of cases, they come out for dinner, have a few beers, and then they take up their places in the big room, knowing they have saved themselves the trip into Ottawa, and they are here to be entertained.

The Neat Coffee Shop is a believer club. I think these folks hit the mark square on, I'd say better than anyone. They built it from the ground up. It is a unique experience, and this is not the main drag of a large city, this is rural Canada. According to the perceived wisdom of the music industry, this show should be worth nothing. This is not Toronto, there are no music labels here, and there is no press in the audience, just folks. These folks live out here, and Kim and Adam have been serving them coffee for a while now and have been talking up this band and that band. Those bands' music will be playing in the café, and the posters are up all over the walls. So come that night of the month, it could be a Tuesday or Saturday, but when that day comes around, the folks get off the couch and come out. The other thing the folks from around Burnstown do is pay to see the show. They figure if these folks are going to come all the way out here to play for us, I'm guessing they are going to need to get paid, so they reach in their wallets and pay. They saved the gas money that it would take to drive into the big town, and they saved the hassle. They all know, as most people do, that bands generally don't play Ottawa except for maybe the festivals, so they come here instead.

It's comfortable like a house concert, but unlike private homes, this place has the necessary equipment while still managing the intimacy that those house shows give. The Neat Coffee Shop is the guiding light in today's music scene. Almost every venue in Canada, from the stadium show to the 500-person venue to the struggling bar in a B town, can take a page from Burnstown. You have to be part of a community if you want it to work, if you want it to mean anything and be a success. If your place isn't bringing the folks in, it's 'cause you opened your doors and just expected folks to show up 'cause you are awesome. It doesn't work like that. To pry them away from Netflix, you have to go out and get them to come to your show. You start by opening the door, and you put up a sign that says *coffee*. Everybody in the free world drinks coffee, and you can do it while you drive. You come in to get your morning coffee, and while you wait, you are listening to music, and reading the poster on the wall. You ask the staff about it, and they say, "Yeah, these guys are good. We've been listening to them all week, and, oh, they are playing here as you can see in two weeks. It's only twenty dollars a head." You are thinking, "What? Twenty dollars? Man, that is like two months of Neflix. If I take my wife, that is $40 that I could pay my Internet bill with." They kind of grumble a bit and go out and get in their car and spend the next hour driving into Ottawa to work or just to go get something they need from the big city. They spend $35 on gas getting there and back, and by the time they get home, they are thinking, hell, driving into town was really not worth it. Then they sit at home for another week, and maybe they repeat this experience a couple more times, and then show night comes, and they are, "Hey, man, $20 to get into a show that is just up the road. I could maybe even hike the mile into town on foot, have a couple of beers, see the show, buy the CD, see my neighbours, and talk to that band in person probably." It's the slow pitch that does it.

This is how the Neat does it. Your bar on a B street in a B town maybe isn't going to find the commuting crowd, and maybe you don't want to sling coffee at seven a.m., but the idea is the same. Give folks a reason to come in often, inform them, educate them, and then drop the hammer on them and give them a good show. It is the constant interaction with your community that is going to fill your room up, that is going to get them to come out and pay for a show and get them to seek out these bands and become part of this unique experience that travels the country. This is the meat and potatoes of the Canadian industry, we are out there selling CDs and paying the bills. This is how you get big in the scene. Yes, getting on a label is great, maybe getting in the paper, playing an "it" show at one of the festivals, but you will be denied all of that if you are not out selling CDs and building your audience. It is places like Neat where you will actually build your career, playing shows in front of seventy-three people and leaving your disc in the hands of many, those individual CDs fanning out across the country, making people know who you are. It's stark, realizing that is how it works, knowing you are going to have to play a show for everyone in all of Canada, fifty to 150 people at a time, before you will get known enough to be anointed with an appearance on *Q with Jian Ghomeshi*. The scene and the industry have nothing to do with your being good, or witty, or talented, it is how much exposure you have managed to attain and how much success you have garnered on your own, and that is all. Yes, it does help if you are very good at songwriting, play a memorable show, have craft, but that is not actually completely necessary. Nope, it's the work, and how many times are you going to play these shows. The entire music industry, from big rooms, agents, record labels, media, and lawyers, will completely ignore you until you are making money, paying people, and showing to all who manage to see you that your band is viable. They will come on bit by bit as you move up the ladder, but the old rule of thumb is they will come on board only after you don't really need them. Until then, you will need places like the Neat Coffee Shop to help make sense of your realities.

From the stage of the big room of the Neat, I weave a tale of our travels, and we jump into the usual song and dance. The lights are bright, and the audience is front row, shoulder-to-shoulder, attentive. The song ends and folks applaud. They respond to the stage banter, and we are off on a new journey. This continues, there is a smoke break, and everybody refills their drink glasses, and we dance again for another hour. At the conclusion of the show, the good folks line up at the merch table and dig deep into their pockets. You shake hands, it's friendly, both they and you are comfortable. You were on the stage where you are used to playing shows, but the stage wasn't so high or so far from them as to separate you too much, just enough to give you room to perform. If you worked the room, you will find at the end of the night you have made a king's ransom from selling CDs and T-shirts. The folks from here probably have a music collection that would rival the average hipster who lives in the artsy part of the major cities. The farm guy is wearing a Luedecke shirt as he plows the fields, and the parents are slightly more in tune than their kids. It is a topsy-turvy world, this Burnstown. These believer clubs, they get the bands, and they put them in the touch with the folks, one band and one fan at a time.

The show over, the merch sold, the folks dispersing, Kim takes food orders from the band. They have a wonderful pizza oven, and it was our pleasure to make our own pizzas. This is a big thing for me. I never eat before a show, and I really can't sing if I'm even a little weighted down, so post-show I'm hungry as f. Getting to eat, and getting to eat real food, and getting to make my own pizza is just awesome post-show. We have a couple more beers while the pizza is cooking and get a good sit-down with the staff and owners. They pump us for info on the touring scene. Who is out there who is worth seeing, who would fit this venue, who wouldn't? We eat pizza, there is a drunken dance party, and our designated driver drives us back to our accoms. I'm not saying this is necessarily going to happen to you, but having won the coin toss among the band, I have actually slept in Kim and Adam's king-size bed, while they grabbed floor back at the café. That is hospitality. Keep in mind, it's a two-way street. I believe the band the Unsettlers actually got rooked into gardening with massive whiskey hangovers for a couple hours the day after playing their show. Work is done by everybody at the Neat, and it's nice when everybody's work actually is for everybody's benefit.

Ottawa, Ontario

Arriving in Ottawa in the late afternoon, you wind your way through town following the signs for Route 5. This town is a mishmash of roads. The locals say it makes sense, and perhaps it does if you spend enough time here to get to know it. You won't if you're a travelling band. There are precious few shows here. Other bands have said that there are some good shows to be had at the Avondale, but we never made it there. We have played the Bluesfest twice, which is a rock-solid gig. It's a big fest that goes on for ten days, it pays well, the accoms are great, the rider not bad, and an afternoon show will leave you wandering the streets of Ottawa wondering where the night life is and where to buy a sandwich at ten p.m.

Driving through town, you make your way through the impossible traffic and find yourself speeding up as you hit the bridge, the King Eddy, that will deposit you in Quebec. Don't forget to honk. Now you will have to pass back through town on your way to Montreal, so maybe it won't have that conquered feel that other provincial border crossings have. But you have rightly or wrong just snubbed Ottawa, which should be seen as your birthright as a Canadian, not only a Canadian indie musician. *Bonjour Québec, encore.*

Wakefield, Quebec

Rolling up in front of the Black Sheep Inn, it's late afternoon, and the parking lot is filled with the afternoon crowd. You back up as close to the front doors as the parking situation allows, fling the doors open, and start loading into your last out-of-town show of the tour. The gear gets tossed up on the long, low stage, the individual pieces set down by whoever in the exact place they are needed. The entire band by this point knows where every piece goes and the individual requirements of each of your bandmates. It's a dance you have now done fifty times in and fifty times out on this tour. Most days, this is a slog, but tonight you are playing your last show. There is a mix of "we will be home tomorrow!" and "oh, we will be home tomorrow." Either way, the one worry right now is not the show. You are tight and you are at the Sheep, so you probably don't have to worry about the crowd showing up.

Paul walks in with his pug dog in tow. You shakes hands, and you pass the time of day for about thirteen seconds, and he is off to attend to one thing or another. Paul is a busy guy, and Paul is well known for being either abrupt or intensely interested in whatever he is doing, and it switches around a lot. The key to Paul is not to worry about whether he is shaking your hand or walking away from you. Paul generally knows what he is doing.

Paul is the guy. He invented the believer club idea. The Canadian music scene was falling apart: bands had ceased travelling long distances, touring for small bands was dwindling, and the closure of the hotel bars was eating away at the number of live music venues. Even a city like Ottawa, which is a thirty-minute drive south of Wakefield, was having more than a hard time keeping live music going in the face of dance clubs and DJs. Along came Paul. Paul once told me, "I've never been to Toronto, and I hope I die having never made it." That is how this place came together. The utter gall it took to imagine that you could be part of the Canadian music scene and never step foot in Toronto. His take was, "I'm going to buy this old hotel and put shows on. I'm going to put the bands upstairs, I'm gonna hang posters on the walls, I'm going to harangue the press, I'm gonna go out there and get people to come to shows, and I'm gonna make folks realize that music is worth paying for, and I'm gonna give them a good show for their money, and I am gonna have it all happen at my place thirty minutes outside the city. You just see if I can't." Obviously, I'm paraphrasing a little.

The short answer is, he did. Years later, with this room that holds maybe 120 folks, in a small town with no real industry, and no great population base to fall back on, the Black Sheep gets every successful band touring Canada. Now, I don't mean Nickelback, but bands out on the club and small-venue tour, and even getting up to the bands that are pulling pretty big soft-seat gig, as well, successful bands, and getting-to-be-successful bands. There is a steady stream of talent. If you want to know who is on the road in Canada, check Paul's website. As well, there is a steady stream of music fans beating their way into town from the surrounding area and Ottawa and as far away as Montreal. I know our band has played Montreal on a Thursday night with a $7 cover, and the next night beat it on up to the Sheep to play a $15 show, only to find thirty Montrealers in attendance having passed up the cheaper and more convenient show to see us at the Sheep. It's a weird place that way. Folks like coming up here to see this place with the history of the bands that have passed through, the small-town feel, and the beautiful surroundings of a quaint town that make it one of our favourite out-of-town shows.

The years have left it a less-than-perfect show. The sound can be a little touchy, the stage lights can be a little dark, and Paul has, after some bad experiences, quit allowing bands to stay upstairs. The overall success of the place also makes it hard to get a booking here. So all of this adds up to its not being a hippie breeze of a show but always worth it. The fans who travel to see you are enthusiastic, the room is rife with good mojo, and the crowd can be right there for you to jump down offstage and lie on their table tops if need be. The money is always good. Paul has gotten these guys used to paying for shows, and he passes it along to the bands. Along with that, he staffs the merch table for you, and his staff give you a good breakdown of your sales. Those sales are usually very much on the high side of any show you are gonna play, even when you have played town several times and thought that everyone coming must have already bought your gear. They buy more. It's the promised land, built on the original idea that you can build these things almost anywhere. If it is somewhere near the main road of the touring scene, you can eventually find the audience to fill it. It takes work and it takes bands, lots of both.

Sound check squeaked and squawked through, you await the show. I remember the first time we played the Sheep. It was way, back for us, our first Ontario tour. The fourteen in fourteen tour, busting from one end on Ontario to the other, twice, I think, in a real pinball sort of way. It was just Ontario, but we put a ton of miles on a rental that trip. I remember we slogged through this pretty dismal tour, because touring in July without festivals is generally not going to be a great trip.

Here we were on the back end of the road, the final show, and we had this gig at the Black Sheep Inn booked for the Sunday afternoon 4:20 show. We were green. We didn't know the club, and we figured we'd just bust in there on the way home, play a set or two, and walk out with $50 and be home by nine p.m. We arrived at 3:30 and loaded in, did a quick line check. We sat on the balcony out front smoking, all worn out and not really feeling an afternoon show at the end of this grueling tour. Ten after four, and there were a couple of old guys hanging around inside drinking Labatt's 50. By now, we had just done thirteen shows, so we had an, "Oh well, let's just knock this last one off" sort of feel to it. Then 4:15 hit and twenty cars pulled into the lot, and the folks got out and just headed straight for the door. They lined up to pay, grabbed a beer, and at 4:19 Paul yelled, "Let's go, folks. If I put up a poster that says 4:20, then we start the show at 4:20. This ain't Montreal. We do our shows on time."

We hit the stage and played for an hour and a bit to, say, fifty-five-plus people, and then we finished up and did a two-song encore to folks banging on the table. We climbed down off the stage and made our way to the bar to get a much-deserved beer as we watched a line form for the merch table. This was back on the first album, and we had one disc and no shirts. We had never seen a lineup at the merch table before. CD in hand, the folks mostly headed out to make it home for Sunday dinner, with the knowledge that there would be another show next Sunday, and the band would be good, and if they didn't like the look of the Sunday band, they could come by Thursday night 'cause there are always good bands touring Canada, and they are all playing the Sheep.

Paul liked us that afternoon, and as he handed us a fat envelope, the first we had seen on that tour, he bought us a bunch of beer and sat down with us and truly wanted to know who we were and where we were going, what we wanted to happen to our career. Paul is enthusiastic, and Paul has good ears and a good sense of the Canadian scene. I can't remember who had said they were going to be the designated driver that evening for the final leg home, I guess thinking, "Hey, it's an afternoon show. It's not like we are gonna get drunk after, because everyone wants to head home," but Paul gave us a bunch of beer, and we drank it before we headed out. On our way home, we definitely realized that we had been given a shot at a good gig. We were lucky that we played well, because there were a few shows on that trip that we didn't, and to be honest, we had even talked about blowing the gig off. We didn't, and from that show on, we had a great anchor show that was part of every tour we took after that. Paul taught us and a lot of folks about the future of what is now becoming the Canadian scene, its salvation and its blood.

Whenever we had the Sheep on the back end of our tour, we would always head for home after the show. It's only a two-and-a-half-hour drive back to Montreal, so we would save the motel fees because the Sheep no longer provides rooms, 'cause of some dick band, or probably a couple of dick bands. That aside, if the Sheep was on the front end of our tours as we headed west, we would put ourselves up at the Alpine Grouse Motel. All things being equal, I really have to say that I was always really miffed at the band for always, without exception, voting to head home right after the show. These trips were always terrible, although not as terrible as the Fredericton-to-Montreal grind, but the Wakefield shows always found me unloading gear into my house at 5:30 a.m., probably an hour after the first guy that got dropped off was already in bed. It sucked, and it was a downer that always coloured my enjoyment of the final show on a tour. So for the purposes of this book, I get to rewrite history and bad ideas, and we stay at the Alpine Grouse for the night and return to Montreal, the way we should have after every trip, in the afternoon we rested. And without even going home to change, we pull up in front of a Montreal bar and play a proper homecoming show, our friends and loved ones showing up to see us play like motherfuckers all tight from the road, and those friends and loved ones saying, "Welcome back. We missed you, and you, got better."

The Alpine Grouse, owned by elderly Germans, sort of looks like a ski chalet as you drive up a very steep driveway and round the back to find a two-storey motel located on the backside. The rooms are pretty old but mostly clean, the beds creak, and the decor is everything I remember from my childhood. My parents had friends named Inga and Irwin, and we used to go over to their place a lot. They had a boy a couple of years older than me named Dieter. I lived in rural Ontario, so I was always glad to go anywhere. It's the Grouse's motel rooms that remind me of a prepubescent angst. Germans who built homes in the seventies and eighties built homes that look just like this, dark brown wood paneling, exposed decorative faux beams, tan ceramic tiled floor, cheap light fixtures, and robust furniture.

Lying on an empty bed pushing the remote control that is rumoured to activate the gas fireplace, to no avail, power drinking your way through the last two-four of the trip. Wandering outside onto the balcony to have a smoke, you realize tomorrow you are home, and Monday you have to go back to work. You probably won't have a specific reason or that looseness to life that will afford you drinking until maybe even the following Friday. The question arises: "Will I get the shakes this time after a couple of days, or will things just return to normal?" You will get to see the family, the wife, and in some cases the kid or kids. You'll see friends, and life will not be all frenetic, insane. You might even get through a whole day without having an argument with somebody. Obviously, it will be better than being on the road. It will be normal, and all you have been craving for weeks is normalcy. At last, it is in your grasp. It sometimes takes a bit of time to let that sink in, so you down a half bottle of Lakeport and reach for another one as you light another smoke. Now that the tour is over, you will have to reanalyze your tobacco addiction, adding that to the list of things that you have to change back to normal when you get home. The road is about keeping it together. When you get home, you will have to get used to keeping it together without all of these crutches or the relentless structure of touring, just like you always did. The more seasoned you get, the less difficult this transition becomes, and always the draw of home brings you back there, so you stub out your thirty-second smoke of the day on the flat board that passes for a handrail, glance up at the moon, bidding it a good night, and wander back in to a night's sleep, which in the walk from the front door to the bed you realize you need.

The quiet drive

The gear is packed one last time, dropping into the Sheep to grab the gear off the stage, having eaten at the Alpine Grouse. The Quebec fare breakfast souring in your stomach, a coffee to go awaiting in the cup holder, you play Tetris one last time, making sure all the gear has made it. With the exception of several ¼ to ¼ guitar cords that crapped out, one XLR lost, and a blown amp in Hamilton, you have safely gotten all the gear from one end of Canada to the other and back. You have left fifty empty guitar string packs strewn across green rooms, and stickers, tons of stickers, have marked your travels. You left CDs in the hands of countless paying fans, and so you remount your tour van and hang a right off the main drag, stopping a quarter mile up the road to refill ten one-litre bottles at the roadside spring, the bottles thrown up on the dash to replenish the van's occupants, screaming blood cells with badly needed fluids.

You make your way back out to the main highway, a four-lane that is slowly encroaching on Northern Quebec, having gained twenty kilometres since you first started playing up this way. With the van up to speed and on cruise control, you hear that an eerie silence has taken over the van. This is the road home silence. Conversation is hard to maintain on this trip: half the van is drifting between sleep and coma, and the other half is lost in thought. I know for me this is always when the summation and planning are at their height. The biggest fear always for me is the return home: the doors of the van swing wide, your bandmates bid a hasty goodbye, grab about half their gear, and bound for parts unknown. The question is always there: "I wonder which one of them is not going to show at rehearsal next week?" The long tours are the hardest on membership: three months gives a guy a lot of time to work out different plans. Folks come home to find they have no job, or have been demoted, or some busboy is now their boss. The rebuild after every tour is immense, a constant reshoring of finances, work shifts, careers, relationships. In a lot of cases, it's bounding out of the van and straight into a bar shift, desperately trying to pick up a $100 shift in hopes of adding that to your meagre tour pay and having the rent only three days late.

There are several different ways to run a band in light of this problem. I suppose the first way, and I have seen it a couple of times, is that a band just hits the road and never comes back. Everybody stores their couch and boxes of pots and pans and couch-surfs their way across the world. It can work to some degree, but the constant touring really does hamper the proper management of one's career. Without a home base and two or three months in one place in which to rehearse, record, plan, fill out grant apps, do PR campaigns, answer email, book a tour, and generally get a chance to get everything running in the right direction before going out again, bands can really get lost out there, trading off complete wanderlust for success, or at least building their career into a profession. These bands may have a shot if they have worked out their management problems before embarking. A good manager, maybe even one that tours with the band from time to time, can go a long way towards making this type of touring possible and fruitful. I know the band Tequila Mockingbird toured constantly for years, but the fact that Chandler Murray had their back constantly meant that they could keep up this pace, knowing that someone had the time and wherewithal to always be heading in the right direction. I know this from the outside, and I have no real insight into how that band works, but I did see them for quite a few years in a lot of different parts of the country, and Chandler was always the contact and always seemed to be holding it together.

Then there is the mercenary approach: just use hired guns every time you go out. I've seen it work. If you are a good singer-songwriter and have a great sense of organization, it can be a real win-win. But that, of course, could mean a completely different set of problems. You really aren't going to know these folks until about six weeks in, and then it turns out you are touring with heroin addicts and they pawned your radio while you were in getting some Chubby Chicken at the A&W, or worse, you just don't like them, or they groove like shit or quit in the middle of a tour.

I have got to say that the best scenario I have seen to date is the Burning Hell. In a sense, the Burning Hell is Mathias Kom. He writes all the songs, he records all the songs, he books all the shows, he advances the shows, fills out all the applications, rents the cars, sometimes two at a time. He spends three or four months doing all this in either Peterborough or St. John's or East Berlin, and herein lies the part that may be conjecture, but as far as I have noted over the years, after spending three or four months getting his ducks in a row, he then picks up the phone and starting with the first members of the Burning Hell, going back years, he starts booking his band. Depending on whether he is touring Canada or Europe or even Eastern Europe, he describes the tour, he says whether he can pay the airfare, the accoms, and the travel costs. All of this is based on whether he got funding from some grant app, or some anchor gig at a big festival, or just money dropped out of the sky. It is rumoured he gives a pretty good prospectus of how this tour is going to go. Is it sleeping in the car, or on floors, or hostels? Or maybe there might be some hotels here and there. He lets them know what the chances are as far as making any money at all, and then each past member kind of gets a yay or nay as to whether he is going or not.

Now the Hells have had thirty or forty members over the years, so depending on what the deal is and just what happens to be going on with any number of them, Mathias is stuck with the reality that he could be going out with any number of bandmates, in any number of possible combinations of instruments. The ultimate rule here is that Mathias is completely prepared to start and finish every one of these show all by himself, and although a solo ukulele show doesn't quite have the impact of, in some cases, two bass players, an omnichord, a four-piece horn section, two guitars, keys, and maybe a flame-thrower, he is ready to put his ass on the line. If nobody shows or if half the band quits halfway through, he is still going to play every show. His tours are epic. Sixty- show tours are common, touring across Canada, adding band members along the way, and then flying out to do twelve countries in Europe, stop for a two-month hiatus in Friedrichshain, record an album, make a couple of videos, and then run another couple of weeks back across Western Europe and then home. The promise is the entirety of the experience, the shows, the accomplishment, the hero status, and I'm not mocking here. For the moment, this is what Mathias is doing. He is playing shows and seeing the world. He is not rich by any means, and he probably won't get rich, but I hope he does. This guy should write a book. It's a crazy style that he himself has invented, and I don't exactly know how it is he maintains this thrust through life, but he does. He is a gypsy and is in it for the long haul with you or without you. He would always want it to be with his bandmates but does understand that they all can't be there all the time, even though he is.

You can look at our band as another way of doing it. In the beginning, we were all martyrs to the band. We never took any pay, we put all the money from our shows back into the band to record, promote, manage, and make ourselves look good. The first five years saw not a single dollar find its way into the bandmates' hands. In the world of indie, there are more than enough places to spend the band's money: trips, plane fare, van repairs, and the like. A little bit into the fifth year, when we had been doing some touring, we started paying a $20 per diem. Up until then, we had been covering all our own accoms, food, and beer ourselves, and the band paying gas and van payments. You would come home after a three-week trip and owe a couple hundred on your Visa, and spend the next two months getting that paid off and then go again, so per diems helped offset the cost of that. Every step of the way, the band started to move toward professionalizing ourselves, and the idea was to get the band to eventually pay for everything on the road first.

For the next couple of trips, the band paid all the gas, hotels, a two-four of beer every day, and some of the food as well as the van payments, merch replacement costs, taxes, members' tax accountants, and so on. It worked, but after a while, the band got to the point where it was making enough to actually reasonably pay the members. That was the tough part. Once everybody started getting paid, I think they started to realize they weren't getting paid that much. Even though we end up paying the band members the equivalent of $100 a show, a king's ransom when it comes to bands, it didn't take that long for folks to do the math and realize that you would have to play 100 shows a year just to make ten grand, which most adults don't really see as a lot of money, especially if you are out of town five months of the year doing it.

The trouble with that pay scale is it's probably enough to compensate a guy for the time he is on the road, but what the hell does he do for the three months he is at home? The problem is he gets a job, and after getting a job five times and quitting it over the span of two years, he gives up on the band. Man, that's tough, always battling with the return to home, coming back and finding your job gone, or someone has scooped it, or that guy that has been campaigning against you has won while you were gone, and your houseplants are dead. On a more personal note, the bandmates who are getting older are coming home to friends that have babies, and careers. It's all really tough. Sure, you are a star, well, becoming a star, but the people at home are becoming real people while you are away.

There is not really any one answer here. I know my plan, which I took from Maia Davies of Ladies of the Canyon, was always book, book, book. Always have something on the horizon, something to use as a carrot to entice the bandmates back to the next rehearsal, the next, bigger show. True enough, it worked. We always had something better on the horizon, but we also never really had any breaks, and that was pretty tough to hold together over the years. The years passed by quick, and there was always that drive home from Wakefield, that silent ride as this ran through my head, as many things ran through my bandmates' heads, with everybody thinking the same thing: I could just quit.

The Welcome Home Show

Pulling up in front of L'Esco Bar on St.-Denis, the bar located just south of Mount Royal, right beside the Quai des Brumes. L'Esco is a small basement place, and its downside is that it is located right at the bus stop, so parking out front is always tough on this busy street. Having cruised the block twice and finding a space fairly close but never directly in front of the bar, we unload. We unload everything into their storage space at the back of the bar. This is Montreal, and we know better than to leave gear in the van. Our bags go under the specially constructed storage in the back of the van, locked tight, and we enter the bar and prepare for sound check.

L'Esco, as stated, is small, dark, and has dark, rough rock walls. The place is tricked out in local art, and the staff are friendly. The stage is low to non-existent, actually just the corner of the bar, the space marked out by monitors. The great part about L'Esco is the sound system: it's a small place, with a low ceiling and a lot of hard space to bounce sound off of. In most places this size, you would be doing your own sound and probably have a hard time of it, first checking in an empty room and then when it fills up. The cramped space throws your sound all out of whack, which would then have you chasing sound throughout your set, which is distracting and generally annoying to the audience. To address this problem, L'Esco has a big old sound system, probably a lot bigger than it needs to be, and they have a soundman to run it. I'm not saying the sound in this club is stellar, but it is definitely someone else's problem to wrestle.

Sound check done, local phone calls made, computers logged on, final Facebook invites sent for tonight's show, you exit the bar and plug the meter, and head for food.

Heading north up St-Laurent and hanging a left on Mont Royal, on the north side of the street you find the Beanery (*La Binerie*). If you got to town early enough to get sound check done, or at least plugged in, and made it up to this place before it closes at eight p.m., you will find a dingy diner that serves tourtière and beans. This nothing-fancy place sells the stuff that has become known as *Quebec fare*: the meat pie, beans, mash, and maybe some pea soup. It sounds hokey, but it's nice food. The portions are not giant, so you shouldn't be too weighted down by the time the show starts.

Post-dinner, you while away the evening on the terrace of L'Esco, watching the folks walk by on this very busy street. Terraces are what the Montreal bar scene is all about. We get by for those couple of months in the winter when the cold and the snow keep us inside, but first chance we get, we are on the terrace, drinking beer and watching folks walk by. To sit on L'Esco's terrace is to experience Montreal. It's not the best terrace but it is quintessentially the Montreal experience.

I'm not 100 percent sure if this was in fact the terrace that I was sitting on twenty years ago when I first fell in love with Montreal, but I am sure that if not this, then one just like it. This one I'm sure has been responsible for many a traveler being lulled into staying in this city.

The opener fires up their set, probably some band you know from the road who needed a favour here in this rough-on-the-outsider town. This show is, as stated, ethereal. Although we have played this place a few times, this welcome home show never actually happened as such, so for that I'm going to say that we had the Schomberg Fair opening for us and knocking it over the fence to a packed house. They finish up, and the band launches into the tried, tested, and true road set that Matt Watson built the hour before, feet up in the van pre show, as he always did, building a set list for the night. Matt was our set list captain for the last couple of years, and he was magic at getting a bead on the night and laying the tunes out for maximum effect.

The set, which turns out to be one and a half hours long, ends to great applause, all our friends, and folks who have become fans, banging the tables in this small sweaty club and egging us on to continue. It is hot, but we are in shape and cocky, and start running through tunes that had fallen off the set list during the tour, tunes that went bad and then we lost our nerve about playing them. Normally, we would leave town with about thirty tunes on the set list and come back with maybe twenty-two, but the night feels good, we are in front of friends, and we run those tunes, clicking off another half hour. The folks not slowing down on their enthusiasm, we start doing tunes we haven't played in a year, some of the bandmates who have arrived to us recently having never played them before. Looks are batted back and forth, keys shouted out, and we riff through those tunes. We are on fire and start digging into tunes that we haven't played in years. I hear Felicity and myself singing "In Spite of Ourselves" by John Prine, and before we know, it I am singing "Mama Look a boo boo" by Harry Belafonte.

Having reached the two-and-a-half-hour mark, we close the set as we almost always do, with the song "Place St-Henri." At this point, to a crowd of fans, and at that locals, we hardly even have to sing this tune ourselves, because everyone in the audience knows all the words, and they sing at the top of their lungs as they slow dance, every one in the club, even the bar staff dancing. The song grinds to a halt after the big finish, and I hold the final note longer than I've ever held it before.

I always worked hard on the road, always tried to do more than my share of the driving, loading, planning, organizing, bitching, and obviously the taking of credit. As a band, we fought a lot, we bitched, and in some cases punched and wrestled. The tours were hard emotionally, but that all stood in suspension when we played "Place St-Henri" and everyone sang along and danced as we all piled into the mics for the big finish, leaning out over the monitors and touching the crowd. I held that last note, here on the ethereal show, and I held it for longer than I ever had, the band giving me that final moment suspended in time until my breath ran out in the finish of the song, the song and tour over.

The audience explodes in applause, and I count one, two, three, and the band picks up the instrumental as I thank the crowd, the bar staff, our music label. I name the bands we played with on our tour, and start reciting the names of my bandmates, first the ones onstage, and then keep going to cover the folks who were in the band and then showed up to see us tonight, and then continue to folks I haven't seen in years, thanking them all for being part of what got us here to this show. These folks were Felicity Hamer, Shawn 'Gus' Beauchamp, Matt Watson, Flipper Frumignac, Dylan Perron, Steve Brockley, Chris Reid, Eddy Blake, Jessie Enns, Kevin McNealy, Sean B'y Moore, Larry Whittaker, Roger Dawson, Seamus Cowan, Jeff Cowan, Derek Skeie, Sean Scanlan, Dan Ellison, and Niki Hildebrand, and, of course, yours truly, Gern f.

The front step

It's four a.m. on a Sunday morning, and my wife and child sleep in our apartment two floors above my head, here in Little Burgundy. I sit this morning as I always do at the end of every trip we have taken. The band is most likely home sleeping, and I have just loaded the final contents of the van into my office space at the corner of Lionel-Groulx and Vinet. It's a ground floor load in, and it's the easiest place to store gear. The rest of the band lives in second- and third-floor walk-ups, so more often than not, I get the dregs that are left in the van to deal with. I don't presume to know the return home rituals of my bandmates: do they go to bed right away? Do they unpack, and do they eat Kraft Dinner with hot dogs? My ritual is to unpack the van and park it across the street, the Wednesday side of the street, which means I can leave it unattended for the next three days and not have to reenter it for a couple of days and have my nostrils filled with old band and rotting food containers. By Wednesday, I shall take the van out and gas it up, sweep the crap out of it, maybe even wash the rubber floors depending on how bad it got. It will be taken next week to Frank's garage for a once-over. Frank's a good man and a front man to a band himself. He always kept our van in top shape, to the best ability of our finances.

That all rolls through my head as I light another smoke, and crack a beer. Chances are I had to go easy on drinking at the last show, being as I was going to have to drive at least the last of the band home. The beer I took great pains to squirrel away for this moment, maybe a band beer that I found rolling around the floor, having gotten lost mid-tour, maybe from the rider from the previous night's show, but it got tucked away in my bag safe and sound, awaiting this moment. I tuck it behind my leg as a cop drives by, but he spies me with that "What are you doing here at this time?" sort of look and continues his patrol.

I look across the street at the trees in the park. They have leaves on them, small but budding and promising that summer is soon here. When last I looked, they were covered in snow. We left on the ice and came back to terrace weather. I sit and smoke and take stock of the winter's effect on the stonework of my building. Someone is going to have to do some mortar work this year. I take another sip, and my brain returns to the road and I surmise, always with the question, why do we do this? Thumbing through my band pay, enough to make next month's rent and maybe a partial payment on my credit card, tomorrow I will be back behind the bar at Grumpy's, slinging drinks and telling tales. But for the moment this early morning, I make sense of it.

Touring as a band is probably the best way to see a country. I have been a truck driver, backpacker, and a tourist, and none of these pursuits touches that of a travelling musician. No other means of travel takes you down the main highway with as much purpose. The road winds out between towns and eventually brings you to the centre of a city, a city learned by maps and GPS units, scribbled directions, and repetition to a place where you disembark. You learn the parking regulations quickly in each city where you land, you remember the layout of the back alleys and the likelihood of crack-addicted bandits, you remember the back doors, the manager, the barman, and the waitress. You eat badly near the gig, you waste time between sound check and show, skulking in the immediate vicinity of the club, looking for smokes. Before the show, you preen and wheeze. During the show, you get to show off in front of locals, you make friends with them, and after you drink, you sleep in their beds. Nothing gives you the reason to be in a particular place, meeting its people and sampling their lives and their food, like being in a band. International airline pilots wish they had access to this world.

You didn't make money, you probably didn't get laid, and you are probably not going to be recognized soon. Your back hurts, you fingers ache, and you have to go back and see if you still have a job, and see if your wife still loves you. But what you did get is a context of the world that few have. You know folks from one end of the country to the other. You now know the lay of all the towns, and how they play out on the map. Later, weeks later, you will hear a news report about something going on in Calgary, and you will recognize the street names, maybe even have an opinion of the news report based in a conversation you had with the opening band. You will know each part of the world you travel, and you will be added to that list of folks who know cities well: cab drivers, bartenders, news reporters. But it goes farther than that 'cause they know their town, and you know their town, yours, and every other town. You are a touring musician.

A special thanks to Joseph from Café lili & Oli for the table space and electricity needed to make these pages exist. I would also like to thank Rachel Hoffman for her seemingly tireless work helping keep my life, career, and this book going in a straight forward direction. Thank you, Claire Porter, for your belief and encouragement as well as your all too numerous hours spent editing this project in the early days and getting me to the next step. Lee Mellor, thanks for letting me know what I was in for. Thank you, Jon Paul Fiorentino, for, among many things, okay, fourteen things, the most important of which was passing this along to the powers that be. Thank you, Insomniac Press and Gillian Rodgerson, for your skillful expertise in polishing these pages. And to conclude, thank you, Oscar Peterson, you were a good van.